AF655383

TOURISM MANAGEMENT

TOURISM MANAGEMENT

J.P. Sangar

ANMOL PUBLICATIONS PVT. LTD.
NEW DELHI - 110 002 (INDIA)

ANMOL PUBLICATIONS PVT. LTD.
H.O.: 4374/4B, Ansari Road, Darya Ganj,
New Delhi-110 002 (India)
Ph.: 23261597, 23278000
B.O.: No. 1015, Ist Main Road, BSK IIIrd Stage
IIIrd Phase, IIIrd Block,
Bangalore - 560 085 (India)
Visit us at: www.anmolpublications.com

Tourism Management

© Reserved

First Published, 2006

ISBN 81-261-2693-0

[Responsibility for the facts stated, opinions expressed, conclusions reached and plagiarism, if any, in this book is entirely that of the Author. The Publishers bear no responsibility for them, whatsoever.]

PRINTED IN INDIA

Published by J.L. Kumar for Anmol Publications Pvt. Ltd., New Delhi - 110 002 and Printed at Mehra Offset Press, Delhi.

Contents

Preface

"Tourism Managment" as a paper is being taught at Tourism Management Courses at various universities and institutions. This book is designed as an introductory text to the above paper, encompassing vital information on all pertinent aspects. Thus the material presented here would be of interest as well as of great use to the students, teachers and professionals of Tourism Courses. This book will provide complete knowledge of development of tourism and people, goals, scope and nature, tourism promotion and customer needs, environmental and ecological trends, destination planning, marketing, Govt. and Admn. systems etc. to the students.

The major topics dealt in this book are—Growth and Development; Tourism and People; Historical Perspective of Tourism; Goal of Tourism; Scope and Nature of Tourism; Development of Tourism; Tourism Promotion and Customer Needs; Tourism Planning; Impact on Tourism; Role of Hotel Industry; Tourism and Management Strategies; Environmental and Ecological Parameters of Tourism; Destination Planning and Economic Development; Tourism Marketing; Redevelopment of Tourism; Tourism and Govt. Administrative Systems; Structuring the Demand for Tourism etc.

It is hoped that all those will benefit from the contents of this book for whom it is meant. The author will feel amply rewarded, if motive is achieved.

Editor

1

Growth and Development

To UNDERSTAND tourism's growth and development requires analysis of its past, for the seeds of change can be used not only to explain the present but as pointers to the future. Travel is a long-established tradition. It origins can be found in pre-industrial society, but over time the opportunities to travel have increased, changing the picture from one of individual travel to mass tourism. In the pre-industrial era pleasure travel was limited to the wealthy and privileged. The earliest travellers were the explorers but, like many today, they frequently combined business interests with the exploration Marco Polo is an excellent example of such a pioneer, as are numerous explorer-traders of the New World. The most popular form of domestic travel was the pilgrimage, which became a social and recreational event in addition to a religious commitment. Indeed contemporary observations by Chaucer would indicate that self-fulfillment took on a higher priority than self-denial. Another symbol of these early stirrlings of tourism is the security against vandalism undertaken at various shrines.

More extensive reminders of the early days of tourism lie in the spas and seaside resorts whose origins were linked to the pursuit of health, but which eventually became centres of amusement and recreation. In Europe, locations favoured with hot springs or mineral water were strongly recommended for, their therapeutic value by the early medical profession. Since it was mainly the rich and powerful who could seek such advice and follow it, spas like bath and Carlsbad became magnets for society and merchants. As a result the natural resource of the community was supplemented by accommodation and entertainment facilities that became attractions in their own right, as can be seen in the Regency terraces and public buildings in Bath. Furthermore, the prospect of attracting business by developing local natural resources led to the earliest example of city council investment in tourist attractions.

A notable legacy for today's tourism from the pre-industrial era is the Grand Tour. During the seventeenth century "increasing numbers of potential diplomats, men becoming rich through England's growing foreign trade and scholars in search of European learning, began to legitimize gallants' jaunts which thus imperceptibly merged into the educative and political institution known as the Grand Tour". The route prescribed for this tour by John Gailhard in his book, The Compleat Gentleman, was a three-year exploration of the capitals, politics, culture, and society of western Europe. The proposed itinerary was an outbound trip to Paris and Italy. with stop in Genoa, Milan, Florence, Rome, and Venice, followed by a return trip through Switzerland, Germany, and the Low Countries. The motives for the Grand Tour have a lot in common with present day university students who frequently "take a year off" to travel, between leaving school and strating their first job, while the development of a specified route is reflected in our modern package tours.

The industrial revolution brought about major changes in the scale and type of tourism development. The increases in productivity, regular employment and growing urbanization gave more people the motivation and opportunity to go on holiday. In contrast to the earlier dominance by the wealthy, tourism began to embrace a broader social spectrum; and as in other areas of social behaviour, class distinctions became apparent. The emerging middle class combined higher incomes and growing education into annual holidays. To escape from their responsibilities and the congested urban environment they sought relaxation and renewal in areas of natural beauty and, in turn, created the beginning of the modern holiday industry. In some cases established resorts with prestige and notoriety expanded and developed to capture this new market. In others new locations became popular destinations. The working class also experienced. higher wages and more regular work, but their house were longer and their proportion of discretionary wealth smaller. Consequently, working-class involvement in tourism was more gradual, and began in the form of day-trip outings.

The force behind the upsurge in productivity and higher incomes was the development of steam power. This innovation not only stimulated the industrial revolution, but it provided the increased mobility needed by the burgeoning tourism business. Steamers on the major rivers provided reliable and inexpensive transportation that led to popular day-trip cruises and the growth of coastal resorts near large industrial towns. The London to Margate route was carrying over 100,000 visitors by 1830. Steamers were carrying hundreds of thousands of Liverpool residents across the Mersey to New Brighton, Rhyl, and Landudno. and had initiated the Isle of Man holiday industry. The railroads were, however, the major agent of change, and as they began to develop their passenger market, access to a rail system became the prime development consideration in the tourism market.

Examples of this rail-tourism symbiosis can be seen on both sides of the Atlantic. The small fishing village of Whitby. Yorkshire, was transformed into a Victorian resort serving industrial West Yorkshire due to the creation of a rail link with York. The construction of a railroad northward from Montreal to the Laurentian hills during the 1890s made this scenic recreation area accessible for mass tourism for the first time. In the process it changed the recreational and touristic preferences of Montrealers,' which until that time had been manifested by riverine tourism and vacation travel east and west along the St. Lawrence valley (Lundgren 1983). Tourism in the Catskill Mountains started in 1824 with the construction of a large resort hotel on the crest of an escarpment, known as the "Wall of Manitou" overlooking the Hudson Valley. The majority of patrons during the early years were members of the social elite of New York and Philadelphia, who willingly spent 8 hours travelling up the Hudson by steamboat and then endured a 4 hour, 12-mile stagecoach ride in order to experience the splendour of nature while enjoying the hospitality of a first-class hotel (Darlington 1981).

The railroads created not only more business by providing reliable and inexpensive transportation for the first time, but also more competition as various companies and resorts vied for this new business. The new resorts were based primarily on natural resources that appealed to the urbanite wishing to break free from the crowds and pollution of the city. Due to the scale of development and increased competition such amenities needed to be augmented by man-made facilities. Private companies invested heavily in hotels, resort development, and entertainment facilities, but tourism's growth also encouraged municipal investment in parades, parks, piers, and baths notable municipal ventures included Atlantic City's "boardwalk" and Blackpool's "tower."

The scale and mobility introduced by the railroad transformed tourism from a small business catering to the elite into the start of a mass market, where consumers found a growing and complex number of options. The novelty of a holiday plus the confusion of a rapidly expanding travel industry provided an opportunity for the professional consultant, and this era saw the emergence of the travel organizer. The first and most famous of these was Thomas Cook. His first excursion train trip was between Leicester and Loughborough on July 5, 1841, with 570 passengers at a round-trip fare of one shilling. By 1851 Cook was arranging transport and lodging for 165,000 visitors to London's World Exposition at Crystal Palace. In 1866 he organized his first American tour and in 1874 introduced "circular notes" which were accepted by banks, hotels, shops, and restaurants. These were in effect the first traveller's checks. Amongst all these achievements Burkart and Medlik content that his true significance.

The dynamic nature of the market place in terms of technical innovation and the increasing numbers of people who could afford and accept the idea of vacations brought changes to the resorts. Many inaccessible resort areas that had been exclusive through their association with the elite became more cosmopolitan and proletarian as the railroads offered better service and local entrepreneurs responded to the new business opportunities.

Tourism continued to develop in close association with the railroad until the Second World War, after which the technological advances of wartime were transferred to peaceful pursuits and governments faced demands for a new order. The post-war era, like those preceding it, presented a continuation of trends plus some innovations, but in total it has been the most dramatic period of growth so far recorded.

The greatest change after the Second World War was increased mobility. The development of jet engines made it possible to fly large numbers of people great distances at high speed. Furthermore, as aircraft design evolved, airlines were able to do so with increased comfort, because they could fly above the weather, and at very economical rates. A trip undertaken by the author in the late 1960s from the United States to England worked put at 2c a mile, including meals and entertainment. Herman Kahn provides another illustration of the airlines' growing speed and efficiency in a comparison of a trans-American flight between 1929 and 1979. In 1933 a New York to San Francisco flight took 21 1/2 hours (if it was on time, flying against the prevailing westerly winds) and the round trip cost dollars 320 or dollars 1.900 in 1979 dollars. That same flight in 1979 took 5 1/2 hours and was more likely to be on time, but most important cost only dollars 234. despite the upsurge of oil prices. These improvements in air transport not only encouraged greater transcontinental travel but were instrumental in the explosion of intercontinental travel in the 1960s and 1970s. The earth literally shrank for the tourist, bringing distant exotic islands closer and replacing week-long sea voyages with a few hours of armchair comfort.

Increased mobility was not confined to air travel; after the war the western world became a consumer society and the major goal for many was an automobile. The automobile diffused tourism more than any other form of transport. It brought back the true (meaning of the work "touring" for it provided flexible and personal transportation which freed people from the schedules and fixed routes of public transport. Resorts could no longer depend on the traditional two-week vacation but became temporary stopover on family automobile tours. It enabled people to travel wherever there was a road while new recreation vehicles (four-wheel drives and snow mobiles, do not even face this restriction. Any amenity or community can now become a tourist attraction if it can be reached by the automobile or one of its derivatives. For many the purchase of such an expensive item can be justified only through maximum use including that of pleasure driving and vacations.

Although the dramatic changes in mobility after the Second World War many have had the most visible impact other forces were at work which permitted the growth and proletarianization of tourism. More people found they had the leisure time and discretionary income that are necessary prerequisites for a vacation. Thanks to labour negotiations and social legislation the length of official and paid holidays has been steadily increasing. Governments have created more vacation time by incorporating isolated public holidays into the now familiar "long weekends" throughout the year. In addition. the post-war economic recovery provided a major increase in real income, which many people converted into increased recreation and travel. By the 1970s two vacations a year were not uncommon. The enlarged market potential did not escape the notice of travel companies who established tours and created familiar environments for the uninitiated traveller. In this way many working-class people were tempted to break with tradition and replace the local resort holiday with a package vacation on distant shores. These travellers were offered a "guarantee" of sun plus accommodation and entertainment that would not be too different from the familiar resort back home.

The big question now is what direction will tourism take in the future? Over the last few years there have been dramatic increases in world energy prices with resulting repercussions on individual mobility and national economies. Between 1973 and 1982 world oil prices increased from dollar 3.00 to dollar 34 a barrel, and the operating costs for an automobile have risen by 158 per cent since

1973, according to a Hertz report. In addition, the rising price of oil has been blamed, in part, for the combined inflation and recession of the 1970s, which becam known as "stagflation." People found inflation cutting into their discretionary income and the cost of travel rising abruptly, while recession was challenging the notion of job security or leaving a member of the family unemployed.

The prospects for tourism may appear bleak but if we look at the record for the 1970s we find the industry has been resilient and even managed to grow. The industry's phenomenal growth rates of the 1960s have disappeared but there is still growth, even after adjusting for inflation. Like many other consumer industries, tourism may be entering a more stabilized period of operation, following the boom years of expansionary development. Stability, however, does not mean static.

Growth Factors

The reasons for tourism's resilience in the face of adverse conditions lie in its evolution and the hold it has taken on our lives. The major trends encountered in our historical review and groups them under three general headings-motivation, ability, and mobility. These three factors account for past growth and can be used to identify future growth trends.

Motivation to travel is necessary for the development of tourism since if there was no interest in travel or need to travel the tourist industry could not exist. Maslow (1954), in his book Motivation and Personality, identifies a hierarchy of human needs, that uppermost of which is self-actualization and self-realization. The concept is that after our basic psychological needs, security and social acceptance have been realized, we turn to self-fulfillment. The dramatic advance in living standards since the Second World War have enabled more people to indulge in personal preferences. and one of these, according to Taylor (1983), has been to travel. Taylor refers to the observations of Yankelovich and Lefkowitz (1980) who consider Americans no longer limit their priorities to money and status. They feel three other ideas have been appropriated by the majority of Americans:

1. First, the growing conviction that what is regarded as a "nose-to-the-grindstone' way of life is too high a price to pay for material success.

2. Second. the feeling that Americans have devoted too much time and attention to the task of how to make a living and not enough to the question of how to live.

3. Last, the belief that what counts most in life is that "I keep growing" as an individual, "that I have an opportunity to fulfill my potential." and "that I have a moral obligation to do so."

As the world has developed into an industrial and post-industrial society, the means to learn about travel opportunities has increased while the stress and pressure of modern life has transformed the vacation into a new form of therapy. A survey conducted by Psychology Today (Rubenstein 1980) showed the two major reasons for taking vacations among its readers were rest and relaxation (63 per cent) and escape from routine (52 per cent). While the survey's sample is not truly representative of the United States population because it involved a high proportion of young post-graduates, its analysis of leisure priorities is informative because this group of influential consumers has a major impact on the tourist market. A factor analysis indicated that relieving the tension of responsible and stressful jobs was the most popular motive for travel. This was followed, in descending order of importance. by intellectual enrichment, family togetherness, exotic adventure, self-discovery, and escape. Thus, one can see a wide variety of travel motives exists in today's society and many of them can be considered basic needs.

During its heady post-war expansion the tourist industry largely ignored tourist motives and expectations because it was too busy serving the growth to become overlay concerned with those who were disappointed with their travel experience. The recent slowdown in business and increased competition for tourist revenues, however, has created more interest in market research and the needs of the tourist. More countries and states are investigating the motives of travellers and potential tourists. For example, Tourism Canada has explored the perceptions and motives behind French. British. and Japanese interest in Canada and has duly adjusted its marketing to suit the individual tastes of these contrasting markets (Taylor 1983). One champion of such research into motivation and preferences is Pearce. He feels that tourist expectations have been taken for granted in the past but that "one can obtain a social psychological profile of tourists which links roles motivation and social and environmental preferences".

Motivation considerations should now extend beyond individual consensus to include corporate agency and government policy decisions. Each of these groups has become increasingly involved in providing vacation opportunities with their motivation varying from productivity to therapy and preventative medicine. It all results in some form of "social tourism." a term which in itself indicates how far tourism has penetrated our value system.

Social tourism can be described as "the relationships and phenomena in the field of tourism resulting from participation in travel by economically weak or otherwize disadvantaged elements of society" (Hunzinger. "Social tourism. its nature and problems.". It involves the provision of vacations for people who can afford them only with the aid of a third party. Although the aim of social tourism is unitarian in philosophy-to extend the benefits of vacations to a broader segment of society-it is expressed in a variety of forms.

Trade unions in industrialized nations have long sought and won paid vacation time for their members and by example have won similar rights for most industrial and service workers. In Europe and Japan some companies help pay for a substantial portion of vacation costs. Most Workers in West Germany receive *Urlaubsgeld* (holiday money) a bonus that can equal 45 per cent of their regular vacation pay. In France, the state-owned Renault company contributes to the operation of thirty family vacation villages for its workers (Time 1981).

In Europe the emphasis is on families, and many central and local governments are committed to develop and operate facilities for low-income or otherwise disadvantaged families. A good illustration of this is Villages-Vacances-Familles (VVF) in France. This association, created in 1959 by national and regional government bodies, operated 78 family vacation centres with a total capacity of 40, 600 beds in 1974. There are two types of centre, either a village providing full board or selfcatering accommodation, or campsites established near villages so campers can take advantage of local facilities. In Switzerland a Travel Saving Fund (REKA) has been established which permits residents to systematically save for their holidays, offering them a discount on domestic vacations or international travel using local agencies or tour companies. Furthermore, the capital so invested has permitted REKA to construct its own holiday centres, which are oriented to family needs. "Today REKA owns six holiday centres with 254 family units and 1,434 guest beds...In order not to exclude any families from the possibility of REKA holidays, a graded rental discount of 10 per cent to 50 per cent is granted to families with lower incomes".

Social tourism has become a recognized component and legitimate objective for modern tourism. By extending the physical and psychological benefits of rest and travel to less fortunate people, it can be looked upon as a form of preventative medicine. By emphasizing national and regional resources and cultural heritage it can be viewed as a means of cementing the economic, social and political ties of a country. To encourage the adoption of this concept, the International Bureau of Social Tourism (BITS) has been created, with the goal of promoting social tourism at the international level.

The ability to travel depends on a combination of personal circumstances and the tourism industry's initatives to expand its market. There has been a steady increase in discretionary income and leisure time, but recently both of these forces have come under increasing pressure from inflation. As rising prices for basic needs have eroded personal and family discretionary incomes, one response has been to sacrifice some leisure time by taking on a second job, or undertaking one's own maintenance and repair work. However, the industry has continually attempted to lower the price of vacations and expand the number of options, so that a moderate decrease in discretionary income and leisure time does not mean the end of vacation travel.

A driving force behind many industry innovations has been value, and nowhere is this more evident than in the growth of organized tours, which now offer a myriad of options to suit all tastes and pocketbooks. The modern package tour provides value for money through economies of scale and vertical linkage. If a coach, airplane, or hotel can be—assured full capacity then the cost per traveller decline drastically, as the overheads are spread over large numbers of visitors. Add to this the advantages of one company owning the travel agency, the transport system and the accommodation, and tremendous saving can be made by channelling the visitor from one branch to another and ensuring high business volume throughout the system. The savings of such an arrangement can, to some extent, be passed on to the traveller and thus provide an attracti‚e and competitive package. Examples of this trend can be seen in the growth of travel wholesal giants like Amex and Cooks, national networks such as Inter tourist, and mutual arrangements like the "fly and cruise" packages.

In addition to the large-scale solution many individual entrepreneurs and travellers have made personal adjustments to lower the price of vacations. Foremost amongst these is the trend to self-catering. This term is used to describe travellers who provide some of their own services, such as accommodation and meals. It is a far cry from the traditional concept of a vacation, where one is pampered and gets away from the usual household chores, but by washing one's own dishes and providing one's own bed considerable savings can be achieved.

Self-catering takes on many form, but the most evident has been the growth in camping and recreation vehicles. There have always been camping enthusiast of course, people who wished to get away from the crowds and close to nature. These people generally used tents, had few luxuries and favoured isolated campsites. Over the past 20 years or so, however, more people have become campers because of its economic appeal and in the process changed the camping scene. Very often these campers prefer to bring the comforts of home on their vacation, so they purchase or rent trailers and recreation vehicles. There has been a major growth of private campgrounds designed to provide convenient access to the highway and tourist attractions while offering reasonable rates by operating at high densities.

The ultimate development along these lines are the new franchise campgrounds that operate like motel chains, providing a standard format at each camp and offering reservation systems. Kampgrounds of America (KOA) for example, has an extensive franchise of campsites and can offer rates that are a third to a quarter the cost of a hotel room. Each has a standard design which includes a redwood-coloured central complex containing a general store, washroom, and laundry facilities a games room with pinball and electronic games plus a swimming pool which is heated where necessary. These camp grounds provide sites for the tent, and that post-war phenomenon. the recreational vehicle. This vehicle is no longer a simple caravan or trailer to be pulled behind a car but has become a sophisticated mobile home either towed or self-propelled. It requires water and electricity hook-ups, sewage disposal units, and pull-through sites so the driver does not have to back up.

The newest form of self-catering is the time-share concept. where people may purchase a short time period in a condominium or apartment-hotel that is located in a resort area. "Whether it's a hedge against inflation or just a guaranteed getway, throngs of Americans are now buying vacation homes by the slice". The time-share system is a derivative of the European holiday flat or villa, which was leased by its owner during the tourist season. This system has evolved in North America into two systems of timesharing. The more popular is "interval ownership" where consumers purchase a certain time period in a resort condominium, say a two-week Christmas period on

Maui, Hawaii. which can be used personally or sub-let. The second type is called a "vacation licence" or "right to use" which in effect is a long lease. The buyer gets the right to use an apartment. or class of apartment for a designated number of years before it reverts back to the developer. To make these purchase or lease arrangements more flexible, exchange networks, such as Resort Condominiums International, have been created.

The third growth factor in tourism's evolution is personal mobility which is a crucial element for an activity involving travel. Mobility expanded dramatically with the introduction of steampower. but both the steamboats and railroads. were public transport which meant travellers had to travel according to a company schedule and route pattern. The result was an explosion of tourism development along selected routes and at popular destinations in the recreation hinterland of urban-industrial centres. True personal mobility had to await development and widespread adoption of the automobile. When this was achieved after the Second World War the restraints of schedules and routes were thrown off and people began to tour in the true sense of the word. The resulting drop in static holidays saw a decline in many traditional resorts and the spread of tourism activity as people sought out new experiences and unspoiled areas. The development of air travel extended such searching to distant places and tourism became truly international although this component still remained far behind domestic or national travel.

The expansion of personal mobility received a setback with the energy crisis of 1973 and the continuing price spiral for all forms of fuel. The days of cheap energy ended with the creation of the OPEC cartel for its price hikes had an immediate impact on tourism as prices doubled and supplies became unreliable. Of these two consequences, the latter was more troublesome because uncertainty of supply was a big deterrent to long distance travel—no one relished the thought of being stranded in a foreign country or at empty gas stations. In terms of the price increases, however, both the public and the industry were able to make adjustments to meet the new situation.

Individual adjustment and resourcefulness were provided an opportunity to distinguish themselves in such times of crisis. The tourist industry adjusted by promoting more extensive use of tours so that per capita travel and accommodation costs were reduced. One of the prime growth sectors during the 1970s was the increase in sea cruises, which, when combined with air travel to the port of embarkation and bus tours at various stop-overs, meant a traveller spent his entire vacation aboard some form of public transport. Private individuals adjusted by traveling out of season, using package tours and charter arrangements for the first time, or traveling closer to home. Corsi and Harvey (1979), for example, in a survey of shifts in vacation travel between 1973 and 1975 found that households in southeast Wisconsin were willing to experiment with various vacation adjustments. These included greater use of public transport and more local vacations.

People have been able to nullify the higher costs of travel to a greater extent than imagined by making more efficient use of an existing asset—the family automobile. The automobile has a strong hold on people because it offers privacy, status, speed, convenience, and comfort unparalleled in any other form of transport. Added to that the cost of owning and operating an automobile, which was estimated to be 43.28 cents a mile in 1983 for compact-size family sedans, compares very favourably with public transport alternatives if one is carrying a full load of passengers and contemplating regional travel. Furthermore, the move to smaller, more fuel, efficient automobiles has permitted considerable savings. Bryan (1981) calculated that an improvement from 10 to 15 mpg could result in gasoline savings of dollars 333 to dollars 833 per annum, depending on the mileage driven.

A 1980 travel survey by Transport Canada revealed that 90 per cent of all journeys over 50 miles were made by automobile. Air travel was a distant second with 5 per cent of the trips. and buses and trains were insignificant contributors. In the United States it has been estimated that automobiles account for 75 per cent of all tourism related travel (Pizam and Pokela 1983). Thus, the automobile still remains a viable option for many regional or domestic trips, and the move to smaller, more efficient vehicles does not necessarily mean less comfort since the average household size is also shrinking.

Although the three factors of motivation, ability, and mobility have been isolated in the table and examined separately, it should be evident that they are often interrelated and their total impact greater than the sum of individual parts. The fact that all three have grown and interwoven has changed the role of travel and vacations in our lifestyles. Instead of being viewed as a luxury item with a highly elastic demand curve in relation to price, there is evidence to suggest that travel has become more of a necessity and hence less sensitive to price increases, rather like the effect of higher cigarette prices on a chain smoker. When the first energy crisis resulted in a worldwide recession one newspaper reported that a surprising number of newly unemployed people were booking overseas vacations and cruises. For the first time they had the cash in the form of severance pay and time (ability) to fulfill their dreams (motive), and they were not going to let a temporary setback deny them this opportunity. Furthermore, during the early 1970s transportation companies were able to absorb much of the fuel price increase, so international travel expenses (mobility) were still within many people's budget.

Future of Tourism

Tourism is a dynamic and varied activity, where both the industry and public have proven extremely adaptable to new situations. In terms of personal mobility the crises and price hikes of the 1970s have not been catastrophic and have in fact given the transport sector time to adjust. Nowhere is this more apparent than in the aircraft industry where a new generation of fuelefficient plans is beginning to emerge. In August 1981, the first Boeing 767 came off the assembly line, the first new model in 12 years. Likewise, there have been improvements in automobile efficiency and the move to new fuels like gasohol, propane, and hydrogen show the automobile is not going to disappear.

The ability to travel has received setbacks from inflation and rising cost of fuel. but other factors will enable people to adjust to the new situation. Foremost among these is the demographic trend in industrial nations where the post-war baby boom has now become a major consumer group of young adults (Newsweek 1981). These adults differ from previous generations in that they are either deferring or cancelling plans for settling down with a home and family. These people have significant discretionary incomes because they earn high incomes yet have modest expenses for apartments or condominiums; plus they have more leisure time than most because of limited family or housing ties. They form a major portion of the travel market as young people traditionally travel in search of new experiences and socializing. Frechtling, Director of the US Travel Data Centre has estimated that the 35 to 40 age group which "shows one of the highest rates of travel generation." will increase by 36 per cent between 1976 and 1985, and by 1990 will constitute 15 per cent of the nation's population (Frechtling 1977).

Another feature of the west's demographic future that will have an important bearing on tourism is the general aging of our population. Retired people have more time for travel and many, having completed the major expenditures of purchasing a home and raising a family, now have more discretionary funds available for travel. The retired sector of society thought the careful management of its time and financial assets can become an important element of the tourism market; but as Doxey (1983) warns, a lot depends on how society treats its elderly and prepares them for their increased leisure opportunities. He notes we know relatively little about the preferences and consumer demands of this growing group. At present, many retired people have chosen to travel in the off-season to avoid the crowds and stretch their vacation dollar; some have invested in a motor home and become the new nomads following the sun; and others have retired to popular tourist destinations in the sun-belt regions. While the latter are not strictly tourists, they have settled in touristic areas and have become an influential force in the development of these communities.

Finally, one must appreciate that while these demand characteristics look encouraging for the industry the industry itself has not stood still and has continually revised its facilities and attractions. Never have there been so many choices for the tourist. The adventurous traveller can be left on a deserted island with or without supplies and the cautious neophyte can be chaperoned through that first major trip. Innovations such as time-sharing and activity vacations are designed to provide better value through lower-priced accommodation and multipurpose travel. Learning a foreign: language or new skill while relaxing in pleasant surroundings provides added justification and value to a vacation.

In light of continued inflation and a growing demand for public accountability, new elements are entering into the tourism picture in order to achieve more efficient use of their resources and facilities. Farmers, particularly those in the wilder scenic areas where agricultural productivity is low, are being encouraged to supplement their incomes by accommodating tourists. Regular householders in popular destination areas view summer season accommodation revenue as one way of combating ever-rising property taxes. Both of these movements will appeal to those travellers who are tired of the more impersonal hotel atmosphere, or who can no longer afford their prices. In addition public institutions such as universities are being forced into the tourism market to supplement their educational revenues and maximize plant use. Thus, more of them are opening their dormitories to the travelling public during the summer months and offering conference facilities during school breaks.

❐

2

Tourism and People

Mankind's basic, primitive motives are fear, lust, love and greed on the one hand; there is also need for stimulation through change, excitement and novelty by doing different things, on the other. Music, art and literature stimulate the senses but tourism and travel provide that stimulation physically. By and large tourism products are designed for achieving both forms of stimulation. Moving away from familiar places provides divesity and can be pleasantly exciting. Modern art galleries, excursions to concerts and other cultural attractions stimulate the senses and feelings. In brief tourism provides opportunity to escape from their normal humdrum lives.

The human beings need change. Travel provides that change. However, the level of satisfaction received from tourism is based on the age, energy, health, expectations and background of the individual. The younger and educated people travel more than the less educated and elder people, if the time and money are available. Those who are twenty or thirty years of age may be funny and may be overpowering at fifty or sixty years. Thus attitudes to tourism vary considerably and can do so even within the same age group.

Tourism is an activity involving mixture of material and psychological factors. The material ones are accommodation, transportation, the attractions and entertainments available. The psychological factors take into account a wide spectrum of attitudes and expectations. These attitudes and expectations vary from pure escapism to fulfilment of a dream or fantasy, or rest, entertainment educational and other social interests.

DEFINITIONS OF TOURISM

There are a large number of definitions of a tourist. These definitions refer it as a movement and it precisely signifies the word 'tour' which forms the root of the expression 'tourist'. Tourist is one who makes a tour, travelling from place to place for pleasure. The term 'tourist' in the sense of the pleasure tour is, however, of recent origin. The origin of the word 'tourist' dated back to the year 1292 AD. *The International Dictionary of Tourism* published in 1953 points out that 'tour' in English and in French means a journey, a circulative trip. The *19th Century Dictionary defines* tourist as "people who travel for pleasure of travelling out of curiosity, and because they have nothing better to do", and even "for the joy of boasting about it afterwards." The term 'tourist,' the Oxford Dictionary states, was used as early as the year 1800.

In the words of Jose Ignacio De Arrillaga "Tourism in its first period was considered as a sport or rather as a synthesis of automobiles touring, cycling, excursions, camping and Yachting. In the early nineteenth century the term 'tourist' assumed a meaning of 'one who makes a tour or tours, especially one who does this for recreation or who travels for pleasure, object of interest, scenery or the like.'

All the above-mentioned definitions of the term 'tourist' are of general nature. It was, however, the League of Nations which did pioneering work in defining the term for the purposes of statistical measurements. The Committee of Statistical Experts of the League of Nations in 1937 has defined the term 'foreign tourist' as "Any person visiting a country, other than that in which he usually resides, for a period of at least 24 hours." Persons staying for less than twenty-four hours were to be treated as excursionists. The following people were to be considered tourists within the purview of this definition:

(i) Persons travelling for pleasure, for domestic reasons, for health, etc.

(ii) Persons travelling for business purposes.

(iii) Persons travelling to meetings, or in a representative capacity of any kind (Scientific, administrative, diplomatic, religious, athletic, etc).

(iv) Persons arriving in the course of a sea cruise, even when they stay for less than 24 hours. (The latter should be reckoned as a separate group, disregarding, it necessary, their usual place of residence).

The following categories were not to be regarded as tourists:

(i) Persons arriving, with or without a contract of work, to take up an occupation or engage in any business activity in the country.

(ii) Persons coming to establish a residence in the country.

(iii) Residents in a frontier zone and persons domiciled in one country and working in an adjoining country.

(iv) Students and young persons in boarding establish ments or schools.

(v) Travellers passing through a country without stopping, even if the journey takes more than 24 hours.

The above definition of a tourist was accepted by the United Nations in the year 1945. It stated that the 'tourist' was a person who stayed in (another) a tourism country for more than twenty-four hours and less than six months for any non-immigrant objective.

The terms like 'travellers', 'visitors' or 'guests' all mean the same. In the United States, tourists are known as 'guests' in hotels and 'patrons' in restaurants. In most other countries, they are called 'visitors'.

During the year 1960, the International Monetary Fund also recommended on methods in order to calculate travel receipts and payments assuming as a basis for estimating the travel element of a country's balance of payments. They were as follows:

(i) travel includes expenditures in a compiling country by all visitors from abroad and expenditures abroad by all residents visiting foreign countries;

(ii) the five categories of people whose expenditures should be included under travel receipts and expenditures were defined as tourists, business travellers, students, government officials and others;

(iii) travel ought to cover all expenditures in a country which is incidental to travel, *i.e.*, transport and the purchases of goods other than for business purposes. Moreover, payment made to foreign carrier should not be included under the heading of 'travel';

(iv) expenditures by crews of international carriers, military personnel, migrant workers, diplomats and other personnel of foreign governments are to be excluded.

CHARACTERISTICS OF TOURISM

Tourists business is a type in itself. Its several characteristics distinguishes it from other types of business. In productmarket planning for any industry it is essential to consider, and allow for, any features, which are special to the business. Tourism has several characteristics.

1. **Rigidity of Supply Components.** Rigidity of the supply components in tourism, *i.e.*, accommodation units, railways, airports; roads, etc., arise for a number of reasons. First, all these items are capital-intensive and take some time (years) to complete and open after they have been approved and the time-consuming planning stages have been completed. Further, once the facilities have been created, it cannot be converted for other uses. An underutilized international airport will remain an underutilized airport. A hotel which is not in a condition to meet viable levels of occupancy cannot be used as an apartment house successfully. So, once development started, if demand has been overestimated a resort will find itself with substantial underutilized assets.

2. **Instability of Demand.** Tourism also involves instability of demand, creating problems in planning and increasing the business risks. This is due to several reasons. First, there are still seasonal variations in and high elasticity of demand. Secondly, there are the sudden, often unpredictable, impacts of external and environmental factors *viz.*, economic recession or boom, depress or increase demand. Sometimes, certain destinations go out of favour for political reasons. Sudden political changes in host countries can close or open frontiers.

3. **Seasonality of Demand.** Tourism is also a subject to seasonality of demand which may be because of habit, climate or tradition. Seasonal factors may also be caused by institutional factors which are not under the control of the customer. These are school holidays, factory or annual vacation periods of office. It may also be geared to specific events such as Christmas, the Salzburg or Bayrenth Music Festivals and carnival time in Rio.

4. **Elasticity of Demand.** The elasticity of demand in tourism takes place due to income and price elasticity. They are major contributors to instability of demand for tourism products. Income elasticity includes the changes that takes place in the volume of demand due to changes in income of the customers. Price elasticity explains the effect of any changes in price or demand. By and large, demand for tourism products is very responsive to changes in price and incomes. Tourism being considered as a non-essential discretionary consumption by most of the consumers, it does rate as high as other essential expenditure.

5. **Competition.** In tourism, direct competition is found between destinations and resorts and resorts and modes of transport. With distinctions, competition between resorts in the same country, region is strong, *viz.*, the wide choice of resorts of the Costa Brava and other 'Costas' of Spain, the French Riviera, the Italian Riviera, Greek Islands and North African coast etc.

A considerable degree of substitution is available with transport. For short and medium journeys, tourists may choose between air, sea, road or rail. Competition is also strong between airlines serving the same destinations with similar aircraft.

6. **Distribution.** In manufacturing, distribution involves the packing and packaging of the finished product and its shipment to the customer through different channels of distribution. In tourism the product is composed of different supply components. So distribution is concerned with taking the tourist to the product (resort).

   Prior to that there is the need to distribute all the information required by the potential customers to allow them to take decision in favour of the seller making the offering. At the last customer receives confirmation of the reservations. Thus, distribution takes into account the despatch of several paperwork. But the introduction of the computer has simplified this work.

7. **Other Characteristics.** A special characteristic lies in the fact that quality and service standards depend upon the availability of trained and experienced staff. They should be at handling customers efficiently and courteously. This is applicable to office staff as well as couriers and guides. Failure of it can damage the goodwill and image of the tour operator, travel agent, airline or hotel.

   Secondly, there must be 'complementarity' between the different enterprises in order to provide the tourism product and support facilities. Primary resources, *i.e.*, accommodation and transport, can only attract business if the support facilities such as airports, entertainment, etc., are there to back them up. Here a notable point is that there must be a good balance between primary and support resources. If the primary resources are inadequate overcrowding, overbooking to the environment take place and even the most attractive support facilities will be of little use.

Finally, the tourism demand and the attractiveness of a resort are influenced by external factors. Political instability, financial and currency uncertainties and labour unrest often cannot be predicted precisely in advance. Customer response depends on what other motivations are predominant.

TOURISM AND LEISURE

Leisure is a business of 20th century. Leisure and holidays as a contrasting programme to the industrial world have themselves become an industry. Industrial development which has brought us real social achievements and progress, improvements in living standards, higher disposable incomes, reduction in working hours of office/business, higher socio-economic development, demographic changes and increased spare hours (more free time) have led to more leisure time.

In many advanced countries, working hours have been reduced to forty a week. In the post-industrial society, the standard of living of the people will continue improving, generating opportunities and challenges for holiday travel.

Leisure time can be grouped under three categories: After work leisure time, weekend leisure and holiday. The first category of leisure is consumed in activities like watching TV, reading books or strolling. In case of weekend leisure, the two-day (Saturday and Sunday which are off days) weekend leisure is utilized by people for short trips, camping, hiking or just relaxing. This is possible in most advanced countries. In the third category of leisure people in tourism are mainly concerned. People accumulate vacation for one to four weeks and take one or two holiday trips a year.

There is a shift in attitudes towards leisure time. 1960's were known as the U.N. Development decade. Attention of governments and international agencies was focused on developing countries of the world. In the same time period the developed countries became increasingly pre-occupied with leisure and with their own enviroment.

Since the early 1970's there has been marked shift towards active Holidays. The wish to sleep, rest and do nothing was on the declining. In 1975 formation of Leisure Studies Association brought together Academicians, Researchers and Practitioners to discuss:

(i) Issues of Theory, Politics, Planning and Management of Leisure.

(ii) Leisure as a social institution, individual behaviour, or subjective experience, is a product of, and influenced by, more fundamental structures. 1980's four-week paid holidays have become universal. Efforts are to spend a minimum half of holidays time away from home. Efforts to spend more than one holidays away from home have been in practice.

(iii) It was realized that Leisure involves consideration of wide range of fundamental social and political issues.

WHY IS TOURISM GROWING

Tourism is growing due to several economic, cultural and technological factors. Principal among them are:

1. **Increased Leisure.** In most countries of the world how ever, it is now up to two to three weeks a year. This has led to extensive holiday travel.

2. **Industrial Development.** Development coupled with pollution and overcrowding in the cities has led to the people's search for sun, sand and the pure mountain air during annual holidays.

3. **Transport Revolution.** The development of air transportation has resulted in unbelievable low air fares. This has democratized the holiday market. In developed industrial societies, more people can now afford a holiday outside their own country.

4. **Cultural Education.** The spread of education worldwide has led to a natural curiosity among the people in order to travel and discover how others live and work.

5. **Standards of Living.** The rapid economic development has raised standards of living in developed countries with handful income. A part of this income is now spent on travel for fun.

WHY PEOPLE TRAVEL

During the course of history, motivation for most travel has been fairly clear-religion, economic gain, war, escape, migration. What is left is travel for pleasure, which is the most common form of travel in the modern world. The following may be listed as motivations to travel:

(a) To see how people in other countries live, work and play.

(b) To enjoy scenic beauty and cultural sights.

(c) To gain a better understanding of what goes on elsewhere.

(d) To attend special events/festivals/cultural functions.

(e) To get away from the routine of life.

(f) To go to places from where one's family came from.

(g) To visit places where one's family or friends lived in the past.

(h) To have a good time away from home.

(i) To have a romantic or exotic experience.

(j) To enjoy sun, dry climate or to swim on a beach. In other words, to improve health.

(k) To avoid unpleasant weather, for instance, cold winter or very hot summer.

(1) To participate in sports like swimming, skiing, fishing or sailing.

(m) To do in conformity what your friends have done already.

(n) To boast to one's friends what they have not been able to do.

(o) To go to places where living is less expensive than at home.

(p) To undertaken adventure in new areas with new people.

(q) To participate in history by visiting ancient temples, monuments, or historical sites.

TYPES OF TOURISM

Tourism is of two types—domestic and international. Domestic tourism is an integral part of the tourism industry. In a vast country like India, rich in divergent socio-economic and cultural patterns, the promotion of domestic tourism would indirectly encourage 'unity in diversity'. Thus, development of domestic tourism has broader extra-commercial justifications. Now, greater emphasis is placed on domestic tourism in the interest of coordinated economic development of a country or its national integration. It is more and more recognized that a wide, prosperous and active domestic tourism base forms a firm foundation for the healthy growth of international tourism with multiple benefits to the nation. The growth and size of domestic tourism would depend on the per capita income, size of population, rate of growth, cost of travel and existence of national attractions of a country. The increasing sophistication of the domestic tourism industry automatically contributes to the infrastructure required for international tourism and thus domestic tourism becomes a promoter of the later. It is also noted that less expensive international or regional tourists can be directed to utilize facilities normally available to the affluent domestic tourists. Both the traditional and the modern tourism facilities benefit from growth and establish economic and social bridges in many spheres.

In domestic tourism people travel from their normal domicile to other areas in their own country. The tourist activity of residents of a country within their own country is described as internal or domestic tourism. Since the travel takes place within the limits of the boundaries of a country, the various travel formalities are not to be observed as in case of International tourism they are necessary. The barriers of currency exchange, language, passports, visas, health documents, etc., are not to be faced by domestic tourist.

With reference to international travel, a foreign tourist has been defined by the UN. Statistical Commission as "a person who travels to a country other than that in which he has his usual residence, the main purpose of whose visit is other than the exercise of an activity remunerated from within the country visited and is staying for a period of at least one night but not more than one year in that country. Those visitors who do not stay in the country of visit for at least a night are called "Excursionists". India has adopted these definitions with certain modifications to fulfil local requirements. Thus those visitors holding foreign passports are considered as tourists in India.

The evolution of international tourism in India has been faster than the global average mainly due to low base and increased awareness in overseas markets. The foreign tourist arrivals in India (excluding the nationals of Pakistan and Bangladesh) increased from 16,829 in 1951 to 11,63,774 in 1987 which registered an overall growth rate of about 12.5 per cent. The average annual rate of growth during the period from 1951 to 1960 was 24.7 per cent, registering growth rate 8.6 per cent during 1960-70 and 11.0 per cent during 1970-80. However, during the period 1980-87, the rate of growth declined to 5.5 per cent. The period also recorded wide fluctuations in tourist arrivals with growth rates varying from 5.6 per cent to 29.1 per cent.

The most substantive benefit of international tourist inflow is the foreign exchange earning by the country. Over the years this benefit has significantly increased and is now comparable to some of the merchandise exports. In less than a decade and a half, the earnings have gone up from Rs. 32 crores in 1971-72 to about Rs. 1440 crores in 1986-87. Despite this impressive growth, the country's foreign exchange earnings from this sector account for only 0.32 per cent of the world tourist receipts.

❐

3

Historical Perspective of Tourism

The Early history of tourism is the story of development of the mobility of man. Both in the pre-historic era and later, man searched for things he wanted and he travelled for food, shelter or just for curiosity. Adam and Eve could be called the first 'tourists'. In due course, largescale movements were also caused by changes of climate, dwindling food supplies or hostile invaders. The Aryans left their homes in Central Asia due to climatic change leading to dwindling food supplies.

Due to absence of roads or other transport facilities, travel had to be the hard way and this led slowly to development of land routes, as also river and sea navigation. Understandably, travel in the distent past was not a thing of pleasure as is the case now. Trade and commerce was however, the strongest force in the ancient past: it made people travel to distant lands in order to seek fortunes gradually, opening of the new trade routes gave a big boost to travel. Today, too the bulk of the tourist traffic is generated by trade and commercial links. However, the persons who travelled for the love of travel and wanderlust or for increasing their knowledge by visiting other places and countries, were a category apart. They were the 'true tourists' and that is how tourism, as it is understood today, was born.

In ancient Greece, there is evidence of considerable tourist traffic, particularly for the Olympic games and other festivals. Such travel sometimes evoked adverse response and some of the Greek thinkers like Plato did not view these travels with much favour. On the contrary, the contribution made by forgners and visitors to the prospertity of Athens was recognised in the 4th Century B.C. and xenophon, the author of the Athensian Constitution, was favourably disposed towards tourism. He went to the extent for recommending construction of hotels for visitors at public expenses. Tourist traffic was greatly encouraged under the Roman Empire, because of excellent surface transportation system. Romans used to travel up to a hundred miles a day using relays of horses, furnished from rest posts five to six miles apart. They travelled to see the temples in the Mediterranean sea and the famous pyramidas of Egypt. They also journeyed to medicinal baths called 'spas' and seaside resorts. Some of these sea-resorts had developed all the attributes of present day tourist haunts and attracted hordes of people of different walks of life. One of these resorts called 'Baiae' (in the Bay of Naples) with its mild climate, luxuriant vegetation and sulphur springs established for itself a preeminent position for over 400 years as a tourist paradise. Tourist traffic was also greatly encouraged under the Roman Empire because of sea communications and conditions of peace. Some Roman cargo ships carried a few passengers private vessels could be marvellously luxurious. The vessel that carried the beautiful queen Cleopatra to meet mark antony reportedly had billowing scarlet silk sails, silver tipped oars, decks draped with royal purple cloth.

The fall of the Roman Empire in the fifth century a was great setback for pleasure travel in Europe. Also with the decline of the Roman Empire because of in-built causes, came a sharp decline in trade and commerce.

The Renaissance aroused a new spirit of enquiry. Travel became the means of acquiring culture in Europe. Francis Bacon, on of the greatest representatives of the spirit of Renaissance epitomized travel thus; "Travel in the younger sort is part of education; in the older a part of experience." The tradition of the grand tour which started in the 17th century by the aristocracy of Europe was more firmly established in the 18th and the 19th centuries by the emergence of an affluent mercantile class. Another by-product of the Renaissance was the spirit of adventure and discovery as the new motivations for travel.

But until the First World War (1914-18), travel was still the privilege of a small segment of society. One of the early sociologists, Thornstein Veble, called it the 'leisure class' in his classic work. Theory of the Leisure Class published in 1899. Probably, this was the first time that leisure was linked with propensity to travel. The first World War kept the people cabined and confined for four years. As a reaction, there was an outtbrust of travel in the inter-war years. This was the beginning of travel for pleasure and of the transformation of travel into 'tourism'. A great recovery came about in 1937 after the Great Depression of the thirties and a new 'boom' was on the way. In post-World War II period, tourism traffic reached a new 'high'.

The most significant development of the twentieth century tourism has been the growth in air travel since 1930 and the post-1939 era brought in improved, larger and faster flying machines covering not only the transatlantic routes, but biggest step forward in the growth of 'world tourism'. The aircraft did for international tourism what the railways did for domestic tourism and tourist traffic reached dimensions which far surpassed any known previously.

Saga of the growth tourism until today is only a chapter in the life of world tourism and, no doubt, the future of tourism remains assured as a preferred human activity.

Tourism industry is a class by itself, being a significant part of the 'leisure industry'. Its several characteristics distinguish it from other types of industry. It differs from other types of industry in following respects:

1. Unlike other industry tourism involves movement of people and of goods. The industry is essentially a dynamic one. It is susceptible to subjective considerations such as ideas and attitudes and the likes and dislikes of its customers. Political unrest and economic instability caused by inflation and currency fluctuations can damage it. The tourism industry must be prepared to show a much greater degree of sensitivity and willingness to adjust to new conditions than it has done in the past.

TABLE

Year	*International Tourist Arrivals (in millions)*	*World Tourist Receipt (in Million US dollars)*
1980	284.3	97.00
1981	287.8	97.7
1982	287.5	94.6
1983	293.9	96.2
1984	300.0	100.0

Source: Department of Tourism, Ministry of Tourism and Civil Aviation, Government of India.

2. Normally, the products to be consumed are transported to the door of a consumer. In contrast to this in a tourist trade the consumer is required to move (flow) to the product (stock). It also helps in the sale of product which could never have been exported, *e.g.* a view of Taj Mahal, natural scenery of a region, the architectural museums and monuments.

3. The various industries comprising the tourist industry are primarily concerned with 'people'. Indeed, one of the most important motivations in generating international travel. is 'meeting other people' or 'seeing how other people live'. Tourism, therefore, can bring benefits other than the more obvious and direct economic gains of contributing to the balance of payments, increasing national income and providing employment opportunities. Although, these are not always possible to quantify, there are considerable social benefits in the contacts made through visitors who develop new taste and become interested in new activities. Thus, it is highly essential that while promoting tourism emphasis should be on 'people'.

4. Tourism thrives on the natural values. But the number of such natural values are fixed and immobile. This imposes a constraint on the development of tourism.

5. Tourism being a service industry, its product is of a perishable nature Prof. Howard Meek, former Dean of School of Hotel Administration, Cronell University, has very rightly observed:

   "There is no commodity more perishable than a hotel room. If it is not sold tonight, it can never be sold.

   To this is added the rigidity caused by heavy investment in fixed like roads, accommodation and transportation. In the short run, the supply of this infrastructure is inelastic. Further, the 'underutilisation' of some of these resources poses a serious problem. Tourist trade is also not very responsive to price changes. Dissemination of information regarding price changes also takes a long time and is not very effective.

6. The spread of tourism among the sector of the population, among the lower income strata has necessitated a change in the marketing strategy and in the education of modern management techniques to improve efficiency and the optimum utilization of the infrastructure so that tourist expenses can be reduced to minimum. It is no longer rewarding to offer sophisticated services to each individual tourist. The tourist attractions should be presented in such a way that a group of tourists can enjoy them collectively. Further, they must be within the reach of a common man. Emphasis from palacious hotel and transport must be shifted in favour of low tariff and Janta hotels and cheaper transport facilities.

7. A few decades ago tourism was confined to rich and adventurous people. It was considered to be a luxury. Since the early 1950s it has developed into a mass migration,

the equivalent to the movement of the entire population of a large countty. A survey carried out by the Indian Statistical Institute during the period from 1st April. 1982 to 31st March, 1983 of the foreign tourists indicates that of those spending the largest sums on their visit to India, more came from the lower income group then the upper as is evident from Table 3.

8. The tourist industry is highly susceptible to 'seasonality'. It is governed both by the climatic conditions prevailing in the tourist's home countty and those prevailing in the tourist receiving country. India, along with other tropical countries, receives the largest number of visitors during the winter months because of the unfavourable climate in summer. We do not attract many of the tourists who take their vacation during the month from March to June because they are uncomfortable (See Table 4) Kashmir valley, however, is an exception to this.

   Seasonality of tourist industry affects the 'utilization-rate' of infrastructure. This unsatisfactory situation could be improved by staggering of holidays, the promotion of second and out of season holidays at reduced prices, and such other measures. Thus, the promotional efforts are to be directed in such a way that tourist traffic would flow in regularly throughout the year.

TABLE 3

Precentage Distribution of Tourist According to Annual Individual Income

Annual Individual Income	*Per centage of foreign tourist*
(1)	*(2)*
(a) Rs. 50,000 or less	31.5
(b) Above Rs. 50,000 and upto Rs. 1,00,000	13.5
(c) Above Rs. 1,00,000 and upto Rs. 1,50,000	11.2

(1)	*(2)*
(d) Above Rs. 1,50,000 and upto Rs. 2,00,000	10.3
(e) Above Rs. 2.00,000 and upto Rs. 3,00,000	11.5
(f) Above Rs. 3,00,000 and upto Rs. 4,00,000	8.2
(g) Above Rs. 4,00,000	13.8

Source: Indian Tourist Statistics, Department of Tourism and Civil Aviation, Government of India. 1984.

TABLE 4

Seasonal Pattern of Foreign Tourists in India

Year	*Jan-March (I Quarter) Oct.-Dec. (IV Quarter) % (Winter Months)*	*Apr. June (H Quarter) July-Sept. (III Quarter) % (Summer Months)*	*Total*
1971	52.09	47.91	100
1972	55.47	44.53	100
1973	56.67	43.38	100
1978	56.1	43.9	100
1979	55.3	44.7	100
1980	56.5	44.7	100
1981	56.3	43.7	100
1982	55.6	44.4	100
1983	57.4	42.6	100
1984	55.6	44.4	100

Source: Indian Tourist Statistics. Department of Tourism and Civil Aviation, Government of India.

9. The industry is marked by a widely differing economic performance; tourism is dependent upon so many varied activities that a situation can arise "where weak links in the chain of services and facilities adversely affect the progress of otherwise healthy sector of the industry".

10. The industry is primarily a service industry and a large proportion of these activity engaged in it find employment in tertiary occupation.

11. Tourism is a complex industry. It is an amalgamation of several phenomena and relationships.

12. The above complexity arises from the movement of people to various destinations and their stay in these destinations. Thus in the former case, there is a dynamic element the journey and in the latter case there is a static element—the stay. Again, the movement of the people is temporary and of short-term character.

13. Tourism is largely non- remunerative strictly from monetary point of view. There is no intention to take up employment and there is no idea for business or vocation.

14. Tourism is a multi-dimensional activity. There are many and varied activities which make their own separate and individual contribution. These activities, although separate, are inter-dependent which require cooperative efforts and common policies.

In recent years a new trend is visible in tourism, which is known as 'mobile camper-tourism' or open airhotels. This form of tourism is most popular in certain European countries which provides a form of supplementary accommodation. These. 'camps' are usually located within the cities in open spaces. They provide facilities for parking, tent-pitching, water, electricity, toilet etc. They are equipped to receive mobile form of accommodations used by tourists. As such, they are within the towns and therefore, it is easy also for the tourists. In some camps, there are cooking facilities also.

The most numerous and best camping sites are found in the developed countries. Camping is only beginning in the developing countries. However, it takes the form of wilderness camping where there are no facilities and the campers themselves have to take care of all of their needs. Camping, as originally practised by hikers on foot is increasingly giving way to car camping.

COMPOSITION OF TOURIST INDUSTRY

It may be noted that the tourist industry represents a small part of the total 'leisure industry'. All told, it is a complex industry of many segments ranging from a giant airline and a huge hotel to a husband and wife guide service of only two employees. As is clear from table the tourist industry comprises the following aspects.

Accommodation and Catering. This is one of the most important segments of the tourist service needed at the destination. The various types of accommodation facilities used by the tourist are hotels, supplementary accommocation, stay with friends and relatives and other private accommodation or their own means of accommodation like caravans and tents.

Transportation. Tourists require transport in order to visit the different tourist throughout the country. It is primary service needed by tourists in order to reach the destination. The passenger transport may be categorised as public or private, inland and international air and surface etc.

Tourist Attraction. Indian tourism has so far been mainly based on culture. Due to the change in the outlook of the tourist, there is an urgent need for the pleasure tourism.

Entertainment. Development of various entertainment forms such as provision of restaurants, music and dance, theatres and shopping is an integral part of the tourism industry. In addition to monuments and memorials, arts and crafts, fairs and festivals etc. the tourists are also interested in a variety of entertainment.

Facilities. It includes house procedures which either help or hinder tourists within the country including all the regulations they have to comply with an departure. The easier the destination country makes it for tourist to arrive, move around freely and deport comfortably the better are its chances of attracting tourists.

Travel Agents and Tour Operations. Travel agents perform an intermediary function between the tourists and the providers of transport and accommodation in particular. The tour operators carryout an organising function in which thy combine the individual component of a holiday into a product. This product is marketed on their account and risk.

Types and Forms of Tourism. The different types and forms of tourism can be discussed under the following rubrics:

Domestic Tourism. In domestic tourism, people travel from their normal domicile to other areas in their own country. No documentation, passport or visas are required.

Ninety per cent of the world tourist movements according to WTO, are domestic. Domestic tourist movements in many countries are twenty five times more than international tourist movements. WTO has estimated that seventy five to eighty per cent of all tourist expenditure is incurred within the traveller's own country. These figures vary widely; ninety four per cent in the US, seventy five per cent for UK, and forty four per cent for Switzerland. According to WTO estimate, the domestic tourist movements worldwide in 1983 were 3000 million. Prof. Wilford Owen, an American, has developed an approach to travel within a country by a system of index called, "passenger mobility". The index is an average of the following:

* Passenger miles per capita
* Passenger car per capita
* Rail lines for 10,000 population
* Surface highways per 100 Square miles
* Surface highways per 10,000 population

The index is based on 100, France being the normative country with 100. It is an indication or the mobility within a country and shows the degrees to which transportation has developed and also gives an idea of the degree of development tourism in a country.

Today, countries like Mexico, Brazil, Malaysia, Thailand have certainly moved out of their 1981 categories. So has France.

The International Union of Official Tourist Organization (IUOTO) General Policy and the United Nations Conference International Travel and Tourism (Rane, 1963) have placed special emphasis on the development of domestic tourism.

International Tourism. Due to the different currencies. international tourism has repercussion on the balance of payments as such country has to balance its transaction with the rest of the world. There are also obstacles put by the authorities for crossing the national frontiers, with the result, there is a need for documentation, passports, visa and other conditions of entry and movement. All this regulates the flow of the tourists.

Thus, in economic terms, the domestic tourism stands on a different footing from international tourism, on the following grounds.

Notably, now-a-days, due to improvement in the language skills, currency and customs and the growing free movement of people between developed countries, the distinction between domestic and international tourism is diminishing.

Domestic Tourism	*International Tourism*
1. Earning from home tourism cannot claim any extra weightage in investment planning.	Earning from international tourism in the form of foreign exchange claim extra weight age in investment planning.
2. Demand for home can easily be regulated.	It is not possible or regulater the demand for international tourism.
3. The demand for home tourism reflects the international distribution of income.	It does not reflect the international distribution of income.

TABLE 5

Index of Passenger Mobility of Selected Countries-1981 (Inded in France=100)

Developing Countries					
2-5	5-10	10-15	15-20	Over 20	
Ethiopia	UAR	Peru	Algeria	Sri Lanka	(22)
Nigeria	Ghana	Paraguary	Malaysia	Mexico	(23)
Iran	Burma	India	Brazil	Chile	(36)
	Philippines				
	Syria				
	Thailand				
	Ecuador				
	Colombo				
	Indonesia				
	Pakistan				
	Developed countries				
40-60	60-80	90-100	Over 100		
Japan	Netherlands	France (100)	USA	(147)	
Italy	Norway	UK	Canada	(149)	
	Finland	West Germany			
	Austria				

Individual Group and Mass Tourism. It may also be useful to define individual and, group tourism. In the former case, the tourist moves about individually or as a member of a group, irrespective of the way travel or stay is arrange. It is further classified into *(a)* independent travel and *(b)* inclusive tours. In the case of independent tour, transport, accommodation and other elements of travel are arranged separately either by the tourist himself or by his travel agent. The technical word for such a traveller is FIT-free independent traveller. As a member of the inclusive group, the tourist buys a trip, for which he is unable to distinguish the prepaid cost of his fare, accommodation and other elements. Inclusive tours are also called package tours.

Another term mass tourism refers to the participation of a large number of people in tourism which is generally a notable feature of developed countries. Travel for holidays is part of their life style. In fact, the introduction of paid holidays can truly be associated with development of modern mass tourism. India for instance, does not have mass tourism nor it seems to be possible in the near future, due to absence of disposable incomes with a vast majority of the population.

Social Tourism. Social (Subsidised) tourism has also gained greater importance in recent years. Although there is as yet no agreed definition of social tourism, there has been considerable study on the subject. Dr. W. Hunziker at the Second Congress of Social Tourism held at Vienna and Salzburg in Austria in May 1959 proposed the following definition:

> "Social tourism is a type of tourism practiced by low income group and which is rendered possible and facilitated by entirely separate and therefore easily recognizable service.

From this definition of social tourism the following elements become clear. The first is the idea of the limited means. Manual workers are thus included in the scope of social tourism. Secondly social, tourism is subsidised. Thirdly, it involves travel outside the normal place of residence, preferable to a different environment.

Thus, 'social tourism' as we understand today, owes its origin to annual paid holiday. Social tourism is a practice more prevalent in

Eastern European countries. Soviet citizens coming to India and other friendly countries for tourism fall in this category .

FORMS OF TOURISM

The main purpose of travel determines the form of travel and tourism could be classified accordingly. Though, motivations may vary and travel-desire may have been activated by a great diversity of human wishes and mental attitudes, the purpose and resultant action could fall within the following forms:

Rest and Relaxation Tourism. This type of tourism includes tourists who wish to combine physical and mental relaxation with the temporary change of their location to get away from a society of tension.

Cultural Tourism. The cultural tourism envisages travel for purposes of widening one's knowledge about other places and people, their ways of life, their culture and includes journeys to places of art and heredity treasures, religious shrines and other civilization. Contemporary developments in various spheres of human activity and progress in scientific, technological, educational, sociological and other fields are also a few may combine rest and relaxation, with culture as the basic purpose of their travel.

Sports Tourism. Travel for participation in sports activities including local, regional or international events, is an important aspect of tourism. The great variety of sports activities widens the scope for tourist and participation.

Social and Sociological Tourism. Social tourism relates to journeys undertaken by people of limited financial means, whose travel is subsidised and for whom special concession and facilities are provided.

Sociological tourism on the other hand, deals with journeys undertaken to visit friends, acquaintances or relations as well as journeys for reasons of social prestige or as a status symbol. This last factor has considerable importance in many societies, particularly the more affluent ones.

Convention/Business Tourism. Travel for trade or professional reasons, though not strictly a tourist journey, does involves use of tourist goods and services and expenditure in other countries. Journeys to fairs, trade exhibitions, technical seminars, conferences and conventions, involve tourist and social events like sightseeing, entertainment, shopping and as such, result in tourist expenditure which accrue to the host countries.

These conferenes and conventions provide opportunities for considerable publicity for a country and its facilities and became a vanguard for a regular tourist flow.

Political Tourism. This form of travel envisages participation in special events or big national celebrations and the consequential festivals atmosphere generated by such occurrences. Typical examples are the wedding of the British Prince of Wales or coronation of the Queen. Economic and political conferences or commemorations of anniversaries of celebrities attract larger number of tourists; an interesting example is the rush to Elba on the commemoration of Nepoleaon's 200th birthday in 1969. Affiliation to different ideologies may also prove a magnet for travel.

In this connection, another form of travel, which though not strictly tourist in nature, has attracted attention is government travel. According to one estimate, nearly 6.8 per cent of total travel in 1981 worldwide was accounted for by government officials. In reality. this form of travel also consumers goods and services for tourists and as such, should be treated as a form of political tourism.

In classifying the above forms of tourism, the intention is to explain the basic purpose of travel for guidance but it may be noted that there is, as such, no official sanction behind this classification. On entering a country, where immigration cards are used, the purpose of the visit is generally indicated as business or business-cum-tourism or tourism or returning resident. The first three, as will be seen, are included in the above classification.

Motivations Behind Tourism

Having referred to the form of tourism and classification according to the purpose of travel, it may now be of interest to study what motivates travel and what stimulates people to choose certain attractions and activities rather than others. MCIntosh has stated that basic travel motivators may be grouped into the following four categories:

Physical Motivators. These are related to physical relaxation and rest, sporting activities and specific medical treatment; all are connected with the individual's bodily health and well being.

Cultural Motivators. These motivators are connected with the individual's desire to travel in order to learn about other countries, their people and their cultural heritage expressed in art, music, literature, folklore etc.

Interpersonal Motivators. These are related to a desire to visit relatives, friends or to escape from one's family, workmates or neighbours, or simply to escape from the routine of everyday life.

Status and Prestige Motivators. Finally, there are status and prestige motivators which are identified with the needs of personal esteem and persomal developments. Surely, these are related to travel for business or professional interests, for the purpose of education or the pursuit of hobbies.

Apart from the above principal motivating forces, there are other derivative factors also behind the growing significance of tourism.

Pleasure. Getting away from all the humbug of everyday life is perhaps the most importance motive these days. An individual likes to have fun, excitement and good time whenever possible. Various brochures and folders particularly emphasis the pleasure aspect of the holidays and travel. The latest survey undertaken by the Indian

Statistical Institute during the period from 1 April 1982 to 31 March 1983 of the foreign tourists indicate that 43.0 per cent of the tourists visited India for the purpose of 'pleasure'.

Business or Professional. "Business tourism" has gained great importance in recent years. Attending conventions and conferences related to the professions, industry or commerce or to some organisation to which the individual belongs has become very popular. The above-mentioned study of Indian Statistical Institute reveals that as much as 25.2 per cent tourists visited India for the purpose of "business".

Visiting Friends and Relations. This includes visiting one's relatives and friends, meeting new people and seeking new friendships. The Indian Statistical Institute survey mentioned above shows that 11.2 per cent tourists visited India for the purpose of meeting friends and their relations.

Study and Curiosity. Another category of tourists has study and curiosity motives behind the visit to other places. For them tourism provides an opportunity to widen horizons. In the present

TABLE 6

Percentage Distribution of Tourists According to Purpose of Visit

Purpose of Visit	*Per centage of the Total*
(a) Pleasure	43.0
(b) Business	25.2
(c) Visiting Friends and Relations	11.2
(d) Study	4.6
(e) Pilgrimage	3.1
(f) Others	12.9

Source: Indian Tourist Statistics, 1984, Government of India.

day world technological developments in the area of mass media have made it possible for people to read, see and hear about different places. International events like Olympic Games, Asian Games, national celebrations, exhibitions, special festivals etc. attract thousands of tourists. The above survey records that 4.6 per cent foreign tourists visit India for this purpose.

Pilgrimage. Travel for pilgrimage has been taking place since ancient time. A large number of people have been making pilgrimage to scared religious or holy places. This practice is widespread in many parts of the world. In the Christian world, for instance, a visit to Jerusalem or the Vatican is considered to be very auspicious. In the Arab-Moslem World, the pilgrimage to Mecca or some other holy centres is considered to be a great Act of faith. In India there are many pilgrimage centres and holy places of all the major religions of the world where every year a large number of pilgrims from all over the world come. According to the ISI of 1982-83, 3.1 per cent tourists visited India for the purpose of 'pilgrimage'.

In short, one can say that today's tourism combines all the historical factors of motivations for travel which have accumulated from time immemorial.

The main findings of the Indian Statistical Institute, Foreign Tourist Survey during the period from 1 April 1982 to March 1983, regarding percentage distribution of travel motivators are given in the Table 6.

Why is Tourism Growing

The phenomenal growth in tourism. during the last thirty five years has been due to several economic, cultural and technical factors. Principal among these are:

Industrial Development and Urbanisation. The industrial revolution emitting great factory towns is responsible for the change in the economic and social system. The working class is in the beginning burdened by long working hours and poor working and living conditions. Sudden concentration of population in towns and cities and every-increasing urbanisation, have created unhealthy conditions. Thus, large-scale industrial development coupled with pollution and overcrowding in the cities has led to the people's search for sun, sand, unpolluted atmosphere, sea and the pure mountain air

TABLE 7

	Average increase per Decade	*Per cent*
Per capita real income	1900 - 1950	19
Total leisure during	1900 - 1960	20
Population during	1900 - 1960	15
Travel per capita during	1930 - 1960	25

Source: Glawsen. Maria, Economic and outdoor Recreation Baltimore.

during annual holidays. This type of movement is generally from north to south. The Mediterranean are benefiting most from the above mentioned form of tourism.

Education, Culture and International Understanding. The spread of education worldwide led to a natural curiosity among the people to travel and discover how others live and work. One of the world's great historian. Arnold J. Toynbee. has said:

> Since 1911, I have always travelled as often and as long as far as I have been able to. This is the one activity to which I have given precedence over my otherwise paramount activity of writing. Whenever, I have had a chance of intellectually profitable travel, my writing has had to wait. As I see it, travel ought to come before every-thing else for a student of human affairs. To meet someone face to face and see a landscape with one's own eyes is worth more than volumes of letter-press, photographs and maps-glimpses of the world are gleanings of priceless value.

Thus, it is rightly said that "Tourism involves education without class-rooms. Indian culture has also given a great fillip to modern tourism in the country. Cultural tourism has a speical place in India because of its past civilization. Several market surveys of Indian tourism over the last fifteen years show that the most important motivation of 70 per cent visitors to India has been to see country with an ancient civilization, rich in monuments and temples, educational institutions, arts and culture.

Our historical and archaeological monuments continue to be the biggest draw in attracting international tourists. This fact has been confirmed by a survey 1968 as also by the Tourist Reaction Pattern and Reactions Surveys conducted by the Department of Tourism in 1968-69 and in 1972-73. The latter survey placed curiosity (42 per cent) as the major factors influencing travel to India.

Rising Standards of Living. Amongst the economic forces which have greatly influenced the growth of tourism, higher standards of living. the increase in leisure as a result of industrialisation, changes in the demographic picture (resulting from falling death rates and higher expectancy of life), the shift from rural to urban areas. need special mention. The above point would be clear from the figures of showing the average increase per decade per cent in the USA, a highly industrialised country.

In some of the industrialised countries the increase in leisure time has today posed a serious problem as well as opportunity. "Saving the customer time is only one of the marketing opportunities posed by the trend. Another one is to create goods and services for utilising his time. "Nelson Foots pointed out that General Electric has its feet in both doors: "Time gained dishwashers allows more hours at TV. It may be stated that in keeping with Engel's law the percentage spept on travel will tend to increase with a rise in the standard of living.

Revolution in Transport. A rapid increase in automobile through the industrial world, the fast expansion of the aircraft-fleets resulting in unbelievable low airfares. of the worldwide availability of rental cars and the inter-connection of all the sectors of travel industry through modem communication systems have improved transportation facilities and tour packages.

Publicity and Promotion. News publicity is also very effective in creating travel. Newspapers, radios,. televisions, films and magazines are excellent means for promotion of travel trade. Most governments are actively promoting tourism like any other product. Some UN agencies like UNDP, ILO and WTO are assisting the developing countries in various ways to develop tourist facilities, tourist infrastructure and training programme.

All told, the increasing disposable income, rapid urbanisation, increased leisure time with shorter working hours and longer paid holidays, more advanced education, and the opportunities due to the increasing mobility brought about by the motor car and the aeroplanes, have increased the growth-promoting factors of tourism.

Limits to Travel. Many people do not travel and many do not travel extensively. A number of psychological studies have been made in this sphere. In most of these studies, the limited or barriers to travel have been divided into five broad categories.

Cost. Consumers operate within monetary constraints and travel has to compete with other attractions of funds. According to a study, in the United States along over fifty per cent of the people cannot undertake travel due to high cost. In a study conducted by Dr., J.M.S. Negi. 62 per cent of the respondents cited expenses as the reason for not taking a trip.

Lack of Time. This is characteristic of those who are not in a position to leave their business or profession to take time off from work.

Physical Limitations. Poor health and physical limitations keep many persons, particularly oldsters, at home.

Family Obligations. Parents of young children cannot travel because of family obligations and inconvenience in travelling.

Lack of Interest. Unawareness of travel destinations which would bring adequate satisfactions for potential travellers is also a major barrier.

SCOPE OF TOURISM IN INDIA

India has great tourism potential, due to its unique cultural and natural attractions. It has an ancient civilisation at is preserved in its religion, customs traditions and architecture. It has a distinctive culture and a way of life. It abounds in temples that would certainly interest many visitors. Its traditional dances and music are loved by all. It has varied and, spectacular scenery including snowcapped mountains glaciers, geysers, boiling pools, unique glow worm caverns. beautiful lakes, fine beaches and appealing mountains, with exciting wild-life, lovely deserts, a manifestation of history which goes back to more than five hundred years.

This has resulted in historical monuments of great antiquity like stupas of Sanchi, of beautiful monument of love—Taj Mahal and many, other illustrations in art and architecture of fabulous temples, mosques and churches. In this region are represented the great faiths of the world-Hinduism, Buddhism, Islam. This region offers to the tourists the most exciting costumes, foods and festivals. A singular asset of Indian tourism is that there is no shortage of raw materials. India's unique variety of cultural and natural attractions constitute the resources for this industry.

India is the second most populous and sixth largest country in the world. Lying entirely in the northern hemisphere, it covers an area of 32,87.782 sq. kms. The much vast and far more varying landscape of India, stretching spatially from 8°4" to 37°6" north latitudes and 68°7" to 97°25 longitude, and spanning 5,000 years of history has much to offer to the tourist world. It measures about 3.214 kms. from north to south between the extreme latitudes and about 2.933 kms. from East to West between the extreme longitudes. It has a land frontier of 15.200 kms and a coastal line of 6100.

India is an incredibly big country surrounded by deep oceans on three sides and protected by the great Himalayas on the North. It is joined in the North by China and Nepal a series of mountain ranges separate it from Burma. In the East lies Bangladesh in the North are situated Pakistan and Afghanistan. In the south the country tapers off into the Indian Ocean between the Arabian Sea on the West and the Bay of Bengal on the East. The Gulf of Manuar and Palk Strait separate India from Srilanka. The Lakshadweep, Minicoy and Amindivi Islands in the Arabian Sea and Andaman and Nicobar Islands in the Bay of Bengal are parts of the territory of India. Thus, India is cutoff from the main land of Asia by the Himalayan mountains the highest mountain range in the world. Going from West to East along the country's land frontiers are Pakistan. Turkistan, China and Burma. In the South the country is surrounded by the Arabian Sea in the West, the Indian Ocean in the South and Bay of Bengal in the East. Geographically, India consists of three distinct unit:

(a) Himalayas and their associate group of mountains.

(b) The Indo-Gangetic Plains that runs parallel to the Southern foot hills of the range.

(c) Southern peninsula or Deccan Plateau that occupies most of the central and southern parts of the sub-continent.

The peculiarity of the main land is that the Himalayas range is dramatically high, the Indo-Gangetic Plain is a nice plain with hardly a variation in altitudes from sea to shining sea, and the southern peninsula is a fairly high plateau with coastal strips.

The climate of India may be broadly described as tropical monsoon type. There are four seasons in India: *(i)* winter season (Jan.-Feb.); *(ii)* Hot weather season. summer (March-May); *(iii)* rainy season. south-western monsoon period (June-Sept) and *(iv)* post monsoon period. known as north east monsoon period in the so ther peninsula.

From the Himalayas to Kanyakumari the climate varies and so the People their customs and traditions. A bracing could sweeps over most of India from November to February followed by brief spring.

Then comes the hot weather interrupted by the powerful thunder of the monsoon in June, July and August. The clear cool weather arrives again and moves gradually eastward and southwards. The northern part of India lies in the temperate zone. This means that there is more seasonal variation in temperature in the northern part and that the winter are much colder there. In the rest of the country the temperature ranges from warm to hot all year round. April and May are the hottest months. In the inland areas like Rajasthan temperature sometimes goes up to 120 degrees fahrenheit during these months.

The amount of humidity and rainfall also varies a great deal throughout India. The Malabar Coast and the area around Calcutta in the West Bengal receive the heaviest rainfall and have the most humid weather. There are areas which get more than 80 inches rainfall in a year. Nearly all the rain falls during the rainy season. India's prevailing wind the monsoon is responsible for the distinct rainy and dry season. In summer it travels northward and from the Indian Ocean bearing moisture. In winter it travel southward from Siberia and is dry by the time it reaches India.

The rivers in India may be classified as *(i)* Himalayan rivers. *(ii)* Deccan rivers *(iii)* coastal rivers and *(iv)* rivers of the inland drainage basin. The Himalayan rivers are generally snowfed and have continuous flow throughout the year. The Deccan rivers are generally rainfed and therefore fluctuate in the volumes. The coastal streams, special of the West Coast are short in length and have limited catchment areas. The streams of the inland drainage basin of Western Rajasthan are few and far between. The Ganga basin is the largest in India. The Ganga has two main head waters in the Himalayas-the Bhagirathi and the Alaknanda—the former arising from the Gangotri Glacier at Gaumukh. The Ganga is joined by a number of Himalayan rivers as Jamuna Ghagra, Gandak and the Kosi. The Chief rivers of the Deccan are the Mahanadi, the Godavari the Krishna. The Tungabhadra and the Cauvery.

India is more remarkable for her extreme diversity of physical features. Its population is a veritable museum of races representing almost all ethnic groups of the world with their characteristic features. The discoveries of Harappa culture in the early part of this century has placed India on the map of early culture comparable in many of its characteristics to the contemporary civilisations of Egypt and Sumar. The decline of civilisation and the rise of the Aryans may be considered as the turning point of the Indian Geography. Nature and Geography both have made India one of the most attractive tourist countries of the world. It offers every thing in a rich variety-mountains and hills, valleys, highest peaks, sea beaches, landscape, scenic beauty, monuments and memorials, traditional art and dances, fair and festivals and dozens of other precious things which made the country a mosaic of living traditions.

TABLE 8

Places of interest visited by Foreign Tourists

City	*Per centage of Tourists* *1982-83*	*1976-77*
1. Delhi	53.45	62.10
2. Bombay	45.95	50.96
3. Madras	17.91	23.34

Source: Survey conducted by the Administrative Staff College of India, Hyderabad and I.S.I. Calcutta.

Tourism needs variety and India with its vast dimensions and kaleidoscopic diversity offers to every class of visitors something not found elsewhere from the snake charmer to the eternal snowcapped peaks of the Himalayas and system of the folk dances to the big game hills. Unlike other export industries there is comparatively little investment needed for promoting tourism. The scope for its expansion is unlimited. Fortunately, this potent industry has started receiving some focus now.

From the tourist map of India as narrated in the preceding paragraphs it might appear that the whole country is dotted with fantastically rich and varied tourist attractions. But if the question is posed what are the places visited by foreign tourists to India. It is revealed by a cursory look at the figures of actual percentage of foreign tourist arrivals at the various places that there is an extreme concentration of traffic at only certain metropolitan centres like Delhi, Bombay, Calcutta and Madras. A survey conducted by the Administrative Staff College of India. Hyderabad and Indian Statistical Institute. Calcutta of 25 places of interest visited by foreign tourists confirmed the above observations as is clear from the Table 8.

To enlarge this focus, the places of interest and the resources for tourism need to be developed and the amenities and services provided for tourists should be gradually expanded. In this context, the Golden Triangle. (Jaipur-Agra-Delhi) provides a great tourist potential for the country. At Jaipur there are historical monuments like Amber. Jantar-Mantar and City Palace, at Agra the Taj Mahal. Fatehpur Sikiri and Red Fort and at Delhi the famous Qutab Minar. the Red Fort and Jama Masjid and other types of attractions spread all-over India, which are bound to create interest among foreign tourists.

❐

4

Goals of Tourism

The post-war tourism boom lured many nations and individual communities into the business with little forethought concerning a viable tourism product the social and environmental consequences of development or the spillover effects in surrounding areas. Instead the approach to tourism development was essentially myopic both in terms of its economic objective and planning scale. The pursuit of economic benefits has seldom been accompanied by concern over lost opportunities or trade-off situations. Planning for these economic objectives has been conducted by individual entrepreneurs of individual communities with little regard for potential impact on others. Too often the pace of growth and burgeoning opportunities resulted in ad hoc responses to changing market conditions and local opportunities. rather than to coordinated strategies working toward preconceived individual and community goals. The outcome of this frenzied activity and patchwork planning has been inconclusive at best if we are to believe the titles of various academic surveys. Titles like Tourism; Blessing of Blight? (Young 1973). Tourism; Passport to Development? (de Kadt 1979) and Tourism: The Good the Bad and the Ugly (Rosenow and Pulsipher 1979) indicate the contentious nature of post-war tourism development. It is evident that tourism has the potential to become a destructive force as well as a benefit for destination communities. Furthermore 30 years of mass tourism experience has led to a more cautious approach to development by existing and potential destinations.

One reason for caution is that the period of unending growth appears to be coming to an end and individual or community planning and investment mistakes cannot depend on a general rise in activity to minimize or obliterate such errors. The immediate cause of the showdown in tourism growth is the recession but in spite of these difficult times the industry has proved to be remarkably resilient. A recent survey of tourism in OECD nations revealed "tourism is holding up." International tourist arrivals were up by 0.7 per cent between 1981 and 1982 and receipts in real terms fell by only 0.3 per cent (OECD 1983). By themselves these figures do not appear impressive but when one recalls how many other industries have suffered severe declines in activity and revenue generation over the same period holding tourism at the same high level can be viewed as a success.

Such resilience lends credence to the view that tourism has taken hold on our lives (Yankelovich and Lefkowitz 1980) and become a component of the post-industrial age. In fact tourism is probably maturing entering a natural period of stability after its rapid postwar growth as new economic circumstances and demographic trends revise travel needs and patterns. This has major implications for both existing and aspiring destination areas for it means the industry is entering uncharted waters. One implication noted in the OECD report is that while "the recession has not kept people from travelling it has changed their destinations and shortened their stay in some countries". Such changes can lead to more emphasis on domestic tourism within the tourism generating nations of western Europe and North America along with international travel to their sunbelt neighbours. Existing and potential destinations in these areas will need to prepare for new travel pattern and demands brought on by changing economic and life-cycle circumstances.

The response to changes in the tourism market will require increased input and involvement by the community at large. In addition to using public goods the industry increasingly requires public funds for infrastructure facilities and marketing. Residents of industrial nations are accustomed to being consulted on development proposals that affect their community and wallet. Furthermore as experienced travellers and witnesses to 30 years on more of mass travel these residents have developed some degree of expertise and experience concerning tourism.

Goals for Tourism

Planning is concerned with anticipating and regulating change in a system to promote orderly development so as to increase the social economic and environmental benefits of the development process. To do this planning becomes an ordered sequence of operations designed to lead to the achievement of either a single goal or to a balance between several goals". Thus all planning requires goals to provide a frame of reference for the detailed physical planning and day-to-day management decisions.

Goals are abstract and continuous concepts intended to provide general direction rather than specific guidelines. To be effective goals must be feasible and have general support. In tourism this means a community's proposals must be realistic and attractive to tourists in a competitive market place. To develop a satisfactory tourist product and acceptable image requires the cooperation of many sectors including the public so the wider the support for its goals the more successful will be the industry. For tourism in industrial nations the goals need to be a subset of overall community objectives since it represents but one of several activities within most local economies. Cities frequently look on tourism as a way to bolster their retail and service sectors. and derive greater returns on their cultural and recreational investments. Toronto for example attracted 20 million tourists in 1979 who spent over $US1 billion. Many of them were attracted to the city by its museum science centre, zoo art galleries and other facilities (Well and Sinnoff 1980). Small communities in rural areas are interested in diversifying their economic base and providing employment for their women and youth. who cannot find work in the traditional primary activities.

The exception which proves the rule, concerning the development of tourism as one of several activities, occurs when tourism has become the dominant activity—as in a resort. Under these circumstances the community goal becomes one of reducing the dependency on tourism, with its seasonably and low-wage limitations. Many resorts are attempting to entice manufacturing or reseach establishments to their scenic and amentity-rich areas, but find it difficult to overcome the problems of isolation and lack of industrial linkage. Some have experienced success, however, in catering to the growing retirement market. The presence of retired people helps to even out the seasonal peaks, and provides major revenue and capital infusions as the elderly bring their pensions and equity to the destination community.

To date most tourism goals and planning have been oriented toward business interests and economic growth. The prime motive for tourism development and planning has been commercial and economic gain, both on the part of the private sector entrepreneurs and governments. Entrepreneurs, companies, and major land owners have provided for a growing market: local governments have encouraged growth and development though the provision of leisure and cultural facilities (Heeley 1981: Lundgren 1983). Senior government interest and support has been motivated by the employment, taxes, and foreign currency which tourism can create. Tourism has been used as an agent of economic development in depressed peripheral regions and as an export activity.

In the United States, the 1981 National Tourism Policy Act created the United States Travel and Tourism Administration whose basic mission "is to promote US-inbound tourism as an export" and thereby assist in reducing the national travel budget deficit. In Canada, several provinces have joined forces with the federal government in an effort to encourage more domestic tourism and develop attractions of international standing. Again the prime purpose is to reduce a hallmorrhaging travel deficit, and to spread tourism revenues into undressed peripheral regions.

In the *Laissez-faire* atmosphere of western societies and a tourism industry dominated by small business, economic considerations have been slow in relinquishing priority to other concerns. But the very success of past development has necessitated relating tourism's economic, social, and environmental impact with wider public interest objectives. One example of this gradual modification in an economic approach to destination planning can be seen in Gunn's treatise on designing tourist regions in North America.

His first goal is to provide for "user satisfactions" on the grounds that it is the tourist who must be attracted and satisfied if a destination is to develop and prosper. His second goal is to provide for "increased rewards to ownership and development" for those entrepreneurs who risk their capital in destination development, for without such venture capital the industry would be stillborn. The third goal is "protection of environmental resource assets," such as historical and archalological sites. While Gunn's first two goals remain distinctly business oriented his final goal recognizes the symbiotic relationship between a successful tourism industry and a protected environment—the early stirrlings of a renewable resource philosophy.

Communities must start to appreciate the fragility of certain resources and protect their resource base if they are to develop a long-term industry. Potential tourist attractions can be spoiled by industrial development or urban renewal, while established amenities may be destroyed through over use. Dearden (1983) maintains that too many resource industries have developed the capacity to harvest and sell to a fine art, but unfortunately this expertise frequently exceed their capacity to grow or replenish consumed resource stock. He reports that British Columbia's "1982 herring quota was reached in just 36 hours of fishing". This reveals a serious neglect of the fish stock, and leads to a situation where it is no longer possible to provide an adequate investment return-which was Gunn's second goal. Likewise, the British Columbia lumber industry is rapidly running out of accessible mature timber thanks to over-harvesting and under planting. It is vital therefore, that a resource-based industry like tourism does more to protect its interest in scenic landscapes, wildlife protection and heritage conservation.

McIntosh goes further than Gunn, encompassing his goals for tourism development within a community framework. This permits some form of local control and direction to be placed upon the still business-oriented emphasis. His first goal is to "provide a framework for raising the living standard of local people through the economic benefits of tourism." Second, to "develop an infrastructure and provide recreation facilities for both visitors and residents." Third, to "ensure that the types of development within visitor centres and resorts are appropriate to the purposes of those areas." Finally, to " establish a development programme that is consistent with the cultural, social and economic philosophy of the government and people of the host area."

This concern for community input and self determination can be seen in the recent planning objectives of destinations which are either being overwhelmed by tourist volumes or are considering a greater commitment to this activity. Those national parks in Britain which receive large numbers of visitors have created plans to tackle the problem of reconciling tourist traffic with the preservation of a local environment and way of life. For instance, the Snowdonia National Park Plan attempts to integrate tourism with the economic and social well-being of local people. Among its objectives it includes several of the goals suggested by McIntosh.

(i) to maintain the traditional pattern of agriculture,

(ii) to encourage those forms of tourism with the greatest local benefit.

(iii) to create jobs at most of the existing settlements within the Park, and

(iv) to safeguard the identity of local communities by seeking to retain and develop the cultural heritage. (Snowdonia National Park 1977, author's italics)

Even in North America. where free enterprise and minimal government interference are still championed, there have been occasional strongish of a more community-oriented approach to development. In British Columbia, where recent emphasis has promoted tourism in small resource-based communities, an attempt has been made to develop socially acceptable guidelines for future expansion (D'Amore 1983). In the Yukon. with its small population, a planning team of consultants and government planners was able to reach most residents through the distribution of a brochure/questionnaire and public meetings. to obtain their views and input for its 1978 tourism development strategy (Graham 1979). Despite such public participation, however, the prime goals remain oriented to the development aspirations of the government and industry rather than the communities involved.

Tourism and the Planning Process

The move toward a more balanced goal formation and planning within a community setting has prompted some preliminary attempts at integrating tourism into local plans, but so far with limited success. Heeley reports that the British ,statutory planning reforms "created larger and more powerful authorities which, allied with the trend towards corporate management and organization within local government, promised to root tourism more securely within the local government machine." However, after reviewing the actual planning experience he concludes tourism has received "little heavy-weight expression in the post-reorganization authorities," a feeling supported by the observations of Veal (1975) in the Midlands and Palmer and Probert (1980) in South Wales.

In Canada the emphasis has been to integrate tourism planning into a provincial strategy of general economic and social development. The province of Ontario created a "Framework for Opportunity" strategy which focused on seventeen "development zone," each with its own identity and potential (Ardagh 1977). These zones cannot be contiguous in such a large province, so they are linked by touring corridors and bound together by hinterland environments. In British Columbia the provincial tourism strategy is based on nine major tourist regions and is designed to facilitate regionally destinctive themes reflecting the economic and physical diversity of the province (British Columbia 1979). In both provinces a major concern is the coordination of tourism development with existing economic activities and a multitude of administrative boundaries.

In response to the need for a more comprehensive and integrated approach to tourism planning at the local level two tourism consultants have proposed a community emphasis to tourism planning. Rosenow and Pulsipher believe a principal advantage of possessing a place that residents believe is special is that planning can begin from an agreed-upon point of reference. Consensus, always elusive in land-use planning, is more attainable when special qualities have been commonly recongnized. Consequently, they have developed a personality planning process which attempts to identify the elements that make a community unique and assist in formulating specific action programmes to enhance that uniqueness and its tourism appeal.

The process involves four steps. First, the delineation of distinctive community features, including its historical and natural resources, ethonic and cultural features, and dominant landforms. Second, the plotting of critical zones. These are areas where the visual quality is especially important, such as entranced routes, major travel corridors and areas which attract large numbers of people. These critical zones are seen as "the community's public face" and may be equated with MacCannel's front setting. Third, the establishment of use objective within each critical zone. These may involve preservation, modification (development that is compatible with the zone's appearance), or enhancement (altering or concealing obtrusive elements). Fourth, the formulation of specific action programmes based on the use objectives. These can include such things as zoning, the purchase of scenic easements, landscaping, and the preservation of historic buildings or dominant landforms.

In practice the sopecific action programmes can be as varied as the individual community's resources and creativity. Rosenow and Pulsipher provide an example of this planning process at work in Heber Valley, a mountain valley near Salt Lake City, Utah.

With such a planning process a community can retain its own sense of place and develop it according to its own priorities and capacity. From this short review of tourism's planning goals it is evident that though the industry's focus has been changing it is still far short of establishing itself within the general planning framework of industrial nations. It needs to continue to restructure its priorities so that environmental and social factors may be placed alongside economic considerations. The growing emphasis on a community responsibility should continue, since this industry uses the community as a resource, sells it as a product, and in the process affects the lives of everyone.

❐

5

Scope and Nature of Tourism

Tourism has grown from the pursuits of a privileged few to a mass movement of people, with the "urge to discover the unknown, to explore new and strange places, to seek changes in environment and to undergo new experiences". During the postwar period tourism grew into a mass tourist industry. The number of international tourist arrivals rose from 25 million in 1950 to 183 million in 1970, an average growth rate of more than 10 per cent (lUOTO 1970). Since 1973 the effect of fuel price increases has merely moderated the rate of expansion. According to estimates by the World Tourist Organization (WTO) international tourist arrivals in 1982 reached 280 million; but even more remarkable is the fact that these members reflect only the minor, and more easily measured, aspects of the tourism picture. Domestic tourism, which involves travel within one's own country, is more difficult to quantify but generally accounts for 75-80 per cent of all tourism activity. According to the WTO there were over 2 billion domestic trips in 1981, representing a 240 per cent increase over 1975 figures.

Such mass movements of people have been described as contemporary migration patterns. Migration can be seen as a response to stress, and Wolfe (1966) identifies three migration patterns in our society. The first, migration to the city, is a continuation of the nineteenth-century phenomenon, and in the opinion of some, may have run its course in the developed world. The second, the journey to and from work, is a result of our large-scale urbanization and spatial separation of workplace and home. The third, recreational travel, is the newest migration and a function of the other two. It has been stimulated by the stress and uniformity of urban life and been accommodated by the standard of living and mobility provided by the same urban-economic system. Being the newest migration, recreational travel has experienced phenomenal growth rates—rates which cannot be maintained but which led to a major change in our lifestyles. Like the other migrations before it, tourism will peak and probably decline, but it will remain a part of our lives and probably change in form and emphasis in the process.

The multifaceted nature of tourism, its various links with the manufacturing and retail sectors, and its numerous seasonal or unofficial businesses make it extermely difficult to assess its market size. One estimate, however, suggests that worldwide travel spending reached $488 billion in 1978. This represented 6 per cent of the world's 1978 Gross National Product (GNP), which in turn was the equivalent of West Germany's GNP at that time. A more recent WTO estimate places the 1981 expenditure on world travel at $919 billion. The growth in tourism revenues has been substantial since the Second World War, but as in the case of visitor volumes the rate of growth has slowed since the oil crisis and inflation of the 1970s. When calculated in real terms the revenue increases have declined from the post-war region of 10 per cent a year to 3 per cent, but it is still growth nevertheless (OECD 1980).

Despite the short-term setbacks of the energy crises and recessions of the late 1970s and early 1980s, tourism is seen as a growth industry of the future. Toffler's Future Shock (1971) described the modern businessman and vacation traveller as the "new nomads" and foresaw:

> a revolutionary expansion of certain industries where sole output consists not of manufactured goods, nor even of ordinary services, but of pre-programmed "experiences" The experience industry could turn out to be one of the pillars of super-industrialism. The very foundation, in fact, of the postservice economy.

His more recent work, The Third Wave (1981) predicted the breakup of industrial society, as we know it, through a process of "demassi-fication," breaking up large units of government and industry into more individual and flexible litestyles. Among the changes which will relate to tourism he foresaw:

> Large numbers of workers already do paid work for what averages out to only three or four days a week, or they take six months or a year off to pursue educational or recreational goals. This pattern may well grow as two-paycheck households multiply.

The appeal of this industry for the transitory period from an industrial society to whatever future awaits us is not limited to futurologists. Nations, such as Spain and Austria, have based much of their post-war development on growth in their tourism sectors. Earnings from the international tourist account contributed a significant portion of their export earnings in 1977. 22.5 per cent for Spain and 21.7 per cent for Austria. This compared with a European Community average of 4.7 per cent. and created a major source of "hard" currency for other development projects. Furthermore, in a time of growing automation and rising unemployment, tourism as a labour-intensive industry has proved to be both economically and politically appealing. As the then Prime Minister of England, James Callaghan, once described the situation:

> Now new plants in manufacturing and new investment and new methods bring greater efficiency but it does not necessarily mean more jobs and for this reason we need to look at the service industries of which tourism is a notable example as an additional and important source of income and work.

The development of mass tourism has created a powerful and influential recreational travel industry. For example, in England it is estimated that "some 11/2 million jobs were generated either directly or indirectly by tourism in 1975, equivalent to about 6 per cent of total employment". In Canada tourism is permoted as big business which is important to all Canadians because it employs one out of ten workers and is the seventh largest earner of foreign exchange (CGOT 1982). In the United States the tourism industry grosses an estimated $105 billion annually and employs over 5 million workers (Pizam and Pokela 1983). With such impressive statistics and employment opportunities it is little wonder that this industry has become a powerful political lobby. In Britain and Canada the industry has received generous development grants, and in Canada a private sector task force is cooperating with the government to produce the first national tourism plan (Powell 1978).

Definitions

The raison d'etre of the industry is the tourist, so all development and planning must be predicated on the understanding of who this person is, if it is to succeed. The term "tourist" is derived from the work "tour," meaning, according to Webster's Dictionary, "a journey at which one returns to the starting point; a circular trip usually for business, pleasure or education during which various places are visited and for which an intinerary is usually planned." As this definition indicates, there are several motives for travel, each requiring its own facilities and having a different impact. Thus, government agencies in search of a comprehensive definition of tourist, and one which will facilitate the measurement of this activity, have resorted to the more general term of "visitor." The definition most widely recognized and used is that produced by the 1963 United Nations Conference on Travel and Tourism in Rome. Which was adopted by the International Union of Official Travel Organizations (IUOTO) in 1968. It states that a visitor is: 'any person Visiting a country other than that in which he has his usual place of residence, for any reason other than following an occupation remunerated from within the country visited.'

Thus, tourism is concerned with all travellers visiting foreign parts, whether it be for pleasure, business, or a combination of the two. The only exception is someone who is setting up a new residence in a foreign country and will be earning a salary and paying taxes in this new country. The IUOTO definition was intended for international travel but it can accommodate domestic tourism by substituting region for country.

Visitors have been subdivided further into two categories to assist the measurement of tourist traffic and the assessment of its economic impact.

(1) Tourists-who are visitors making at least one overnight stop in a country or region and staying for at least 24 hours.

(2) Excursionists—who are visitors that do not make an overnight stop, but pass through the country or region. An excursionist stays for less than 24 hours, and includes day-trippers and people on cruises.

This division has the practical value of using overnight accommodation records (registrations) as the basic source of tourist information, which can be used in conjunction with border crossing records if international movement is involved. By focusing on the accommodation sector of the industry, however, it also produces conservative estimates of the travel picture. There is no way to count overnight visits with relatives and friends and it is often impossible to obtain accurate records from small or temporary establishments like guest houses and farms.

The excursionist, or day-tripper, can be viewed as a special tourist. Such a person visits a destination for a day or spends some time there while passing through as part of a tour. In either case, he or she is a visitor, spending time and money while utilizing space and facilities in the destination area.

Types of Tourist

There are as many types of tourist as there are motives for travel. Each type makes different demands cf a destination, and has its own particular impacts. Business travel can range from convention and trade fair meetings to vacations that include self-advancement courses or permit the traveller to update certain areas of his profession. Leisure travel can incorporate activity packages where the tourist learns a new sports skill or craft, as well as developing a tan. The impact of tourists' demands will vary according to the demands they place on destination's physical and human resources.

Tourist typologies can be grouped into two general categories (Table 1). Interactional types emphasize the manner of interaction between visitors and destination areas, whereas the cognitive-normative models stress the motivations behind travel. Both approaches indicate the strong links between visitor expectations-motivations and the structure of destination areas. Thus it can be seen immediately that no destination appeals to all tourists and each can develop its own segment of the tourism market.

Among the interaction models are those of Cohen (1972) and Smith (l977b). Cohen classified tourists according to the degree they seek familiar or strange settings and whether or not they were willing to be institutionalized (organized) in their travel. Smith's mode detailed breakdown incorporates recent market developments such as the unorganized "hippie treks" to Nepal and the social implications of a highly structured charter business. Smith, like Cohen, views explorers and elite travellers as having little impact upon indigenous cultures. Their small number requires little in the way of special accommodation, and their desire to gain insight into local customs is aided by a sympathetic attitude to the local way of life. In constrast, the charter tourists travel in their own environmental bubble, viewing everything from the security of their pre-paid and price-guaranteed package tour. To accommodate the large numbers and organizational structure of charters a community must become commercial in its dealings with tourists, and often' needs to import foreign capital and expertise.

In contrast to the interaction models which focus on the market characteristics and symptoms of travel the cognitive-normative models attempt to reveal the causes of travel. Plog (1972) and Cohen (1979a) both look at the sociological concept of "centre," which considers that every society possesses a centre representing the charismatic nexus of its supreme, ultimate moral values. Plog develops a polar continuum consisting of those who differ from the normal (centric) values of society and follow their independent vacation desires (allocentrics), and those who conform to society's norms and values and thus become part of the mass market of tourism (psychocentrics).

Plog suggests that tourist destinations are attractive to different types of visitors as they evolve from untouched discoveries to popular resorts. A community can enter the tourism business with the arrival of a small number of adventurous allocentrics, but their impact would be small because no special facilities would be desired or required for this type of traveller. As the areas becomes more accessible, better serviced and more widely known an increasing number of mid-centric would visit. They in turn give way to large number of psychocentrics as the destination becomes a popular resort dependent on foreign investment and labour. The new visitors are made to feel at home, with a full range of facilities and attractions that may now be divorced from the natural geographic and social attractions which first attracted the allocentrics.

Cohen elaborates on this theme making further reference to people's "spiritual centre, whether religious or cultural—the centre which for the individual symbolizes ultimate meanings". Those travelling on vacation believe there is some experience available elsewhere which cannot be found at home and which makes the travel worthwhile. The spiritual centre of this quest may be purely hedonistic, such as in the case of diversionary and recreational travel or it may be a new type of pilgrimage, with travellers seeking answers through experiential. experimental or existential forms of travel. Cohen notes that these three levels of tourism represent different depths of meaning for the individual, but unlike traditional pilgrimages they involve movement away from the center of the tourist's culture toward an "elective center," which he has chosen or converted to.

Destination Areas

To satisfy the variety of motives outlined above and to accommodate overnight or passing-through visitors, a physical setting is required. "tourism as an industry occurs at 'destination areas'- areas with different natural and/ or man-made features, which attract non-local visitors (or tourists) for (a variety of) activities". This definition by Georgulas possesses two key aspects which distinguish a destination area; it must contain features that will attract and it must appeal to "non-local visitors."

Tourism is a voluntary activity, therefore a destination area must have attractions which appeal to at least one type of tourist. These attractions can be as varied as the tourist types, but they are generally divided into two categories, natural or man-made. Natural attractions include such features as sunshine or scenic landscapes, while man-made features can be primary attractions like Disneyland and the Edinburgh Festival, or support facilities like hotels and restaurants. A third category, which is now receiving more attention, would be a destination area's hospitality record. The manner in which visitors are received, and the quality of service provided, forms a major component of a destination's tourist image.

To be a destination an area must attract non-local visitors, people who have travelled some distance from their home town to see the attractions or use the facilities. This is an important feature because it differentiates recreational travel, where travel is an important and possibly the most important component of the experience, from outdoor recreation, where the activity is the prime objective and travel to a recreational site is of secondary importance or even an inconvenience. Furthermore, the emphasis on non-local visitors is a major economic consideration. Money spent by non-local visitors to an area becomes basic income, or earned income, for that community. If the money was spent by local people it would be redistributed income and thus not so beneficial to the destination area.

To determine whether an area can be classified as a tourist destination has traditionally required criteria to distinguish whether recreational traffic is local and not touristic, or non-local and therefore touristic. Burton (1971) identified five periods of recreational time which may help to distinguish local from non-local recreational travel. The five were *(i)* very short (up to one hour), *(ii)* short (a few hours), *(iii)* a full day, *(iv)* several days (usually a weekend), and *(v)* a week or more (usually the annual vacation. Using this classification, those periods extending beyond a single full day would produce a full-fledged tourist because of the need for overnight stops, and it would provide sufficient opportunities for travel on a regional or national basis. Thanks to our increased mobility, however, it is possible to move beyond the physical limits of a home town in a matter of hours, thus making travel on a regional or non-local basis feasible in time periods *(ii)* and *(iii)*.

Attempts to operationalize such a classification system have produced a rough guide by which to differentiate between local and non-local recreational travel. Wall (1972) in a study of recreational car trips in England classified a traveller as a "pleasure tripper" if he travelled 5 miles or more from his point of origin. Therefore, any village, stately home, or country park beyond this range can be considered a tourist destination if it was included in a day's outing or afternoon drive. Likewise, Clawson and Knetsch in their classification of North American recreation areas have indentified "intermediate areas" which they described as being "used for all day outings and on weekends." Such areas include state parks, reservoirs and lakes which can be reached within two hours or so of driving They possess no, or limited, accommodation yet they are definite. destination areas for nearby urban centres. Such empirical classifications indicate that any community or area outside of a local recreational and economic hinterland can be considered a destination area.

In North America where freeways and emptier roads allow greater mobility. Wall's 5-mile radius to delimit destination areas—needs to be extended considerably. Statistics Canada uses 80 kilometres (50 miles) as its break point between local and non-local recreational travel. British Columbia defines domestic tourism as "the travel, activities and services used by any British Columbia resident beyond a 40 kilometre (25 miles) radius from home for the purpose of personal enjoyment and travel."

In addition to concerns over the non-resident tourist and his generation of basic income, there is a growing awareness of the importance of resident tourists. Those who are making new uses of there local settings. In economic terms it can be just as vital to keep more residents vacationing at home, rather than see them and their money disappear on external trips. Concern over the travel budget account is most frequently expressed at the national level, but since this is the sum of individual community accounts some areas have become anxious about their own deficits. Interest in attracting residents to vacation in their own town or area goes beyond economic considerations, however, to include a growing sense of pride in local heritage and amenities. The growing emphasis on a community's quality of life has encouraged many areas to invest in conservation and facilities that can create a viable, if occasional, tourist destination for residents.

Travel

A common theme in all definitions of tourism is travel, and Peters went so far as to declare "the tourist industry is an industry concerned with movement." As we have seen, the journey must take a traveller beyond his home turf and because of this unfamiliarity it becomes an important part of the travel experience. "Getting there is half the fun" when people travel through different areas on their way to a destination. This fact has been recognized by tourism agencies in their attempts to develop scenic and circular routes that will stimulate the senses and curiosity of the traveller.

Travel and time are interwoven and it is necessary to be aware of both in order to appreciate their significance to tourism. Hartmann (1981), in a paper entitle "Tourism, travel, and timing," notes:

> Whether we decide to travel by package tours where we trust in a fixed route and a pre-arranged time frame, or if we time our stay and change of place completely (by)

ourselves, we need to know the principles of timing or at least to appreciate them.

Since tourism involves travel it requires greater blocks of discreationary time than much recreational activity. Thus, Burton's first recreational time period which accounts for much of our urban-oriented recreation has been discounted in the tourism context. The major blocks of discretionary time are the weekends and annual vacations, which account for the peaking of tourist travel in these periods and the problems of seasonality in the industry. Time also affects the demands for travel and structure of the industry. As people grow older their travel demands change. Young adults and elderly couples are considered a prime travel market because they have relatively large amounts of discretionary time and income. Between these two states the cost of buying a home and raising a family tends to reduce the discreationary aspects of a family budget. Likewise, the tourist industry can age and get out of step with technological innovations and consumer tastes. Lundgren (1983) illustrates this travel-time link in his temporal analysis of the Laurentians, north or Montreal, one of Canada's oldest tourist destinations.

Tourism

Tourism is a sum of the above elements, resulting from the travel of non-residents (tourists, including excursionists) to destination areas, as long as their sojourn does not become a permanent residence. It is a combination of recreation and business. Mieczkowski (1981) notes that while most tourism is recreational in nature, some tourism, such as business, professional and personal travel is not associated with recreation. Recreation falls entirely within leisure since it is an experience during free or discretionary time which leads to some form of revitalization of the body and mind. Part of this recreational activity takes place outside of the local community and as a result travel becomes an important, component leading this form of recreation to be classified as tourism. Tourism's orb extends beyond recreation to become associated with business trips and family reunions; and beyond leisure itself into personal and business motives for travel, such as health and professional development.

To move from the conceptual level to reality requires a system; therefore tourism is frequently referred to as a business or industry. The tourism process combines a demand (tourist), suppliers (tourist industry), and a product (attractions), which Chau (1977) has summarized as the subject, means and object of tourism.

Most economists and compilers of industrial classifications argue that a tourism industry does not exist because it does not produce a distinct product (Chadwic 1981). One problem is that certain industries which sell a large proportion of their output to tourists, such as transport, accommodation, and entertainment, are not exclusively tourism industries, for they sell these services to local residents as well. Kaiser and Helber maintain that it is not "properly" an industry, but more a cross-section of a regional or national economy. This does not however prevent them using the "industry" nomenclature throughout their book. Opposing this view, Mawhinney and Bagnall take the position that tourism is an industry, similar to other industries like agriculture and mining in that it is dependent on the continued availability of those resources upon which it is based. In other words, it is a resource industry, on which sells to local and non-local markets but one whose success and future depend on careful management.

Whether one classifies tourism as an industry or not, one cannot ignore the resource base which is its raison *d'etre*, or the delivery system which permits people to utilize those resources, if tourism is to be understood and managed for the benefit of society. Modern tourism must develop and protect its attractions, whether they be natural or man-made, and become a hospitality industry to make visitor experiences as enjoyable as possible. The tourism industry is highly fragmented with many types of businesses and many levels of industrialization, but they all have a common purpose and that is to help a visitor enjoy his trip. The travel experience is this industry's product, but unlike other industries it is the consumer who travels and not the product demonstrates the supply and demand characteristics of tourism and how the industry attempts to bring these market forces together.

The Industry's Structure

Demand Factors

Some understanding of basic demand motivations is necessary if the industry and planner are to fulfill tourists desires. Four basic travel motivators have been indentified by the industry (Figure 2). Physical or physiological motivators, such as relaxation and medical treatment are major reasons for a vacation, and the quality of food, drink, and comfort frequently represents an important criterion in assessing the travel experience. Cultural motivators have long been associated with the desire to learn about foreign countries and customs. Social motivators include visits with relatives and friends, meeting business associates at conferences, and pursuing activities associated with status and prestige. Combinations of cultural and social motives could be seen in the early tours of China, where influential people vied not only to see this previously closed society but also for the prestige of being one of the first to report on this great unknown. Fantasy motivators form an important element of travel demand and illustrate its individualistic nature. Dann notes "holidays are essentially experiences in fantasy."

A good deal of this fantasy takes place before the trip itself:

> a certain picture is built up of a world that marks an escape from present reality, and environment for acting out psychic needs, and the playing of certain roles which cannot be fulfilled at home, and it is this which forms part and parcel of tourist motivation.

He goes on to identify two types of fantasy, the "Anomic" where the average city dweller desires to transcend the monotony of everyday life, and "ego-enhancement" which provides psychological boosts through such activities as gambling holidays or sexual adventures—real or imagined.

To convert such motivation into a trip requires knowledge about the conditions and opportunities that exist within our reach. Unfortunately as consumers and geographers we are flawed, we have fragmentary information and distorted images (mental maps) of the real world (Gould and White 1974) these images are our perceptions. Studies have shown that some regions have very favourable images while others have relatively negative ones, and the differentiation is fairly consistent (Mayo 1973). The dominant attributes people use to sort out these mental images are often related to cost, climate, scenery, personal safety, and sanitation, and thus can have an important bearing on their choice of destination (Anderson and Colberg 1973; Crompton 1979).

Perception of holiday options and various destination areas is conditioned by three important elements. Individual preferences, reflecting an individual's personality, will direct the search for specific forms of gratification. They will dictate whether a person wishes to indulge in the gastronomic delights of a cruise or pit his skill and stamina against some mountain. Perceptions will be coloured by past vacation experiences, with a satisfactory experience tempting repetition and possibly encouraging more adventurous pursuits. These two elements reflect the two schools of thought concerning image causation (Kotler 1975). One school suggests that images are largely person-determined whereas the other approach suggests that people's mental image is largely destination-determined.

The third element in image creation is hearsay, information from friends and relatives, the media, or travel agents. A study by Henderson and Voiland revealed "communication or second-hand sources seem to play the strongest role when a person assesses an area's recreational utility." This conclusion supports the general communication and marketing models regarding a two step flow of communication. According to this theory, ideas flow from radio and print to opinion leaders and from them to the more conservative sections of the population (Lazarsfeld et al. 1944; Cox 1964). Within the opinion leadership are two groups, the innovators and influentials. Much of the promotion for new destinations or experiences is directed at the adventurous and innovative market, and word of their pioneering experiences is channeled to the influential opinion leaders with the hope that they will adopt this new vacation and spread the concept by example to the masses. As we will see later this two-step theory of communication fits in very well with the general evolutionary pattern of resorts.

Motivation and perceived options build an image of each tourist destination (Figure 2). This image may be defined as the sum of beliefs, ideas, and impressions that a person has regarding a destination. It is a personal composite view of a destination's tourism potential, and where prices are comparable it is often the decisive factor in a tourist's selection process. The images are not necessarily the same for each visitor and this makes it difficult to allocate resources and plan for future land use in destination areas. To cvercome this problem many areas attempt to appeal to a specific group through extensive and expensive promotion presenting themselves as a family-oriented resort, a place or rugged outdoor enthusiasts, or a swinging locale for night people.

Supply Factors

Such a question is pertinent to an industry which regards itself as a host industry and is dependent on local goodwill, but it also needs to develop the resources and product which will substantiate the image. With such diversity of tourist demands and interests destinations need to focus on a particular market subset one they can satisfy in terms of resources and facilities. When the supply side of the tourism market is considered the twin foundations of the industry are its destination area attractions and hospitality.

Tourism is a resource industry, one which is dependent on nature's endowment and society's heritage. Visitors are attracted to areas of outstanding beauty and this beauty can take many forms. In some areas it is the climate which is the major attraction, as can be seen with the sunbelt and Mediterranean resorts. In others it is landforms such as the Grand Canyon the Rockies, or Alps, or specific terrain within these areas which may facilitate certain activities like the skiing in Vail, Colorado, or mountaineering around the Matterhorn. Water has always appealed as a source of relaxation whether it be associated with a seaside beach, a waterfall or lake and river fishing. Flora and fauna provide idyllic setting and as such enchance a visit, such as the host of daffodils in the English Lake District at Easter, or provide a specific purpose to the visit, as with walks through alpine meadows or observing game in national parks and game reserves. Wherever an accessible area processes several of these natural attributes it becomes a major attraction and in many cases has been designated a national park, so as to conserve these resources for future generations.

In addition to nature's resources, people are attracted by the cultural attributes of society and its heritage Centres of learning (Oxford, Heidelberg), of culture (Stratfor-upon-Avon, Athens) and of entertainment (London, New York) have long been magnets for travellers. Likewise, the splendor and history attached to various buildings and locations have created major attractions. Numerous castles (Windsor, Caernarvor), palaces (Versailles, Blenheim), stately homes (Woburn Abbey, Mount Vernon), ruins (Colosseum, Parthenon), and battlefields (Gettysburg, Pearl Harbor) feature prominently in the tourist literature. As the significance of heritage and its conservation has spread whole city districts have been preserved because of their architectural merit, historical significance, and potential tourist value. "Venice is an extreme example of a tourist-dominated city." where the original city on the islands has become a tourist Mecca and the scene of an international restoration rescue while its mainland twins of Marghera and Mestre provide the bulk of the region's industry and housing, and local life.

As important as the natural and cultural resources, which combine to form the major attractions, is the welcome which is accorded to a visitor. Public goodwill is an essential ingredient of any trip for if the host community is antagonistic to visitors no amount of attractions will compensate for the rudeness of hostility. It is for this reason that various governments feel obligated to remind residents of the value of tourism to local economies and encourage local people to be hospitable and friendly toward the visitor.

There are three facets to note about tourism's resource base. First, it is a combination of physical and human resources which form the basis of the industry. Nowhere is this more important than in the case where the major attraction is a public amenity either publicly owned or subsidized by the public purse. Under these circumstances the industry's foundation is a public good (a beach, a plaza, a park, or museum), and as such the industry should be cognizant of its special relationship with local community. It has a responsibility to foster what is in fact a community resource, and has no right to enclose or destroy it for its own purposes. Second, the physical resources often possess a seasonal element that encourages variations in visitation patterns. The most obvious is the climatic variation experienced in northern latitudes which encourages most people to consider vacations during the sunny summer weather. This climatic variation also affects the flora and fauna and attractiveness of various locations, providing each with a periodic climax. Thus many of its attractions ensure that tourism will remain a seasonal activity, and any attempt to extend the seasonal life of a destination will need to consider supplementary activities. Finally tourism has frequently been described as a search for the four S's—surf, sand, sun, and sex. If this sarcastic description of the industry has any truth in it, it is that prime attractions can be found in many areas of the world. This makes the industry very competitive and flexible for it can often find substitute resources and locations if an original destination turns sour because of growing residential hostility or changing fashions and economic circumstances. As Peters (1969) has noted the optimum situation for a destination is to offer "an asset so outstanding and unique that the tourist industry can largely depend on and be prompted by this feature." Since this situation occurs rarely the industry and communities often attempt to supplement the natural tourist resources of an area with other facilities and man-made attractions.

To make a destination area more appealing and diversified in the competitive tourism market the industry often creates support facilities and artificial attractions. The objective is to create a more enjoyable and comfortable visit and thereby earn more revenue by inducing visitors to stay longer. An old maxim in tourism is "the longer they stay the more they spend," thus the industry continues to pursue the objective of enticing visitors to stay.

Ideally, the support facilities and attractions will supplement and complement the natural resources of the area. Hotels and motels should blend with the local architecture and landscape. Stores should emphasize local customs and handicrafts and where possible, visitors should have access to local markets where informality and daily bustle add an air of authenticity and local flavor. Likewise, attractions are hopefully in keeping with the natural resources and customs of the area, providing complementary educational and entertainment themes. For example, coastal cities are developing marine exhibits to show sea-life, historic centers develop museums and tours, industrial centres are stressing industrial heritage as in the case of Stoke-on-Trent's renovated Potteries and Dayton, Ohio's National Air Museum. Unfortunately, as we will see, such ideals are not always met and uncoordinated development can result in montonous homogeneity and garish low-quality tourist traps, which clash with the destination's ambience.

In some cases the quality of the facilities and created attractions has been high enough. however, to rival to the original tourist resources as a major destination attraction. Famous examples of this are Disneyland, California, and Disney World, Florida. They attract millions of visitors to what were previously agricultural areas, with Disneyland recording nearly 11 million visitors in 1978 and Disney World attracting over 14 million visitors in 1978—only 6 year after being opened. In the process, these Disney parks have set the standards by which all other thematic parks are judged.

Artificial attractions take many forms. A decommissioned battleship, the USS Massachusetts, was introduced to the non-tourist area of Fall River Massachusetts, to help boost and diversify the local economy. It has more than fulfilled those expectations, for the ship has over 200,000 visitors a year and generates over $2 million into the local economy annually. Such success has encouraged similar ventures in Long Beach, California (Queen Many), and London (HMS Belfast), and now competition for retiring famous vessels has become intense. Newsweek (1980) reported a battle between the US Naval Academy in Annapolis, Maryland, and the submarine base in Groton. Connecticut, over who would have the honour of putting the world's first nuclear submarine, the USS Nautilus, on display.

Facilities designed to improve accessibility are a key capital investment for destination areas since the industry is based on travel. Investment in various forms of transport is considered desirable in order to remain competitive and flexible with ever-changing transport technology. Each new form of transport changes the accessibility equation for tourist destinations, especially those in peripheral regions.

Similarly, development of the freeway system has brought certain scenic peripheral areas closer to urban-industrial centres, in term of time, with dramatic increases in visitor volumes being the result. In the United States, Interstates 75 and 81 bring people from the Midwest and Atlantic states within a few hours of Gatlinburg and the Great Smoky Mountains National Park. As a result, this park receives over 8 million visits a year, more than three times the number of any other national park in the United States.

Although transport links are seldom built solely for tourism purposes, the tourism market potential plays a major role in upgrading existing facilities and creating new ones. Competition for international tourists has encouraged various governments to build new airports or operate national airlines. Development of Hawaii's airport enabled it to take advantage of new generations of jet aircraft and their associated economies. In some cases the importance of a tourist link becomes so important that governments will protect it with special legislation. British Columbia's government, for example, has promised to incorporated the ferry connection between Vancouver Island and the main-land into an Essential Services Act, to ensure it is not disrupted by labour disputes. A major factor in bringing this about is the importance of tourism to the Island in general and to Victoria, the Island's provincial capital, in particular.

The creation of a product that is noticeable and marketable in a competitive business world appear to be a simple task for most industries, but for one made up of numerous individual businesses and entrepreneurial spirits, it is a major challenge. In a free enterprise system there is little control over market entry or quality. As Disneyland in Anaheim experienced, there is no way of influencing the quality and type of neighbouring facility, there a carefully planned and developed attraction is surrounded by a jungle of neon lights, garish architecture, and snarled traffic. Not only is it difficult to develop a harmonious product within a destination, but it is even more difficult, with the competition for visitors, to get various destinations to combine their development and promotion into an effective regional product. Yet regional cooperation is required as the public become more mobile and is no longer content to spend its entire vacation in one place. Therefore, the need for government coordination and promotion has become more essential in drawing businessmen and destinations together in order to form regional product units, where the whole has more appeal than the sum of individual parts. This approach can be seen at the national level in England where the English Tourist Board has divided the country up into 12 regions, and, at the state/provincial level, with British Columbia's strategy of developing and promoting nine geophysical-tourism regions.

Market Place

To be successful, an industry must sell its product in the market place. Since tourism's product is immobile and its potential customers need to build and compare destination images before they travel, some form of intermediary is required. This is the function of the travel agent who must successfully match a tourist image and tourist product if the travel experience is to have any chance of success. Four phases in this process have been identified. First, the development of a tourist product and promotion of an image is the role of tour wholesalers. Three of the biggest companies are Thomas Cook, Amex, and Intertourist, and they send out representatives to find new destinations or combinations that can be put together as a saleable package. Second, the actual selling of individual vacations is the responsibility of the store front travel agent. These people act as advisors and consultants, and a sense of geography is vital if they are to match their customer's wishes with suitable customs and climate. Third, the travel agent either arranges accommodation directly or leaves it to the destination area to provide such services and supplementary information concerning local attraction and events. In this way it is hoped that most tastes and budgets can be satisfied. The final objective is to have a satisfied customer, who is likely to make a return trip and act as a goodwill ambassador, for this is the most effective way of nurturing the industry and fulfilling the goals of tourism.

Community Approach

The product and image that intermediaries package and sell is a destination experience, and as such creates an industry that is highly dependent on the goodwill and cooperation of host communities. Many destination area attractions are public property or public goods, and the hospitality needed for a memorable visit must come from members of the public as well as employees of the industry. Increasingly, development of new facilities requires public investment in infrastructure and shared facilities; and many festivals or events that evolved to fill local needs are being commercialized and promoted as tourist events. It is the citizen who must live with the cumulative outcome of such developments and needs to have greater input into how his community is packaged and sold as a tourist product on the world market.

❑

6

Development of Tourism

There has been increased awareness of the economic importance of tourism in the 1980s and this stems from a number of sources, including appreciation of how long-term structural changes in demand are leading to expansion of the service economy. With increasing real incomes and leisure time there is growing demand for recreation and holidays, and this benefits tourism. Not surprisingly, therefore tourism is often considered to be one of the economic sectors which has realistic potential for growth beyond the short term. The importance of this trend for employment is strengthened because of the relatively labour-intensive nature of tourism and the limited substitution up to the present, at least of capital in the production of tourism services. Given the growth of large-scale and long-term unemployment thoughout Western Europe in the 1980s, it is hardly surprising that policy makers have seized upon tourism as a source of employment creation. At the same time, the increasing share of services in international trade has focused attention on tourism as a major contribution-either positively or negatively-to the balance of payments. In short, tourism-along with some other select activities such as financial services and tele-communications has become a major component of economic strategies in many parts of Western Europe.

As tourism emerges from the shadows of economic policy to a centre stage position, it has become imperative to evaluate its role in economic development. The industry is shrouded with myths and stereotypes, and there is a need to examine critically recent trends in tourism, its economic organisation and its contribution to economic development. There have been previous attempts to question whether tourism is 'a passport to development' or is 'a blessing or blight' as well as more broadly based assessments of the economic, social and environmental impacts of tourism.

Western Europe is a coherent unit for analysis for many reasons. Although, of course, there are international flows out of and into the region, Western Europe actually accounted for 68 per cent of all international tourists in 1984. Compared to all other macro regions, there is a very intense level of international tourist flows within Western Europe, so that the fortunes of the tourist industry in particular countries are heavily dependent on movements from-and events in other countries within the continent. The major exception to this is the quantitatively important (and economically even more significant) inflow of tourists from the United States. The event's of 1986 testify to the importance of North American tourists because the sudden reduction in arrivals following the Chernobye incident and the US bombing of Libya had a notable effect on the tourist economies of several European countries. To some extent, emphasis on international tourism tends to overstate the importance of Western Europe because the geographical scale of the United States and Canada means that, in comparison, similar-length tourist journeys are recorded as domestic tourist flows in these two countries. Nevertheless, it is also important to study Western Europe as a unit because there is a communality of policy interests. Most obviously, the European Community (EC) constitutes a single market for tourism and, while EC policy initiatives in this field have been limited the very existence of the Community affects the industry. At the level of demand, it facilitates international tourist movements while, at the level of industrial organisation, the free movement of international capital and labour is eased. There are also some instances of EC-wide policy measures for tourism, notably in Social Fund assistance for training and European Regional Development Fund (ERDF) grants for infrastructure. However, most tourism policy is formulated at the national rather than the EC level. Even so, the countries of Western Europe are interdependent in respect of state interventionism. Policy measures in one country-whether to stimulate new forms of tourism, to influence the holiday destinations of nationals or the attract more foreigners-impinge upon competing tourist industries in other countries.

Having considered the geographical parameters of this volume, we now turn to a consideration of tourism itself. The definition of tourism is a particularly arid pursuit. It is sufficient to note that in this volume tourism is understood to constitute travelling away from home for periods of more than 24 hours; the principal purposes are recreation or business activities, but may also include visiting family, educational motives or health reasons. Excursionism involves visits of less than 24 hours. Although the major focus of this volume is on tourism, its development and, indeed, its economic impact are linked with excursionism. and so the latter cannot entirely be excluded. While the definition of tourism may be an arid exercise, the definition of the tourist industry is crucially important. In most countries tourism is 'statistically invisible' and usually, only the most obvious sectors or those exclusively devoted to tourists are enumerated in official tourism data. Inevitably, this tends to be the accommodation sector and perhaps, cafes and restaurants. Yet the tourist industry is far larger than this. Tourists also spend money directly on recreational facilities, tourist attractions, shops and local services. In turn, these have indirect effects on agriculture, wholesaling and manufacturing, while secondary rounds of spending of tourism income create induced linkages in the economy. This, indeed, is the basis for the research which has been undertaken on tourism multipliers. In this volume, we have sought to encompass as broad a definition as possible of tourism but the constraints' of space and of data inevitably mean that much of the discussion is centred on the accommodation sector.

This volume seeks to analyse the major changes which have occurred in Western European tourism in recent years. This is justified by the emphasis we wish to place on domestic versus foreign tourism. and by the concentration of policy-making powers. at this level. While space precluded the inclusion of chapters on all seventeen major Western European countries. The ten which have been selected represent the major types of tourism economies. While each chapter has been written so as to take into account the particular characteristics of tourism in each country certain themes recur throughout. The most important of these are changes in the demand for tourism (international and domestic by region by season etc.).

The organisation of the tourist industry and its responses to demand changes and the contribution of tourism to economic development.

The case studies concentrate on two levels of analysis the national and the regional and on the relationship between these. Any analysis which ignores either level is likely to be incomplete. National developments affect regional developments and vice versa. For example the effectiveness of national marketing programmes of national investment schemes and of international currency fluctuations influence the ability of regional tourist industries to attract tourists and to restructure in the face of changing market conditions. However, these interrelationships are not unidirectional for the attractiveness or effectiveness of the national tourist industry is in large part a sum of its regional components. Furthermore the national and regional levels are also linked by capital and labour movements both interregionally and internationally. This is illustrated in a case such as Austria for the national performance of the industry is usually an aggregate of decline in some regions and of rapid expansion in others.

Tourism and Development: National Perspectives

The importance of tourism to national economic development can be measured in a number of ways the most important of which are its contribution to the balance of payments income/GDP, employment and other sectors of the economy (via indirect effects). The balance-of-payments contribution has received most attention. The importance of tourism in the 'invisibles' account in international trade has long been obvious in countries such as Spain where. indeed it was promoted as part of a long-term economic strategy. It helps to pay for imports (whether of food, technology, capital or consumer goods) and this can be important both in economies in development (Greece, Spain, Portugal, etc.) and mature economies (such as the United Kingdom), which have a negative balance on merchandise trade. In this respect, the importance of tourism is usually greatest in small open economies, such as Cyprus or Malta but it is also a source of vulnerability in such countries especially when as in the latter case its is heavily dependent on a single foreign market.

Estimates of the contribution of tourism to the balance of payments are usually based on direct tourist expenditure. However. this is a rather narrow (if relatively easily measured) indicator, for it excludes the indirect transactions.

TABLE 1

Components of Tourism's External Account

Expenditures	*Receipts*
Expenditures by tourists abroad	Expenditures 'at home' by foreign tourists
Transportation	Transportation
Investments (outward)	Investments (inward)
Dividends, interest and profits paid out Commodity imports (tourism induced)	Dividends, interest and profits received Commodity exports (tourism induced)
Capital goods	Capital goods
Consumption goods	Consumption goods
Salaries repatriated abroad	Salaries sent from abroad
Training	Training
Publicity and promotion	Publicity and promotion
Miscellaneous services	Miscellaneous services

Source: Baretje (1982)

Which follow from tourism. Baretje (1982) therefore recommends the use of the broader concept of 'tourism's external account' (see Table 1). which includes a variety of economic linkages but, it must be emphasised, there are practical difficulties in seeking to operationalise this. The breadth of the definition makes it equally difficult to estimate the contribution of tourism to national income or GDP. In addition to the linkages suggested by Baretje, calculations of income or GDP also have to include the effects of domestic tourism which, in Northern Europe at least, sometimes exceed those of foreign tourism. There is also the even more intangible consideration of how tourism impinges on general lifestyles and expenditure patterns. International tourism can have a demonstration effect leading to increased indigenous demand for new types of goods or services, and these may be produced by domestic or by foreign companies.

While there has long been an interest in the contribution of tourism to the balance of payments, this has been surpassed in the 1980s by a concern for its potential employment creation. Again, there are practical difficulties involved in any evaluation of this role: some jobs in shops, recreation centres, etc., are only partly dependent on tourism, while there are considerable difficulties involved in tracing secondary linkages. Furthermore, jobs are not a homogeneous category to be measured in simple units as with income or net foreign exchange earnings. Instead, there are a variety of job types and these can be classified as seasonal/all-year, parttime/full-time, family-Iabour/waged-labour, voluntary /waged-Iabour, manual/non-manual, skilled/unskilled, etc. According to some stereotypes; tourism employment tends to be low-waged, seasonal, non-unionised, parttime and the preserve of family and/ or female workers. This may hold true in some cases but, in most instances, it is at best a partial description. Jobs in tourism may be jobs in hotels, shops, government administration, air transport or factories, amongst others. The need to be critical of the quality of jobs generated by tourism, and to resist the political 'hype' surrounding its potential for job creation. The variety of experiences outlined in these chapters also emphasises the need to avoid stereotypes and excessive abstraction. Consideration of the tourism-related demand for manufactured goods underlines this point, for the impact depends on where the goods are produced, whether it is by craftmen or factory workers, on the alternative work opportunities available locally, and on the evaluation of these jobs by the individuals and by the community.

While the previous discussion has stressed the need to examine individual cases in detail, it does not preclude identification of the key elements which condition the relationship between tourism and development. Amongst the most important of these are the type of tourism, the structure of the national economy, and relationships with capital and labour movements.

Types of Tourism

There are many different types of tourists but, in terms of their contribution to economic development, the critical considerations are per-capita spending power and the forms of tourism in which they participate. The most important distinction is probably between domestic and foreign tourists, although there are also important differences within both categories. For instance, American tourists tend to have a high spending capacity so that, in most countries their economic contribution is far greater than their absolute numbers might suggest. In addition, there are also other differences between national groups and, indeed, amongst domestic tourists, depending on their incomes, duration of stay, mode of travel, range of activities and type of accommodation. Much of the debate on whether to pursue strategies of mass-tourism or quality tourism is based on these differences. This is a debate which is common in such diverse locations as Venice, the Algarve and South-West England.

National Economic Context

It is also important to see tourism in context of the national economy for, as de Kadt (1979) stresses, 'tourism is not a unique devil'. Instead, the ability of the national economy to benefit from tourism depends on the availability of investment to develop the necessary infrastructure (hotels, golf courses, etc.) and on its ability to supply the needs of tourists, whether for food, souvenirs or hotel beds. While the types of demand are conditioned by the types of tourism, there are also important differences in the capacity of particular economies to respond to these demands. In general, small economies are more likely to be dependent on imports, and the same is also true of economies where tourism is not very well developed and where, therefore, there are poor economies of scale for suppliers.

There is also an important relationship between development and tourism in that the former conditions the level of domestic demand. Increasing real incomes result in growing demand for tourism but this is distributed between domestic and foreign destinations. One hypothetical scenario whereby domestic tourism is overtaken in relative importance by a considerable expansion of foreign tourism. This shift can lead to a stagnation in domestic tourism. However, with further increases in income and leisure time, there may be a growth of second and third holidays-including short breaks and there may be sufficient demand for domestic resorts, to renew growth in this sector. If, having reached saturation point, the growth of foreign tourism also slows down, the gap between this and domestic tourism may close. Elements of this relationship can be found in the experiences of several northern European countries, including the United Kingdom.

The Organisation of Capital: Domestic Versus Foreign Sources

The role of tourism in national development also depends partly on the organisation of capital and, in particular, on the penetration of international capital. This assumes a number of forms and, although foreign investment initially may assist the development of tourism, it also leads to leakage of income abroad through payment of royalties, profits and dividends. International capital can be involved in tourism development in a number of ways, including direct ownership of facilities by large companies, individual ownership of second homes, and ownership of the means of transport (especially airlines). In terms of the ownership of foreign facilities, hotels have been the most obvious recipient of direct foreign investment. The largest hotel groups are enormous and in 1986, for example, Holiday Inn owned 1907 hotels world-wide, followed by Quality Inns with 801 hotels. The largest European groups were the United Kingdom's Trust House Forte (793) and France's Accord (534). Many of the major tour companies also have interests in hotel chains. While direct ownership of hotels and of other facilities is important, of even greater significance is the bargeining power of a large foreign tour companies such as Thomson, Tjaereborg or Schaernow- Reisen. For example, Thomson had 3.75 million overseas holidays on offer in 1987 and its sheer size allows it and other major groups to secure very low pieces from sub-contracting to nationally-owned hotel chains. Given the oligopolistic position of the tour companies in the delivery of tourists, especially when faced with large numbers of relatively undifferentiated hotels, their bargaining power is considerable. International migration also plays a role in the tourist industry and in this, the experience of tourism is not dissimilar to that of other economic sectors, including manufacturing. The dominant international migration flows in Europe are from the South to the North (King 1984), and from less developed countries to Northern Europe (Castles et al. 1984). Countries such as the United Kingdom. France, Switzerland, the Federal Republic of Germany. the Netherlands, and Sweden rely on the labour of an estimated 6 million immigrants. They occupy a variety of jobs including less well-paid posts in such services sectors as hotels and restaurants. Their role is twofold: the supply of a flexible labour force contributes to depressing wages in the tourist industry, while their remittances to their home countries contribute to the balance of payments and to the levels of consumption in those countries (King 1986). There is also an important link between tourism and the generation of emigration. Tourism contributes to familiarisation with foreign culture and lifestyles (Lanfant 1980) and this may encourage emigration. There are some instances where tourists or at least foreign settlers have found jobs for locals abroad. Moore (1976) reports such a link in the Canaries where immigrant Swedes found jobs in Sweden for some of the local people.

Tourism and Development: Regional Perspectives

The distribution of tourism is inherently uneven: not only is this polarised but traditionally it is concentrated in less urbanised area. Therefore, as Peters states, 'tourism, by it nature, tends to distribute development away from the industrial centres towards those regions in a country which have not been developed'. There are many studies which have illustrated the extent of such regional polarisation and the rapidity of the process. Quite apart from every single case study in this volume, previous studies of the United Kingdom (Duffield 1977). Greece (Buckley and Papadopoulos 1986) and Yugoslavia (Allcock 1983) reinforce this argument. What is surprising is not that tourism has featured in regional policy and regional development strategies but that it has featured so little in these. Belatedly, however, local authorities are awakening to the possibilities of using tourism as a basis for regional development, as is evident, for example, in urban tourism projects in the United Kingdom and France.

The contribution of tourism to regional economies is measured in similar fashion to that for national economies. Its share of regional income or output can be estimated either in terms of direct effects or, *via* multiplier studies, or direct and indirect effects. The levels of interlinkages and dependency identified depend on the spatial scale of the analysis (Henderson 1976). Smaller tourist region are more likely to be dependent on tourism than are larger regions, which are more likely to have more diversified economies. As tourism can be developed in a short time-span, and with only moderate levels of investment, its impact on a regional economy can be very rapid as, for example. Diem (1980) reports in the Vald Anniviers in Switzerland.

Tourism is also a major source of employment at the regional level. However, as Pearce and Grimmeau (1985) have shown for Spain, the numbers and types of jobs vary considerably between regions in relation to the structure of the tourist industry, especially its seasonality. The year-round tourism of the Costa del Sol provides more permanent jobs than does the summer tourism of the Costa Dorada. Seasonality is but one aspect of employment in tourism, and there is also a need as at the national level to consider whether jobs are full-time or part-time, and whether they provide professional or manual work. There is also a need to consider how jobs in tourism interact with other household employment: whether tourism wages are supplementary to or the principal source of income, and whether they are used to support another enterprise such as a farm or a small workshop. Alternatively the employment effects can be negative, and tourism may destroy the basis of other activities as, for example,

Greenwood (1976) describes for an agricultural community in the Basque region. There is also the very real problem for many communities of the generational gap, so vividly described by Fraser (1974) in his study in southern Spain, but also evident in may Alpine communities (Kariel and Kariel 1982). Younger members of the family, lured by the easier wages and more glamorous lifestyles of tourist areas, may turn their backs on the traditional economy and, sometimes, society.

At the local level tourism can also have a very considerable impact on land markets. Tourism is highly polarised spatially, along the coastline, in a few cities or in some of the more picturesque inland areas. This is particularly evident along the Mediterranean coast where there is near-continuous urban sprawl largely as a result of tourism (Gonen 1981). The demands of tourism may force up land prices providing a windfall for local landowners and farmers as, for example in the Alps (Vincent 1980). However rising land values can also cause difficulties for those locals who are not in the tourist industry but who need to build homes or establish businesses in these areas (see Andronicou 1979 on Cyprus, and Boissevain and Inglott 1979 on Malta). The highly polarised nature of development also generates intense environmental problems such as water and air pollution, water shortages, traffic congestion and destruction of traditional landscapes. This reduces the quality of life for locals as well as for tourists and ultimately, may threaten the viability of the tourist industry itself. This is vividly illustrated in the Alps where the scars left by winter sports reduce the attraction of the landscape for summer visitors.

Types of Tourist

As with national development, care must be taken not to overgeneralise about the role of tourism in regional development. This role is conditioned by a number of considerations. One important element is the number of tourists and whether they exceed the 'tourist carrying capacity' (de Kadt 1979) of a region. There are usually critical numbers of tourists which can be integrated into regional economic and social structures and, beyond this any increase will result in a transformation of these structures. The regional economic effects are also dependent on the types of tourist attracted and; for example, Middleton (1977) shows the uneven regional distribution of (highspending) foreign tourists compared to domestic tourists in the United Kindgom. Only a few cities and small regions benefit substantially from foreign visitors while other regions such as the far South-West suffer from their inability to attract foreign visitors. Similar trends can be observed in the Mediterranean countries where foreign tourist are usually much higher spenders per capita, than are domestic tourists, although there may also be differences in consumption behaviour between groups of foreign nationals.

Regional Economic Context

The structure of the regional economy is also important in conditioning the economic impact of tourism, and two elements are important in this. First, there is the question of whether the tourist development is integrated into an existing settlement or is on a greenfield site and, also whether the scale of the development is such that it can be absorbed by or overwhelms the existing economy. In the Alps for instance, there is a major difference between high-level ski villages, built beyond the traditional settlement line, and low-level centres where tourism is better integrated with existing villages (Barker 1982). Each of these types makes different forms of demands on local labour, capital and suppliers a large specialist. high-level ski centre may be developed almost entirely by capital and labour from outside the local region.

This leads to the second question which is whether the tourist industry is able to utilise local resources. For example, farm tourism by its naturemostly utilises local resources, in terms of capital, labour and food supplies (see Beteille 1976 on rural France). However, with the rapid expansion of farm tourism in Europe (Dernoi 1983), there is a tendency for the marketing and, therefore, some of the control of farm tourism to pass into the hands of tour companies. The critical importance of regional economic structures in the utilisation of local resources is highlighted by Loukissas's (1982) comparative study of Greek islands. The economic impact of tourism is most beneficial in the larger islands because these have more diversified economic structures leakage effects are limited and the pressures on the local population are reduced because tourism tends to be concentrated in specialised villages. In contrast, tourism tends to dominate the economies of the smaller islands but may lead to unstable, short-term and dualistic development.

Sources of Capital

Capital in tourism development tends to be highly polarised between a few large groups and a mass of small, family-owned enterprises. The former will have access to the capital resources of large groups (for example Thomas Cook to it parent, Midland Bank) or to banking or institutional capital (for example, Accor financed its 1987 expansion programme through a share issue to French banks). However, venture capital has been notoriously loath to invest in smaller tourist businesses which sometimes wrongly have been considered higher-risk activities than manufacturing firms. Instead, small tourist businesses may have to rely on public sector grants or loans or, more commonly on personal or family sources of capital (see Shaw, Williams and Greenwood 1987 on a Cornish case study); this can be a major constraint on business expansion. The polarisation of capital can also be a potential source of conflict between the different interests of small-scale and (often externally owned) large-scale segments of the industry and their labour forces as Werff (1980) reports in the case of Pescara in Italy.

The sources of personal or family capital can be diverse but usually involve a transfer of resources from another economic activity, such as a small farm, fishing or transport business. One particularly important source of such capital at least in southern Europe has been the savings and remittances of emigrants and turned migrants, as King et al. (1984) and Mendonsa (1983a) report for southern Italy and central Portugal respectively. One final point to be emphasised with respect to capital is that most studies have concentrated on the accumulation of capital and new rounds of investment in tourism, while there has been little research on the restructuring of capital in existing tourist areas.

Regional Labour Markets

The type of local economy and of tourist development also condition the impact of tourism on regional labour markets. It may be possible if the development is small enough to rely entirely on local labour but. failing this a system of labour migration will develop. This can involve daily movements (from surrounding towns and villages), seasonal migration. or permanent in migration. These have very different impacts on the local economy depending on whether extra housing and services are required and also on how the migrant labour force distributes its expenditure between the locality and its home area (see Bernal et al. 1979 on the marked variations which exist between regional labour markets in Andalusia). Given that tourist regions often attract labour from less developed rural regions (see Cavaco 1980 on Portugal), the remittances they send back to these areas can ameliorate some of the features of uneven regional development.

Tourist Development

Tourist development might be defined specifically as the provision or enhancement of facilities and services to meet the needs of the tourist. More generally it might also include associated impacts such as employment creation or income generation.

Tourist development takes many forms. Classic examples include coastal, thermal or alpine resorts such as Benidorm, Bath and Chamonix. On a different scale, Tokyo, London and Paris each year attract millions of tourists who must be catered for. Then there is the second home phenomenon, be this in the form of converted farm cottages in the Auvergne or massive condominium construction in Colorado. The building of Disneyland and the opening of British stately homes or Canadian national parks to the public together with their conservation measures constitute other forms of tourist development. Often less apparent alongside hotels. restaurants. marinas and ski-fields is an accompanying infrastructure—airports, motorways. sewage treatment plants-which may be developed wholly or partly to serve the travelling public. Moreover, all these different developments can occur in different ways, at different scales and at different rates.

Tourist development also takes place in many different contexts. Modern mass tourism has its origins in the affluence of the industrialized nations of Western Europe, North America and more recently Japan. Tourism has also expanded significantly in Eastern Europe and is becoming an important sector in many developing countries in Asia, Africa, Latin America the Pacific and the Caribbean. Thus tourism has developed in liberal Western societies under highly planned socialist regimes as a relatively small part of large industrial economies or again as the leading sector of small developing countries. Likewise, tourism has developed in a wide variety of physical environments on low islands of the Pacific in the heart of Alpine Europe, in the countryside of the English Lakes District and along the Mediterranean coastline.

As a result the form tourist development may take can vary enormously from situation to situation, from one context to another. There is no more any one type of tourist development than there is a single model of agricultural, industrial or urban growth. However. this has been ignored by many writers, particularly those examining the social or cultural impact of tourist development. Summing up the 1976 symposium on tourism and culture change held by the American Anthropological Association, Nash noted: 'In these papers generally, the causal agent (tourism or some aspect of tourism) tends not to be well delineated or explicated. We have to dig to find out what it is.' At the same time it is possible to identity the various factors involved in tourist development and to describe general relationships among them. That is the aim of this book, to examine tourist development systematically in order to provide the reader with a general appreciation of the subject and a basic framework and methodology with which he may then address particular problems. The aim is not so much to provide the technical details for the planner (Cf. Lawson and Baud-Bovy, 1977) but rather to present a general overview of tourist development, outlining the different factors involved and emphasizing the nature of the relationships between them.

❐

7

Tourism Promotion and Customer Needs

In the dynamic world of leisure and tourism, promotion is the most visible of the four Ps. Promotion is used:

(a) to make customers aware of the availability of leisure and tourism products.

(b) to inform customers of the benefits of one product over another. To stimulate demand for products.

(c) to provide incentives to purchase or use products.

(d) to remind customers of the existence of a product.

The leisure and tourism industry uses a number of different promotional techniques (sometimes referred. to as 'the promotional mix). The most important are:

1. Advertising. Advertising is the most obvious of all the promotional techniques in use today. We are all subjected to advertising on our TV screens, on buses and trains, on commercial radio, at the side of the road and in newspapers and magazines. These are known as advertising media; the precise choice of media will be dictated partly by cost and partly by the type of product.

A new museum aimed at local people is unlikely to use national TV advertising but will rely on advertisements in the local press.

Advertising in leisure and tourism is directed either at the customer or at those working in the industry. Travel Trade Gazette and Leisure Management are two examples of trade magazines that carry advertisements.

Many people believe that leisure and tourism organisations put nearly all of their promotional effort, and budget, into advertising, over and above other types of promotional activity. This is far from the case, since many small and medium-size organisations find it hard to justify the expense of advertising campaigns. They rely much more on methods such as direct marketing and public relations, which can be just as effective with less investment.

(2) Direct Marketing. While advertising is sometimes criticised for not always hitting its intended audience, direct marketing is able to target particular customers very successfully. Direct mail is the best-known method of direct marketing, a technique used extensively in leisure and tourism. Using a mailing list, which may have been bought, borrowed or compiled from its own records, a leisure and tourism organisation can mail existing and prospective customers with a personalised letter or brochure giving details of its facilities. If planned carefully, a direct mail campaign can bring excellent results for a whole host of leisure and tourism organisations, ranging from hotels, leisure centres and travel agencies to tour operators, visitor attractions and art galleries. Direct mail is one of the fastest-growing types of promotional activity in leisure and tourism today.

Telemarketing is a growing method of direct marketing in the UK. Already widespread in the USA, its use in this country in leisure and tourism is fairly new, and is limited to activities such as selling time-share and selling services to businesses.

(3) Public Relations. Public relations, or PR as it is often known, is used a great deal in leisure and tourism. Organisations sometimes think of it as 'free publicity', particularly when associated with a newspaper or magazine article that features its facilities. In reality there is usually a price to be paid for such editorial coverage, even if it is just the cost of entertaining the journalist who wrote it!

Public relations is more than just keeping the media informed of your organisation, however, although this can undoubtedly pay dividends. PR is also about making sure that all staff and functions of an organisation which come into contact with the public, *e.g.* promotional literature, telephone technique, staff at reception, uniforms, etc., are well managed so as to gain maximum publicity and goodwill. PR is also about leisure and tourism organisations helping in the local community and getting involved in work for local and national charities. As well as providing much-needed cash, sponsorship can also bring PR benefits to leisure and tourism organisations. The image of a football club, for example, can be enhanced by being sponsored by a company that is regarded as successful in its own particular field.

(4) Personal Selling. Being a service industry, leisure and tourism relies heavily on the selling skills of those employed in order to achieve success. Selling is all about helping people to buy rather than selling them something they don't really want. Training in selling techniques is important for leisure and tourism staff, particularly in the commercial sector. Planning prior to a sales interview is essential as is being able to recognise buying signals, such as nodding of the head and signs of agreement from the customer. Closing the sale can be achieved by the taking of a deposit, credit card details or simply noting the customer's name and address.

(5) Sales Promotion. There are many different sales promotion techniques used in the leisure and tourism business. Some of the most common are:

(a) Discount vouchers and coupons.

(b) Brochures and leaflets.

(c) Price cuts and 'sale' offers, *e.g.* 10 per cent off all brochure prices of summer holidays.

(d) Extra product, *e.g.* a 'three for the price of two' offer at a restaurant.

(e) Free gifts, *e.g.* free sports bag with every ten aerobics sessions booked.

(f) Prize draws.

(g) Competitions.

(h) 'Giveaways', *e.g.* free carrier bags, pens, balloons, hats, T-shirts, stickers, etc.

(i) Free demonstrations, *e.g.* of sports and fitness equipment.

(j) Free membership of a new club in the area.

(k) Displays and exhibitions.

The main features of all sales promotion techniques is that they are temporary and aim to stimulate demand in the short term. The fast-moving nature of leisure and tourism means that managers are constantly having to react to fluctuations in demand from customers on a daily, weekly or seasonal basis. Unlike advertising, direct marketing and public relations activities, which are essentially long-term promotional tools, sales promotion gives an organisation the flexibility needed to be able to respond quickly to such changes.

Sales promotion techniques are not limited just to members of the general public; it is common for many staff working in leisure and tourism, especially in the private sector, to be offered incentives and rewards for achieving predetermined sales targets. Travel agency counter staff, for example, may be given Marks & Spencer or Boots vouchers by tour operators in return for selling a certain number of holidays. Indeed, incentive travel is a growing sector of leisure and tourism. Started in the USA, incentive travel is the reward of, say, a fortnight's holiday in Florida for an employee who has achieved sales success within his or her organisation.

IDENTIFYING CUSTOMER NEEDS

In order to be able to put the customer as the hub of all activity the organisation will need to have certain basic information on the characteristics of its customers, such as:

1. How many are there?

2. What ages are they?

3. Are they male or female?
4. How far do they travel to get to you?
5. What level of income do they have?
6. What is their attitude to your facility?
7. How long do they spend at the facility?
8. How much money do they spend at the facility?

Why is This Sort of Information Important?

Without this basic data, any leisure and tourism organisation, be it a leisure centre, museum, art gallery, country house hotel or visitor attraction, will be basing its management decisions purely on guesswork; sometimes referred to as 'seat of the pants' management! Decisions on pricing, design of promotional material, advertising media used and choice of menus can only be carried out effectively with accurate knowledge of present and future customers.

Customers and Markets

In the leisure and tourism industry, the term 'customer' means different things to different people. In the private sector, customers are quite obviously those individuals and groups who buy leisure goods and services; anything from a meal in a restaurant to a two-hour bingo session or a two-week holiday in the USA. In the public and voluntary sectors, the definition of a 'customer' is not quite so easy. Those who pay to use a local authority leisure centre are certainly customers, but so are those who use services for which there is no charge, such as the playground at the local park. Although there may be no direct charge for the playground, the people will have indirectly contributed to its cost by paying central and local taxes. Members of voluntary bodies, such as the RSPB or YHA, are again 'customers' of their particular organisation. They too must be treated with courtesy and respect, since without them, the organisation would not exist.

The size of the market for a particular facility, for example a theme park, can be calculated reasonably accurately by using population statistics readily available to the general public. Census data will indicate numbers of households and numbers of people by age groups. By calculating the population within different travel time zones, the attraction will have a good indication of its total market. Private sector operators in leisure and tourism are constantly trying to increase, or at least maintain, their market share in an increasingly competitive environment.

Are all Customers the Same?

If we start from the point of view that everybody is unique, then the number and range of customers for any leisure and tourism product is immense. The characteristics of customers (*e.g.* their age, social class and income level) will be different at different leisure and tourism facilities and their habits, tastes and even moods will change constantly over time and in different locations. Customers' expectations will also differ depending on, for example, their education, religion and cultural background.

An important group of customers are those with special needs; the elderly, young children, disabled people and ethnic minorities, will all need particular attention. Because customers are so different, a number of attempts have been made to classify them or put them into different categories in order to simplify the process of providing data for marketing purposes. Three of the best-known classification techniques are:

(1) Socio-economic Classification. For Many years, this JICNARS classification based on 'social class was the only one available to marketeers. Individuals were placed into one of six categories according to the occupation of the head of the household.

The underlying principle of the socio-economic classification is that those in each category will have similar values, display similar patterns of buyer behaviour and have similar levels of disposable income. It is assumed, also, that those at the top of the scale will have the highest level of disposable income. Clearly, there are a number of anomalies in this classification system:

(a) It is too much of a generalisation to expect all those in a particular category to have similar characteristics for example, a surgeon may choose to read the Daily Mirror, a newspaper read mostly by working class people.

(b) If the Managing Director of a large PLC loses her job, she will immediately move from social grade A to social grade E.

(c) Many skilled manual workers (C2) may well have a higher disposable income than those in the Cl, B or A social grades when payment for items such as private education and private health care are taken into account.

(d) When the whole social fabric of the nation is changing so rapidly, it is even questionable who the head of household is. Today, the heads of many households will be unemployed and in receipt of state benefits.

(2) Life Cycle Classification. The shortcomings of the socio-economic classification led marketeers to investigate if there wasn't a better way of categorising segments of the population. The life cycle concept puts an individual into one of nine categories, which are based not on income but on where that person is on his or her life cycle. The categories, with an indication of their likely demand for leisure and tourism products are:

(a) Bachelor stage young single people with few ties and a resonable level of disposable income. Likely to frequent clubs, discos, bars and buy CDs and tapes.

(b) Newly-wed/living together possibly a higher disposable income with leisure pursuits such as going to the cinema, eating out and going to clubs.

(c) Full nest 1 young marrieds/living together with youngest child less than six. Beginnings of family orientated leisure including visits to the park, tourist attractions and family holidays.

(d) Full nest 2 as above but youngest child over six. Falling disposable income, less spending on leisure.

(e) Full nest 3 older couples with dependent children, perhaps still studying. Disposable income low. Leisure centred on the home.

(f) Empty nest 1 older couples, childless or children all left home. Level of disposaple income likely to be restored. Demand for short breaks, overseas travel and active leisure.

(g) Empty nest 2 older couples, chief breadwinner retired. Income again restricted. Avid watchers of the television and listeners to the radio.

(i) Solitary survivor 1 single/widowed person in work. Home and garden likely to provide most leisure activity.

(j) Solitary survivor 2 as above but retired. Little spare cash for leisure.

(3) Lifestyle Classification. A further refinement of the process of categorisation came with the introduction in Britain during the 1980s of the concept of lifestyle classification, a technique which had been previously used in North America. One of the first British companies to test the concept was Young and Rubicam, a well-known advertising agency, who developed a lifestyle classification known as the '4 Cs'; four classes of people who were categorised according to their innermost needs into one of the following:

(a) Mainstreamers people who are looking for security and who live a conventional lifestyle. They usually buy wellknown brands of products, such as Heinz, Daz and Fairy Liquid, rather than 'own brands'. Mainstreamers do not want to 'stick out from the crowd'. They are by far the largest of the four groups, accounting for around 40 per cent of the British population. Their leisure habits are rather conventional including reading, gardening, knitting and walking in the country.

(b) Aspirers these are people looking for status and who like to be thought of as being 'at the cutting edge' of society

They buy status symbols such as fast cars and expensive jewellery and generally like the good things in life. They are risk-takers and many aspirers run their own businesses. Leisure interests include hang-gliding, motor sports, power boating, karate and listening to hi-fi music.

(c) Succeeders these are people who have already achieved status and who ultimately like to be in control of their lives. They have no need for status symbols but value quality in all that they purchase. Leisure interests include gardening, entertaining, taking short breaks and playing golf.

(d) Reformers these are people who consider that 'quality of life' is more important than status and status symbols. They are the best educated of all four groups and tend to join groups to influence decision making in society. They buy many natural products and 'own label' products; they are sometimes referred to as 'the Sainsbury shoppers'! Leisure is often family orientated and includes camping, walking, cycling, reading and playing games.

Why do we Need to Classify People at all?

This technique of subdividing the market into different groups who share similar characteristics is known as market segmentation. One of the main benefits of segmenting the market for a particular leisure or tourism product, for example, is that it allows an organisation to target particular individuals or groups within the segment. These people then become the focus of all the marketing effort, with the design and promotion of products and services that they will want.

Segmentation within leisure and tourism happens at a number of different levels:

(a) The whole leisure and tourism industry can be segmented into a range of different sectors, *e.g.* tourism, sport, arts, entertainment, community recreation, heritage, etc.

(b) An individual sector can be segmented, *e.g.* tourism can be divided into accommodation, transportation and attractions.

(c) Individual elements of a sector can be further segmented, *e.g.* accommodation can be broken down into serviced and self-catering.

(d) At a fourth level of segmentation, serviced accommodation can be divided into hotels, guesthouses, inns, motels, etc.

(e) Further segmentation of hotels by the type of guests, *e.g.* business clients, groups, short break clients, conference delegates, overseas visitors, etc.

Market segmentation is, therefore, a tool that the marketeer can use to satisfy the requirements of his or her particular customers. Being concerned with the needs of customers, however, does mean that segmentation relies heavily on market research to help match the product exactly to the clients' needs.

Market Research

Market research is the collection and analysis of data about customers and its use for management purposes. The term marketing research has gained favour in recent years and is an allembracing phrase to include product research, promotion research and price research. Research into customers, which is the subject of this particular section, is rightly called market research, and this is the terminology which will be used.

Market research data, from whatever source, is invaluable to the manager in providing a sound base on which effective marketing decisions can be made. All leisure and tourism organisations need feedback from their existing customers and many will want to know why people are not using their facilities but prefer what a competitor is providing. It is the job of market research to provide such data in as objective a form as possible, in other words with no bias. This is why many leisure and tourism organisations will employ outside specialists to carry out the research on their behalf. Not all market research activity is a costly or elaborate affair. The proprietor of a small hotel will constantly get informal feedback from his guests on their opinion of his facilities and service level and will make the necessary adjustments.

Types and Sources of Market Research Information

There are many different sources of market research data available to those managing and planning leisure and tourism facilities, some of it very general, such as statistics on trends in the population structure, and some specific to particular sectors of the industry, for example data on the number of visitors to tourist attractions. Material that is already available, through many different published sources, is known as secondary data. If the particular information is not available from existing sources, then it will be necessary to collect primary data. Much of the information that an organisation needs for marketing purposes may already be held within its various departments; this is what is meant by internal sources. Information found outside the organisation (external sources) is useful in giving a general picture of the state of a particular market or sector of the market. Collecting primary data about customers in leisure and tourism generally involves either direct observation, such as counting traffic or observing visitor flow patterns at a tourist attraction, or conducting a survey of one kind or another, *e.g.* asking hotel guests to complete a questionnaire to find out if they were happy with the facilities and service.

Collection of Primary Research Data

If an organisation wishes to collect information not already available, or wants to update previous information, it will need to collect primary data, either through observation, by carrying out a surveyor through the use of focus groups.

Observation. Observation is a very useful, and often neglected, form of primary data collection in leisure and tourism. It does not always involve people actually watching what others do and recording the details systematically. Nowadays, there are sophisticated techniques available for counting and recording customer and traffic flows, such as time-lapse photography, closed circuit television

(CCTV) and electronic tally counters. Particular examples of the use of observation in leisure and tourism include:

(a) A tourist information centre using an electronic tally counter to record the number of people using the TIC.

(b) A large visitor attraction using CCTV to record visitor flows around the site.

(c) A museum using time-lapse photography to examine visitor movements.

(d) A large sports complex installing an electronic traffic counter to help traffic management and ease congestion.

Clearly, such equipment can be very useful for security purposes as well. When people are employed to carry out observation, rather than relying on electronic means of collection, they are often able to collect useful information on customer attitudes to a particular facility by 'mingling' with them but not revealing their identity or purpose.

Carrying out a Suruey. There are three main types of survey used to collect primary data, all of which involve the recording of responses on a questionnaire:

1. Face-to-face interview survey this is usually the most effective way of gathering information on customers. As its name implies, a trained interviewer will ask questions of a respondent and record the responses on a questionnaire. Although one of the best methods for getting in-depth information, since the interviewer can prompt the respondent if he or she is unclear as to the meaning of a particular question, face-to-face interviewing is very labour intensive and, therefore, expensive place in a number of different locations: The interviews can take place in a number of different locations:

   — At home.

   — In the street.

— At the facility.

— En route to a facility.

— At work.

Leisure and tourism organisations will often employ specialists to carry out an interview survey on their behalf so that any bias is kept to a minimum.

One of the most useful face-to-face interview surveys, which is used extensively in leisure and tourism facilities, is the visitor survey. Leisure centres, hotels, tourist attractions, catering outlets and entertainment complexes all use the information from visitor surveys to help develop products and services that will appeal to their customers. By asking the relevant questions, a visitor survey can also indicate which media to use in promoting the facilities.

2. Self-completed questionnaire survey this is a cheaper method of data collection since respondents are asked to fill in the questionnaires themselves, meaning that there is no need to employ and tràin interviewers. A self-completed questionnaire does have the disadvantage, however, that if the respondent is unclear about a particular question, there is nobody to prompt him or her. With this type of survey, there are again different locations and methods by which the data is gathered.

3. Postal survey this is a very common method in leisure and tourism involving the posting back of a completed questionnaire that may have been distributed in a number of ways:

   — Through the postal system some tour operators mail a questionnaire to clients soon after they return home.

   — Given out on the return journey from a holiday, perhaps on the flight home.

   — Picked up 'on-site', *e.g.* at a sports centre, hotel or tourist attraction and posted when completed.

4. Full 'on-site' survey this is the cheapest self-completed survey of all since the respondents are asked not only to complete the questionnaire while they are at the facility, but also to leave it behind, often in a sealed box, before they leave. Cost is minimal as there are no postal charges involved.

5. Telephone survey while not widespread in leisure and tourism, telephone surveys are growing rapidly as a way of getting a quick response to an event or activity. In the leisure and tourism industry they are most commonly used in the commercial sector and often on a business-to-business basis. For example, the organisers of the annual British Travel Trade Fair use the technique to contact exhibitors and trade visitors immediately after the event to gauge their reactions and comments. Hotels and other conference venues will often use telephone surveys to get feedback on the standard of service and facilities at a particular venue.

Focus Groups

Focus groups are the bringing together of a small group of individuals under the guidance of a facilitator, often trained in psychology. It gives the facilitator a chance to delve into people's innermost thoughts and values with a view to exploring the influences that affect their purchasing decisions, *e.g.* what makes them go to restaurant A rather than restaurant B, and so on. Focus groups often produce very valuable information that cannot easily be gathered from either a face-to-face interview or self-completed questionnaire. British Rail used the focus group technique in the early 1980s to investigate ways of improving its Inter City rail services.

Survey Methods

There are a number of important points that relate to how surveys are carried out using any of the methods just described. These include:

1. Qualitative versus quantitative data an organisation must be clear about what it hopes to achieve by carrying out a survey. If it is only interested in factual information, then a simple visitor survey based on a self-completed questionnaire would be sufficient. If, however, more in depth opinions are sought, face-to-face interviews and focus groups would be more appropriate.

2. Sampling in most cases it is not feasible to survey everybody who uses a particular leisure and tourism facility or buys particular products. It is, therefore, necessary to select a proportion of the total number known as a sample. Large samples produce more accurate results than small ones, but the increase in accuracy becomes less and less significant as the sample size is increased. Sophisticated statistical procedures are used to ensure that the sample is representative of the whole group and that there is no bias in selection.

3. Questionnaire design It is important to remember that it is an acquired skill best left to the professional! Questionnaires generally include a mix of factual and opinion questions and a number of 'profile' questions to give a clearer picture of the respondent.

Having made the decision to adopt a culture that puts the customer at the heart of all its activity, any leisure and tourism organisation, whether private, public or voluntary sector, will be well aware of the need for good customer feedback using one, or a mixture, of the market research techniques described above. Once it has this data, it can then begin to develop products that satisfy customer need, and it is this area of leisure and tourism products.

❐

8

Tourism Planning

Reflecting on the entire concept of planning supply side development at the three levels-regional, destination, and site—an over all summary of conclusions and principles seems appropriate. Grouped into five categories for easier understanding and application are basic principles, processes, the environment, policies and goals, and challenges of the future.

BASIC PRINCIPLES

Tourism Planning Must Encompass All Travel-Business and Pleasure

Even though definitions of tourism vary, from a planning perspective all travel (except commuting) should be included. This principle is based on the fact that all the components of the supply side actually cater to all travellers, not just vacation or pleasure travellers. Although plans and designs for the business market segment may be slightly different from those catering to pleasure travellers. the basic functions are generic to both. For example hotel guests may have quite different travel objectives but accept lodging in the same hotel. If plans for tourism development are to be comprehensive and meet the needs of both travellers and hosts, virtually all markets should be included in the scope of planning.

Planning Objectives, Processes and Outcomes Vary from Macro-to Microscales.

Because the term planning has so many popular meanings it is necesary to consider what is meant when planning for tourism is proposed. Suggested here are three levels. At the regional (federal, state, and provincial) level, the outcome of planning is primarily guidelines, not project construction. At this level planning can provide policies, guide destination identification foster integration of destinations, coordinate action, and resolve issues for the region Destination planning however has narrower scope including focal communities and their surrounding rural areas. Much stronger local participation in planning is required at this level. Destination planning involves new cooperation among governmental jurisdictions—city, county, surrounding municipalities. The outcome may include indentification of many site project opportunities. Finally, site scale planning is also called design and utilizes principles and processes that guide actual construction of supply side development. It is helpful to discriminate between these three levels in order to meet desired objectives for the best tourism.

Planning of the Supply Side should Meet the Needs of Market Demand

Because tourism is driven by supply side development as well as market demand, both should be in balance. As plans are laid for tourism development, there should be clear understanding of travel market trends. This understanding is required of planners, designers, owners, developers, and local citizen groups affected by tourism. Knowledge of potential market origins and the interests, habits and other travel characteristics of the population is needed in order to plan the several components of the supply side. For example there is not need to plan attractions and services for youth activities if market analysis shows market origins are dominated by older people.

Integration of Planning at all Scales is Essential

Although there are differences in sponsors and techniques at the three scales-regional, destination, and site the overall success of tourism depends on how well these three are integrated. Regional planning provides guidance for destination and site locations as well as for the region. This principle of integration requires constant communication among the tourism leaders of regions, destinations, and sites. National, state, and provincial tourism organizations and agencies (public and private) can play a major role in integration of plans and planning at all levels.

Supply Side Planning Must be Directed Toward the Three Developer Sectors

There is prevailing misconception that supply side development is performed exclusively by the business sector. Although the commercial enterprise sector usually products the greatest economic impact tourism also is developed by non-profit organizations and government developers are included alongside business. Non-profit organizations own plan and manage many natural and cultural resource areas. They are prime actors in future establishment of historic sites nature preserves, museums, and places for cultural events such as festivals and performing arts. Government agencies have a large stake in future planning, such as for parks highways, camp-grounds, wildlife preserves, interpretive centres and infrastructure (water supply waste disposal, fire and police protection. and health and safety).

Planning Must Integrate all Components of the Supply Side

The five components of the supply side-attractions, transportation services, information and promotion-need to be planned in concert. For example plans for new lodging can be more meaningful if plans for new attractions and transportation are known. The success of lodging depends greatly on decisions made by developers and managers of the other four components. In fact, all developments within all components are influenced greatly by one another's plans and decisions. They are in a very dynamic relationship that requires new communication, cooperation, and even collaboration. All plans for tourism must be directed toward integration of development in all components if owners are to be successful and market needs are to be met.

Urban-rural Planning Must Be Integrated

The dominant mode of tourism development today is focused on two separate geographic areas—cities and rural areas. The planning and development of parks, hunting and fishing areas, resorts, wildlife areas and small town historic sites take place primarily in rural areas. The creation of new convention centres. sports arenas, historic architecture attractions, theme parks and festivals is primarily a city function. Both cities and rural areas are essential to tourism. But, new lodging, food services, transportation, information systems, and promotion depend on the decisions made in both urban and rural areas. In order to meet desired tourism objectives, plans and decisions in the surrounding rural areas must be integrated with city tourism plans.

Traffic and Pedestrian Functions Need Integration

Preoccupation with expanding traffic ways and automobile parking by transportation officials has tended to divert needed planning attention away from pedestrians. Virtually all visitor activities take place after the train, bus, or automobile has been abandoned. Even driving for pleasure produces its greatest rewards at turnout overlooks where people can get out of their automobiles to walk and view the scenery. Although it is essential that new and better traffic handling is accomplished, equally important is planning for people on foot. Urban scenes, natural resource access and culturally significant areas must retain their identity without intrusion from massive traffic ways.

Clustering is Basic Principle of Planning and Design

Clustering-grouping together rather than dispersing has many advantages as a planning principle. All trans portation systems bring travellers to focal points. Expressways lead travellers to exit locations where clustering of services best satisfies demand. When travellers become interested in food service they prefer a variety of restaurant choices favoured by clustering. The same principle applies to lodging. Generally. resource protection is more easily accomplished when traveller facilities and services are not dispersed throughout parks. Clustering favours better visitor control better management, and more efficient engineering of infrastructure. National parks for example can best manage visitor use of resources when major services of accommodations food service shopping areas and traveller services are concentrated in a well planned community nearby.

ENVIRONMENT AND RESOURCES

Global Environmental Deterioration Demands Tourism's Attention

The deterioration of environmental conditions worldwide is of major significance to all tourism planning and development. Certainly, all tourist development must not be detrimental to natural and cultural resources. Successful tourism must have clean air, abundant wildlife, unpolluted water, and freedom from resource erosion. The establishment of, resorts, hotels, restaurants, and roads must not destroy basic resources. Especially fragile are archaeological and historic resources, demanding extreme care in design and management for tourism. Of even greater concern of environmental degradation by others, such as poor practices by industries, muaicipalities, forestry, mining and agriculture-leading to water and air pollution, toxic waste, soil erosion, loss of animal habitat, and acid rain.

Park Protection and Tourism can be Compatible

The ideological premise that tourism is destructive of parks is false. National and state parks would not exist if a vocal public, made up largely of visitors were not strong advocates of their establishment and support. Instances cited of destruction of park resources by visitors are largely due to poor planning and poor management. Better planning involves zoning the park area so that major masses of visitors, primarily at service centres, do not disturb fragile and rare resources. New cooperation between the three developers sectors-non-profit organizations, commercial enterprise, and government resource agencies can result in plans that provide visitor rewards as well as resource protection.

Sustaninable Development is a Planning Principle for Tourism

The planning of tourism, from the macro to microscales, must include consideration of its potential impact on the social, economic, and environmental qualities of host areas. Local area leaders, government officials and general citizenry have the prerogative to make their own planning decisions on how much tourism should be allowed and how it should be developed. The short-range mind set of some developers, such as for resorts, must be tempered by long-range planning and development that can sustain environmental, social, and economic values.

Planning and Design can Resolve Visitor Impact Management Issues

Some recommendations have been made for numerically setting visitor limits not to exceed environmental capacity. However, because of the number of variables, visitor impact issues have not been resolved. Instead planning and management techniques are proving more effective. For example, visitor interpretive centres can be designed for mass tourist use, leaving fragile resource areas untouched. Motorcoach and tram systems are less threatening to environments than private automobile use. For some specific uses, such as forest and wilderness trails, quotas may be necessary. Perhaps the best environmental management comes with regular monitoring of how the planned and developed visitor use is affecting the environment.

Appropriateness is a Planning and Design Fundamental

Much of the objection by environmentalists to tourism development stems from issues of aesthetics. When new attractions, facilities, and services are designed, they can be created and located in ways that respect the quality and dominant characteristics of resources. For example, the architectural qualities of historic buildings would be damaged visually if modern hotels and restaurants were built too close or with incompatible design. Professional designers are especially adept at creating designs appropriate to natural and cultural resource settings. But, owners and investors must be amenable to this fundamental for the best tourism development to occur.

Ecotourism Requires Special Site, Area and Regional planning and Design

The surge in travel market interest in natural and cultural resources can be met with carefuly designed destinations and places. Low-scale, modest, and slow-paced development that is planned in concert with local residents can be good business as well as environmentally sensitive. Especially important are parks and preserves that are managed with both visitor interest and resource protection principles. For example, in coastal areas trained guides can help visitors understand underwater life as well as guide activities in ways that perpetuate coral and other sea life. The planning and design of ecotourism requires the very best of owner-manager principles as well as design creativity.

Ecotourism can Foster Conservation

Eoctourism businesses that depend on government resourcc protected areas have the opportunity to return revenues to the managers of these public areas. Frequently, the major attractions bringing visitors to ecotourism settings are not profitmaking depending mostly on contributions and support from nonprofit organizations or government agencies. Because of the interde-pendency between developers of ecotourism and these resource areas, reciprocal agreements should include funding for the privilege of visitor use.

Economic Success of Tourism Depends on Resource Protection

Preoccupation with promotion in most tourism agencies tends to give low priority to resource protective measures. A planning objective must be the demonstration of how a tourism economy depends on resource protection. Proper planning procedures can bring the environmentalists together with developers to create resource protective projects. Roads, vacation homes, resorts, marinas, and other services can be planned with minimum intrusion of valuable resources. Central sewage treatment plants and other technical solutions, such as water recycling, can eliminate resource damage. Essential is early recognition of the role of resources in creating plans for tourism development. The economic impact of jobs, incomes, and tax returns is dependent upon how well resources are protected.

Placeness is a Tourism Planning Fundamental

Because of the success of some attractions, there is a tendency among developers to replicate them whether or not they fit local settings. Excessive duplication reduces chances of success and denies more competitive development based on uniqueness of place. Every destination has a different set of geographical factors, traditions, relationship to markets, and host characteristics. It is essential, then, for a host area to plan, design, and develop its own special personality based on its special qualities of place.

POLICIES AND GOALS

Economic Development Cannot be an Exclusive Goal

Although economic benefits from tourism are valuable and are a valid goal for tourism planning, there are several other goals of equal importance. Certainly, many communities and regions derive substantial number of jobs, greater incomes, and worthwhile tax returns from tourism. For many areas, tourism is replacing dwindling former economies. But planning also must be directed toward three other goals. Planning must enhance visitor satisfaction if economic improvement is to accrue. Planning must integrate tourism into the social and economic life of communities and destinations.

Tourism Planning Policies should be Directed Toward Quality as well as Growth

In today's competitive tourism world, an increase in numbers of visitors does not always equate with the four desirable goals. It is quite likely, considering today's more discriminating travel markets, that better quality of all development has a much better chance of fostering desired goals. Planning should reveal the need for upgrading the supply side development and the potential for attracting higher quality trade. Better quality trade implies greater sensitivity to more satisfying visitor experience as well as high grade physical plant.

Tourism Policy must be more than Promotion

Although most nations, states, provinces and cities spend the majority of their tourism budgets on promotion newer and more comprehensive policies are needed. Certainly promotion continuous to be needed but it should be balanced with policies on other very important topics. For example, health and safety policies should be in place in order to protect travellers from poor sanitation and other travel hazards. As travel becomes more universal in scope, international agreements on travel regulations need to become essential policies at all levels. Government and private sector tourism policies need to ensure greater support of research training and education in tourism. Increasingly universities are showing interest in adding tourism programmes but lack adequate support from business and government.

Tourism Planning Policy Requires Greater Public-private Cooperation

As more and more nations turn to the private sector for the provision of services and production of products new cooperation with government is needed. Tourism, development is not created exclusively by private commercial enterprise. But an adversarial attitude often inhibits tourism progress. In order for the tourism system to run more smoothly, greater understanding of the roles of both sectors is needed. All private sector actors in the supply side components of tourism-attractions, services, transportation, information, and promotion depend greatly on investment, planning, and management policies of government. Conversely, governments can reduce budgets by diverting many tourism responsibilities to the private sector. New cooperation, between the public and private sectors is essential.

Regional Policies for Development Incentives can Stimulate Business

Government incentives at the regional level can assist tourist business planning and establishment. These incentives could include tax abatement or direct grants contingent upon factors of destination plans and feasibility documentation. Within many government agencies, such aids are available for other business but not for tourism. New legislative mandates may be needed in order for these agencies to broaden their policies to include tourism. Such incentives can stimulate destination to create their own plans.

Regional Tourism Policies can Strengthen all Planning

At the national, state, or provincial level planning policies can foster better development at not only that level but also the destination level. For example, policies for transportation can influence greatly the access from markets and between other destinations. National and destination promotion can be integrated. National policies on uniform visitor information and directional systems can foster the taveller's understanding of attractions at destinations and how to find them. These advantages can accrue from greater cooperation between planners and decisionmakers at both national and destination levels.

PROCESSES

Processes for Plans and Continuous Planning Need Integration

Essential at regional and destination levels is the integration of two forms of tourism planning: plan projects and a continuous planning process. From time to time, an in-depth project is needed that involves essential process steps: setting objectives; researching markets, resources and programmes; synthesizing research; developing concepts for development; and preparing recommendations. Such a planning process not only provides guidelines for development but also (when done properly) stimulates involvement by key developers and decisionmakers. However, such projects are limited by the research information and forecasting abilities at a specific time period. These projects should be updated, probably every five years. But, in order to be most effective, plans should be accompanied by a continuous planning process that is carried out regularly and cooperatively by the public and private sectors.

Geographic Requires Destination Identification

Although areas are not all alike, there is a dominant development tendency toward sameness of development. Universal design styles tend to make all places look alike, reducing greatly the competitive edge of each destination.

Destinations vary greatly in their geographic content and location. Natural resources are not evenly distributed nor of the same characteristics. Even beaches and waterfronts at different locations that seem similar have different physical characteristics of sand composition, wave action, shore-line topography, vegetative cover, climatic conditions, and development. Nor are cultural resources evenly distributed. Some locations were important to national or world events—others are of little cultural consequence for future tourism development.

Process Techniques can Assist Identification of Potential Destinations

Analysis of physical factors can reveal geographic difference within a region that are important to future tourism development. By researching and mapping an overlay map series, computer Geographic Information System programmes can produce composite maps showing areas of strongest and weakest resource foundations. These foundations can be generalized into two main categories-natural and cultural resources. Common to both are the location and significance of cities and transportation systems. Planning processes that identify potential destination zones and their special characteristics can provide: a new perspective for policymakers, a foundation for local tourism planning and development clues for future opportunities, and the basis for project feasibilities.

Destination Planning Processes Encompass Cities and Surrounding Areas

A planning process for destinations cannot stop at the city limits. Research analysis, synthesis, and concepts for tourism planning of destinations must encompass surrounding areas as-well-as focal cities. This conclusion is based on the principle that lands with attraction potential for visitors are located in suburban and rural areas as well as within cities. However, the dominant location for travel serviceslodging, food, shopping and entertainments within the city. Steps for planning destinations must include analysis of development factors surrounding cities as well as within them. New jurisdictional cooperation will be required.

Destination Cooperation of Leadership and Organization is essential

Tourism in contrast to a manufacturing plant, cannot be managed by a single director. It can be guided, stimulated and led, but not managed by a central authority. Especially important at the destination scale is leadership, not dictation.

Leadership implies both guidance and organization. Organization is needed in order to bring together the many entities that develop and are affected by tourism. This approach means more than the organization offered by the typical chamber of commerce or tourism agency. It means the enlistment of representatives of the many facets of community and surrounding life because all are involved in tourism.

Leaders can come from many sources—government, business, planners, environmentalists and educators but their role for tourism will be the same. Their role is not managing in the sense of forced control but rather guiding, stimulating, and regularly reaching toward desired goals. When leadership cooperates with a comprehensive organization, plans and planning can be most productive.

Site Scale Design is Interrelated to All Tourism Planning

Although the design of parks, hotels, resorts, transportation, and other elements of the supply side must'meet requirements of owner-clients, designers must consider interrelationships as well. The traveller perceives and uses such site development only in context with a larger whole. Design for a hotel, for example. must meet all functional needs of lodging but will be inadequate if external factors are not considered. Adjacent land uses, accessibility. relationship to attractions, and adaptation to the destination are among key factors that need to be incorporated into site design concepts for a hotel. Processes for site scale design fall short of their full purpose if they fail to include external as well as internal factors.

New Design Paradigms Require New Kinds of Designers

Traditional design education and practice fall short of meeting today's design needs. Reliance only upon intuition and skill is an incomplete agenda for a design process in modern tourism. To these desirable factors must be added a greater understanding of facts resulting from research of two important subject matter areas. First, designers must become cognizant of studies of traveller characteristics, preferences, and behaviour. Assumptions based only on the designer's experience can provide a false and misleading foundation for design. Second, today the many scientific characteristics and environmental factors of the land are equally important foundations for design. Mere casual inspection of a site and shallow discussions with clients are inadequate in today's planning and design processes for tourism development.

Site Design Must Meet Several Design Criteria

In addition to meeting the requested programme of owners-developers, designers are bound to several other criteria for their design concepts.

1. All designs must function as a system with structural stability to satisfy all use functions, and to provide aesthetically satisfying development.

2. Tourism plans must be integrated into all other plans and planning processes.

3. All tourism designs must meet the needs of the true clients-the visitors.

4. Individuality of design can provide the greatest adaptation to settings and the best competitive edge.
5. Authenticity is an important criterion.
6. All designs should incorporate aestheticlly satisfying appeal rather than see sterile, drab, and ordinary to visitors.
7. All design processes must provide designs that are marketable. Satisfying the interests and needs of the several travel markets is an important design criterion.

Site Design Requires Special Design Processes

Although planning and design processes for tourism may be similar for all scalesuregional, destination, and siteuthose for sites require special emphasis. Key steps include market analysis, programme statement, site selection/revised programme, site analysis, synthesis, conceptual design, feasibility, final plan, and postconstruction evaluation. It must be emphasized that these process steps are not exclusive prerogative of designers. The best designs will result from close collaboration not only with owner-sdevelopers but also marketers, specialists in natural and cultural resources, local residents, and others who can offer constructive assistance.

FUTURE CHALLENGES

Entgrepreneurship is Essential to Future Tourism Plans

Because tourism contains a large component of service businesses, special programmes to stimulate entrepreneurship are needed in all nations. There is not substitute for the establishment of new businesses by individuals with initiative. Entrepreneurship is a product of a culture, and where absent, a nation may have great difficulty in providing the services needed by travellers.

Several qualities are required of an entrepreneur. The ability to visualize a marketable service is essential. An entrepreneur must understand the field of travel well enough to sense and opportunity to fulfil some new or improved traveller need. Essential also is commitment. Full and enthusiastic belief in a business fires the development process form concept through construction and management. Although, rewards from profits may be a major incentive, personal satisfaction form achievement may be equally important. Tourism plans must include strong incentives for entrepreneurship.

Plans should foster Low-Impact Development

The past trend toward environmentally insensitive mega-resort development appears to be giving way to smaller-scale and more adaptable tourism expansion. Although the market for major tourist complexes continues interest in low-key attractions and services has increased. This trend is a reflection of a more sophisticated travel market segment as well as stronger worldwide sensitivity to the environment. Local residents are recognizing that low impact tourism development places much less stress on the community. This stronger local role provides closer scrutiny of new projects. There is increasing questioning of major outside investments as compared to local sponsorship of indigenous tourism. In the future plans for tourism expansion will include closer examination of local impact upon the environment and society.

Much Greater Intersector Cooperation is Needed

In the future, the go-it-alone policy of all development sectors will be modified by greater intersectoral cooperation. This will result not from altruism but from self-interest. Governmental land development projects such as parks and recreation areas will meet their objectives more fully when created in concert with commercial enterprise. Policies of mutual support will supplant adversarial roles of the past. Tourist businesses will increasingly recognize the need to support environmentally sensitive attractions that create markets for their services. Nonprofit organizations will understand the need for new cooperation with governments and commercial enterprise. Future planning for tourism at all levels, macro to micro, will include policies and processes that foster intersector communication and decision-making because of the mutual benefits that they can produce.

CREATIVITY AND INNOVATION CHARACTERIZE

Future Tourism Planning and Design

Review of tourism development over several decades shows the importance of breaking away from repetition of the past. Markets change, demanding inventive solutions to new visitor needs. Equally challenging to the resourceful and imaginative design abilities are the requirements of environmentalism. No longer can designers create tourism projects for only the developer's objectives. Ingenuity and originality must be directed toward all major goals of tourism planning-economic improvement, better visitor satisfaction, resource protection, and integration into the local economic and social setting. This new philosophy places heavier professional practice of planners and designers. But the results will be far more rewarding than in the past.

A New Planning and Design Principle of Land Use Stewardship is Needed

Even though owners of land in a democracy have rights of land use, their short-range objective must be tempered by long-range continues forever. Mankind has a custodial responsibility that reaches beyond today. But, all three tourism development sectors tend to believe such long-range planning limits resolution, integrative planning, public today's potential. Actually, the opposite involvement and sustainable is true as is being demonstrated by other resource exploitation such as forestry and agriculture. Wasted and abused resources diminish opportunities, often even in the short range. It is incumbent upon future tourism planning and design professionals to promote protracted as well as immediate goals and objective. The highest and most noble objectives of society at large must always take priority over occluded self-interest.

Federal to Local Government Roles Need to be Clarified

Tourism plans of the future can ensure better functioning of the system if they clarify roles at all scales, macro to micro. The present overlapping and confusing roles of all sectors waste funds and misdirect effort. For example, the potential traveler is now confused by proliferation of promotional literature produced by federal, state, provincial and city agencies as well as businesses and destinations. Nationwide and regional plans should be integrated with destination and site plans if all tourism objectives are to be met. New policies, revisions in regulations, and new incentives for the private sector should have high priority at all governmental levels if tourism is to thrive.

Tourism must not be Overplanned

To say that tourism must not be overplanned is to place constraint upon excessive manipulation of tourism development. There is much to be said for planning that is open-ended enough to allow spontaneous and innovative growth. The tendency today toward contrived tourism development must be curbed rather than fostered. by new planning concepts and processes.

Paramount is the freedom of travellers to seek out their own rewards from travel experiences. So much of modern life denies this opportunity, only available through travel. Work, duty, law, social responsibility and personal obligation continue to remain but travel offers the one remaining opportunity for emancipation.

Tourism must be planned at all scales with such restraint that travellers can be free to obtain the enriching rewards of discovery, adventure and achievement. Planned physical settings, programmes. politica! action management decisions and promotion can and should foster, not inhibit the individual originality and personal satisfaction that can be derived only from travel. If domestic travel is to break down the barriers of parochialism and if international travel is to stimulate world understanding and peace all policies and practices of planning must be so dynamic and flexible that these objectives are assured. Planning policies concepts and processes are merely tools, not ends.

The financing of tourism development is an essential consideration in implementation. The type of funding needs and possible sources of financing must be understood, and an investment strategy formulated. The funding needs and approach must be specifically identified for each particular country or region. However, there are certain basic considerations that should be made as explained in the following sections.

Funding Needs

There are three types of funding needs that should be considered in developing tourism. Funding is needed for preparation of tourism plans the general national or regional plan; more detailed planning of tourism development areas; and planning and feasibility analyses of specific development projects. Funding the general level of planning is typically the responsibility of the government. Financing the more detailed plans and projects can be either by the government or private sector, depending on the local situation. However the more detailed planning must still be carried out according to government planning standards and reviewed and approved by the government. If financing is not available locally for planning, then international assistance must be sought.

Funding is required for development of the infrastructure necessary for tourism. The importance of developing adequate infrastructure has been emphasized in previous chapters. Major infrastructure is typically the responsibility of the government to finance. However, at least some of this investment, such as for utility services, can be recovered through payment of user fees. As has been emphasized much of the infrastructure can be developed to serve general community and economic needs as well as tourism and thus bring substantial overall benefits to the country. Infrastructure is expensive and many countries need international assistance in financing it, especially for the foreign exchange component of the cost. Infrastructure costs within commercial development sites are usually paid by the private developers of the sites. Private developers may also be required to pay for some of the off-site infrastructure costs that benefit their sites.

Many types of major attraction features such as national parks and museums, typically are financed by the government. However, user fees can help recover the initial investment or at least pay for the operational and maintenance costs of these features. These attractions also serve residents of the area as well as tourists, and the costs can be justified as providing an important public recreational or educational facility.

Human resources development, such as establishment of a hotel and tourism education centre must also be funded usually by the government but often with private sector involvement. A training levy may be applied as a tax on tourists' hotel and restaurant expenditures to help pay for operation of a tourism education centre.

Major funding is needed for development of the commercial revenue producing tourist facilities and services including accommodation, restaurant, tour and travel agencies and shopping facilities. These are typically funded by the private sector but in newly developing tourism areas the government may need to be a pioneer developer until the private sector has developed the confidence to make its own investments. Development incentives may also need to be offered to induce the private sector to make investments. National tourism development banks are often organized. sometimes with some international financial support to make loans to the private sector for investment in tourist facilities. Development corporations and also organized for implementation and operation of specific projects and enterprises. Joint venture international and local financing is a common approach to tourism project investment.

Finally, funding is required for the public management of tourism by the NTA office including for the overall national or regional marketing of tourism. The NTA budget is typically provided by the government. However, if there is a tourism tax such as a hotel and restaurant expenditure tax some or all of this can be allocated to the NTA budget. Thus tourism can directly pay for its own management.

A funding mechanism sometimes used by the government is to establish a Tourism Development fund supported by the hotel tax or other sources such as duty-free shopping facilities. This fund can be used for development, marketing, training and other purposes.

International Source of Funds

There are several types of international funding sources available for financing tourism development as follows:

- **World Bank Group.** The IBRD (International Bank for Reconstruction and Devleopment), although not now directly involved in tourism projects provides major funding for infrastructure environmental and conservation projects which benefit tourism as well as serve general needs. This funding is provided in the form of long-term loans at commercial rates of interest. The IDA (International Development Association) makes loans to low income countries at no interest rates, with ten-year grace periods and very long-term repayment schemes. The IFC (International Finance Corporation) makes loans directly to the private sector for development of revenue producing projects including hotels and other tourism projects. IDA loans are usually for not more than 25 per cent of the project cost and thus serve more as a catalyst to development.
- **UNDP (United Nations Development Programme).** The UNDP is mainly a technical assistance agency. It is an important source agency for the funding of tourism planning and other tourism related projects through the WHO as the executing agency. Many of these projects include provision equipment as well as technical assistance. The UNCDF (United a nations Capital Development Fund) provides smallscale capital assistance in the form of grants or long-term loans for social facilities and services and economic activities.
- **European Union.** The EU is becoming quite involved in supporting tourism projects in the many countries which ccnstitute the ACP group under the Lome IV Convention. These projects are both technical assistance (including planning, marketing and training) and investment oriented.

- **Bilateral Sources.** Bilateral funding sources usually operate on a government-to-government basis and several of these programmes include technical assistance and investment oriented tourism projects. Many countries offer bilateral assistance including countries in Europe. North America and the East Asia and Pacific region. Each bilateral programme has its own particular assistance policy.

- **Regional Development Banks.** The Asian Development Bank (ADB), African Development Bank (ADB), Inter-American Development Bank (lDB) and other regional development banks offer some assistance on aspects of developing tourism in their member countries. The European Development Fund has been established to provide assistance to countries in Eastern Europe.

- **Private International Capital Source.** Many private sector companies including those involved in tourism are seeking to invest outside of their home countries. This type of investment often brings with it competent management resources, marketing connections and desirable international images which can benefit tourism in the countries seeking outside investment. It is important for countries to understand the nature of these corporations and, how to negotiate with them. The United nations Centre on Transnational Corporations can offer countries technical assistance on dealing with international hotel and other tourism-related corporations. for example on negotiating hotel management contracts.

These various funding sources are of course not mutually exclusive. They can be used in various combinations to meet the particular investment requirements of a country.

❑

9

Impact on Tourism

Tourism is of major economic and social significance. More than 270 million tourists spend $92 billion (US) annually in places outside their own countries. This is one of the largest items in the world's foreign trade. With a world growth in visitor arrivals rate of approximately 6 per cent per annum, tourism is also one of the fastest growing economic activities. It is the most important export industry and earner of foreign exchange in many countries. The significance of tourism has been recognised in both developed and developing countries. This can be seen in the establishment of government departments of tourism widespread encouragement and sponsorship of tourist developments and the proliferation of small businesses and multinational corporations contributing to and deriving benefits from the tourism industry. There is widespread optimism that tourism might be a powerful and beneficial agent of both economic and social change. Indeed, tourism has stimulated employment and investment. modified land use and economic structure and made a positive contribution to the balance of payments in many countries throughout the world.

At the same time the growth of tourism has prompted perceptive observers to raise many questions concerning the social and environmental desirability of encouraging further expansion. Do the expenditures of tourists benefit the residents of destination areas? Is tourism encouraging prostitution, crime and gambling? Does tourism rejuvenate the traditional arts and crafts of host cultures? Do governments direct their development priorities to satisfy the needs of tourists rather than residents? Are residents financing expensive tourist facilities through their taxes? Is tourism contributing to the destruction of the very resources which initially attracted the tourists? Are there saturation levels beyond which further growth in tourist arrivals creates more problems than benefits? What is being done to calculate these levels and to ensure that they are not exceeded?

The unprecedented growth of tourism has prompted a host of such questions, and answers and are only now beginning to emerge. As tourism continues to expand, questions concerning associated economic, environmental and social effects will become more pressing. Adequate answers to such questions are predicated upon systematic and rigorous research which, until recently, has been almost totally lacking.

There have been few attempts to integrate the findings of the diverse studies of the impacts of tourism, yet any assessment of the costs and benefits of tourism requires a full consideration of all the likely impacts. The volume is an attempt to synthesize the findings of research on the impacts of tourism, and to present them to the reader in a systematic fashion. The strengths and weaknesses of existing approaches will be identified, and topics which have yet to receive detailed examination in the literature will be pointed out. The materials assembled in this book are largely taken from published sources and emphasise the impacts of mass tourism in resort areas as opposed to the less apparent, scattered effects of individuals travelling in areas lacking a reputation of tourism. The value of this book will not lie in the originally of the ideas which are presented, for it will be necessary to draw heavily upon the work of others. Rather, as one of the earliest attempts to collate and access the numerous studies of impacts of tourism, it is hoped that this work will provide a balanced introduction to the topic. By drawing attention to the diversity and complexity of these impacts, conceptual and methodological difficulties will be highlighted which may be avoided in future research. An objective evaluation of the impacts of tourism is required if government agencies, planners, developers and businessmen are to appreciate the full implications of their actions. If some of the myths concerning the nature of tourist impact can be dispelled then the way should be open for a re-examination of the true potential of tourism as a contributor to the economic, environmental and social well being of reception areas.

Organisation

Widely accepted procedures for investigating the impacts of tourism have yet to be established and few studies attempt a comprehensive examination of a broad range of types of impact. For, the purposes of this work impacts of tourism are grouped into three major categories: economic, physical and social. This distinction is somewhat artificial for, in reality, the boundries between the categories are indistinct and their contents merge. For example, money may be spent in an attempt to reduce unacceptable environmental change. This, in turn, may have repercussions for the availability of jobs and, hence, on social well-being. Similarly, tax revenues earned as a by-product of tourism expenditures may be spent to promote more tourism, to clean up the environment or to improve social services. Ultimately, therefore, this threefold division must be justified pragmatically. However, most studies of the consequences of tourism focus primarily on only one of these three types of impact so that the organisation into three major impact domains reflects the present status of research.

Just as there is overlap between the impact domains, there is also little consensus as to what should be included within them. For example, some economic studies focus upon income generation, others stress the creation of employment, whereas many reports are devoted to balance of payments questions. Such variations in emphasis hamper the comparison of findings of different investigations, frustrate the establishment of a body of theory, and contribute to inconsistency and contradiction of study conclusions.

Research Issues

Rapid growth of tourism has given rise to increasingly pronounced economic, environmental and social effects. However, until recently, attention has concentrated on the more obvious economic impacts with comparatively little consideration being given to the environmental and social consequences of tourism. The relative neglect of these topics has occurred in spite of increasing anxiety about environmental problems evolving from man's continued manipulation of his environment, and in spite of expanding awareness of the increasing significance of tourism. The economic emphasis of much research is a reflection of the optimism with which tourism was generally viewed in the 1960s. Great interest was expressed in the potential of tourism to contribute to economic development. Tourism was widely acclaimed as generating a multitude of beneficial effects upon such economic indicators as balance of payments, income, employment and tax revenues. While there is an element of truth in this perspective, and some types of tourism may stimulate environmental preservation and benefit residents of destination areas, contemporary tourism is on a massive scale which may pose substantial environmental and social risks.

Recognition of the size of the impacts of modern tourism has prompted a reorientation of tourism research. There has been a noticeable shift towards a more balanced perspective incorporating a critical examination of the costs, or negative impacts of tourism. An increasing number of such studies adopt an environmental or a social perspective but the majority of such investigations are of recent vintage. The potentially serious psychological, social and cultural effects of tourism were given prominence in the seminal works of Young (1973) and Turner and Ash (1975). Following these pioneering statements, a number of authors have illuminated some of the more alarming, negative impacts of tourism (Graburn 1976; Smith 1977; Cohen 1978; Pizam 1978). These have included the modification of traditional cultures, increases in prostitution and crime, and the pollution of beaches.

The consequences of tourism have become increasingly complex and contradictory. For example, the commercialisation of culture, through the marketing and sale of artefacts, may revive traditional art forms or modify them so that they are scarcely recognisable. The associated influx of money into a local economy may distort occupational stability and contribute to a breakdown in family and community cohesion. On the other hand the commercialisation of culture may lead to the creation of a 'phony folk culture' but at the same time create jobs and thereby alleviate existing unemployment problems.

Impact Studies

Evaluations of the impacts of tourism reflect the status of impact research in general. Recent environmental legislation and demands by society for environmental impact statements for projects which significantly affect the environment, have stimulated interest in impact research, and emphasised the need for the development of sound analytical procedures. Given the varied requirements of impact assessments and the recency of their rise to prominence, it should not be surprising that there is a paucity of methodological guidelines for undertaking investigations of the impacts of tourism.

Environmental impact statements of any kind are extremely difficult to make. Five reasons for this can be highlighted. Firstly, man has been living on and modifying the earth for thousands of years so that it is extremely difficult to recontruct the environment before the intervention of man and, hence to establish a base level against which to measure changes. In many tourist destination areas public use has existed for long periods of time so that it is now almost impossible to reconstruct the environment minus the effects induced by tourism.

A second difficulty concerns the problem of disentangling the role of man from the role of nature. Even without the intervention of man the environment would not be unchanging, but would be in a perpetual state of flux. This leads to further difficulties in defining a base level. The problem is compounded because many impacts of tourism result from normal environmental processes whose actions are speeded up by the intervention of man. For instance, weathering and erosion are natural processes but they can become major problems when exacerbated by man. The processes remain unchanged but the flows of energy are radically altered.

A related problem is the difficulty of differentiating between changes attributable to pre-existing processes and changes induced by the influx of tourists. Tourism has emerged as a forceful agent of change and creates impacts which are clearly the product of tourist developments resort landscapes, the construction of theme parks and the generation of employment and income are obvious examples. In many cases, however, it is exceedingly difficult to isolate the principal causes of change. It may be difficult to determine whether changes are directly attributable to tourist development or whether tourism is only one among a number of agents of change. In Tonga, for example, the increased demand for imported foodstuffs has resulted from an increasing population, inadequate agricultural production to feed the people, and demands imposed by international tourism. The extent to which tourism has contributed to the deep-seated social and economic problems emanating from this situation is not accurately known. Tourism, undoubtedly, has been one important contributing factor but it may also be a highly visible scapegoat for problems which already existed prior to the advent of modern tourism. It certainly is easier to blame tourism than it is to address the conditions of society and environment.

Thirdly, the complex interactions of tourism phenomena make total impact almost impossible to measure. Many of the impacts of tourism are manifested in subtle and often unexpected ways. In other words, primary impacts give rise to secondary and tertiary impacts and generate a myriad of successive repercussions which it is usually impracticable to trace and monitor. Cross impacts are a direct result of the interactive nature of economic, environmental and social phenomena. Interactions between components of each of these impact domains induce further changes which reverberate through the system, creating a complex array of impact flows. For example, organised safaris to national parks in Africa can modify the feeding and breeding habits of wildlife. Preservation of wildlife may be in the interests of tourist developers and may have economic benefits to countries endowed with this resource. However, the establishment of national parks has forced the rapidly growing African population to farm in areas of low fertility where agricultural production may be barely sufficient to feed the population. Special impacts occur to particular groups of people, such as racial or cultural minorities, or to unique types of wildlife or vegetation.

A fourth obstacle stems from spatial and temporal discontinuities between cause and effect. For instance, erosion in one location may result in deposition elsewhere, destruction of key elements of an animal's habitat may lead to population declines throughout its range, or development of new facilities may divert tourist traffic away from existing locations. A considerable time may elapse before the full implications of an activity are apparent. Thus, there are great difficulties in establishing both temporal and spatial constraints for undertaking impact studies.

A fifth methodological issue is the selection of impact indicators. What indicators should be used and what do they really mean? For example, what is the significance of prostitution and an increased crime rate when compared with traffic congestion or an expanded tax base? In other words, there is a problem in the identification of which variables best indicate the changing situation and in consequence, of what to measure. A related problem is the assigning of weights to the selected indicators as indicators of impact vary in their significance to the impacted system, and devising means of combining disparate measures into a composite index of the magnitude of impact.

Problems, such as those which have been discussed above, have restricted the scope and accuracy of research results and have encouraged investigation to narrow the focus of their research. There has been a tendency to examine impacts from selected specific developments or projects in isolation from the broader tourist phenomena of which they are a part; to concentrate on primary impacts to the exclusion of secondary and tertiary impacts; to measure the more tangible, quantifiable impacts, such as economic impacts to the neglect of the less readily measured social and environmental impacts; and to stress positive impacts or benefits and to overlook undesirable consequence or costs. Future examinations of the consequences of tourism for host communities will continue to be concerned with the types and magnitude of impact and whether they are predominantly beneficial or costly to the destination area. In addition, it will be necessary to give greater attention to the scale of impact for the spheres of influence of tourist development vary and their consequences may be viewed differently depending upon whether they are assessed from a local, regional, national or international perspective. At the same time, it will be appropriate to give greater attention to the assessment of who gains and who loses. Costs and benefits of tourism are not evenly distributed. What may be a benefit to one group or individual within community may be a cost to the neighbours. Investors in tourist developments and associated service industries may gain at the expense of other residents of the destination area who may suffer increased crowding, congestion, noise, pollution and modified lifestyles.

Economic Impacts

Several standard types of economic measurements are made in tourism. Tourism is still not usually listed as a separate sector in national economic tables but is included in the service sector. (The WTO has developed the Standard International Classification of Tourism Activities (SICTA) which has been provisionally approved by the United Nations Statistical Commission. Therefore, it is more difficult to measure the economic contribution of tourism. But, by drawing on various information sources, tourism economists can make calculations sufficient to indicate the general extent of tourism's economic impact. The standard economic measurements are as follows:

Income generated and contribution to Gross National or Domestic Product. This indicates the relative importance of tourism in the total economy.

Foreign exchange earned from international tourism. This includes calculation of both the gross foreign exchange earnings the total expenditure of foreign tourists, and net foreign exchange earnings-the foreign exchange remaining in the country after deducting the foreign exchange leakage factor. This leakage is the foreign exchange spent for imported goods and services used in tourism—food items and hotel equipment and supplies; expatriation of salaries of foreign workers and of profits of foreign-owned facilities; payments made to foreign hotel management companies; and other leakages. At the regional level the gross and net money earned from outside the region can be calculated.

- Local employment generated by tourism. Employment is calculated by type:
  - (a) direct employment—the persons who work in tourism enterprises such as hotels, restaurants, tourist shops and tour and travel agencies;
  - (b) indirect employment-jobs generated in the supplying sectors such as agriculture, fisheries and manufacturing:
  - (c) induced employment—additional persons supported by the spending of income made by the direct and indirect employees;
  - (d) construction employment—jobs generated in the construction of tourism facilities and infrastructure (this is usually temporary but may be places with continuing development of tourism).
- **The Multiplier Effect.** This refers to the stimulus that an external source of income has on an economy. It is the number of rounds of spending in the local economy of the initial tourist spending. This effect measures the way in which tourist expenditures filter through the economy and generate other economy activities.
- **Contribution to Government Revenues.** This includes hotel and other types of tourist user taxes, airport departure taxes, customs duties on imported goods used in tourism,

income taxes on tourism enterprises and employees and property taxes on tourism establishments.

If not carefully controlled, tourism can generate some economic problems. Loss of economic benefits can occur if there is a high import content of goods and services used in tourism, and if many tourist facilities are owned and managed by outsiders. This situation reduces the net income and foreign exchange earned from tourism, and may lead to resentment by residents of the tourism area. For certain types of tourism development. however, there may be few alternative to outside ownership and management. This can be the case especially during the initial stages of development when local capital and managerial capabilities are limited. In small island economies with little local production of goods. it may be difficult to greatly reduce the import content of tourism. But the employment and income generated is still usually considered worth the investment in tourism.

Economic Benefits

There are several techniques that can be applied to enhance the economic benefits of tourism. These should be incorporated into the planning process so that possible problems are prevented or reduced before they occur.

Strengthening the linkages between tourism and other economic sectors is a very important technique. This reduces the import content of tourism and provides more local employment—the indirect and induced employment and income from tourism. Opportunities often exist, for example, to increase the locally produced food items used in tourism. Also the tourism industry should be encouraged (or required) to utilise more local items, including building materials and interior decoration, in its development and operation of hotels and other facilities.

Encouraging in country in region and local ownership of tourist facilities and services is also important so that more of the profits from tourism are retained. This can be done in various ways—

providing investment incentives; organising stock companies with sale of shares to the general public; and requiring joint ventures of local and foreign companies. Certain forms of tourism can be encouraged which will provide opportunities for local small business enterprises. If local capital is very limited then a policy can be taken of initially allowing foreign ownership but requiring purchases by local owners when capital is available.

Foreign hotel management by transnational hotel companies of large hotel properties results in a loss of some income to countries. However, it also offers the advantages of professional management and international marketing and reservation services. Whether to allow transnational management must be decided based on the circumstances of each particular country. It is also important that local tour operators be given the opportunity to handle foreign tour groups and that local ground handling operations are not preempted by foreign tour operators.

Maximising local empioyment in tourism can be encouraged by proper training of persons to work in tourism. In some places there may be some social resistance to service employment. It will be necessary to educate local people to understand that employment in tourism is a respected and worthwhile type of occupation. Training should be extended to the supervisory and management levels so that these higher level positions can also eventually be filled by local staff. When a trained pool of employees exists then tourist facility and service establishments can be required to employ local persons. For the higher level positions, replacement of foreign employees by local ones can be phased in over a period of time.

Tourist expenditures can be increased in various ways. Most shopping opportunities, especially of local arts and crafts, can be provided in many places. Tourist activities can be expanded, for example by organising more attractions and tours, which will induce tourists to stay longer. Tourism product enrichment and diversification is becoming an important aspect of expanding and upgrading tourism in many already developed tourism areas.

Environmental Impacts

Tourism and the environment are inter-dependent. The physical (natural and man-made) environment provides many of the attractions for tourists, and the development of tourism can generate both positive and negative environmental impacts. Developing and managing tourism so that it is compatible with the environment, and does not degrade it, is a major factor in achieving sustainable development. In order to plan tourism environmentally, it is first important to understand the possible impacts of tourism on the environment.

If tourism is well planned, developed and managed, it can generate important positive environmental impacts. These include the following:

(a) Helps justify and pay for conservation of important natural areas and wildlife, including marine environments, and development of national and regional parks and reserves, because these are major attractions for tourists. This is an especially significant benefit in countries with limited resources for undertaking environmental conservation.

(b) Helps justify and pay for the conservation of archaeological and historic sites as attractions for tourists. Otherwise many of these sites would be allowed to deteriorate or disappear. Even entire historic districts in towns and cities are being conserved and developed for tourism.

(c) Helps improve the environmental quality of areas because tourists like to visit places that are attractive, clean and not polluted. Tourism provides the incentive to clean up environments through controlling air, water, noise and visual pollution, reducing congestion and upgrading overall appearance with suitable landscaping and building design. Also, well sited and designed tourist facilities themselves can contribute to the attractive appearance of both urban and rural environments. Improvement of infrastructure, especially of water supply and sewage and solid waste disposal, also contributes to improved environmental quality.

(d) Increases local environmental awareness when residents, and especially young people, observe tourists' interest in conservation. They then begin to realise the importance of conservation in their areas.

If tourism is not well planned, developed and managed, it can generate several types of negative environmental impacts. These include the following:

(a) Water pollution resulting from improper development of sewage and solid waste disposal systems for hotels and other facilities. There can be pollution of river, lake and coastal waters from sewage outfall lines, and of groundwater by seepage of waste material.

(b) Air pollution resulting from excessive use of internal combustion vehicles (cars, taxis, buses, motorcycles. etc.) in tourism areas. Airplanes, used by many tourists for longer-distance travel and for local air tours generate some air (and noise) pollution.

(c) Noise pollution generated by a concentration of tourists and tourist vehicles.

(d) Visual pollution resulting from several factors-poorly designed hotels and other tourist facilities; badly planned layout of facilities; inadequate landscaping of facilities; use of large and ugly advertising signs; and obstruction of scenic views by tourism development.

(e) Waste disposal problems of littering the landscape by tourists, and improper disposal of waste generated by tourist facilities.

(f) Ecological disruption of natural areas by overuse and misuse by tourists and inappropriate tourism development. Coastal, marine, mountain and desert environments, all important types of tourism areas, are particularly vulnerable to ecological damage.

(g) Damage to archaeological and historic sites by overuse or misuse by tourists and inappropriate tourism development.

(h) Environmental hazards and land use problems resulting from poor planning, siting and engineering of tourist attractions and facilities.

Ecological Measures

Concern with environmental protection should be an integral part of the planning process. Application of the environmental planning and sustainable development approach is essential, including establishing and staying within the carrying capacities of tourism areas. Selecting the forms of tourism development that are most suitable for the environment also greatly help limit negative environmental impacts. Application of sound principles, such as concentration of facilities in certain zones with provision of adequate infrastructure, a very important in maintaining environmental protection. More generally development of tourism on a gradual basis allows for sufficient time to monitor its environmental impacts, and make changes in the development approach if any problems have arisen.

Adopting techniques of reducing the seasonality of tourism, especially peak season use or tourism areas, is another very useful technique. Environmental problems often occur only during the peak season when overloading of the infrastructure and overuse of attractions, facilities and services take place.

In addition to these general approaches, specific environmental impact control measures should be applied. These include the following:

(a) Install properly designed utility systems of water supply, electric power, sewage and solid waste disposal and drainage for tourist facilities. Conservation techniques should be applied such as treatment and recycling of waste water and use of solar heating devices. Often these systems can be extended to serve general development in the tourism area, thus benefiting local communities.

(b) Develop adequate road and other transportation systems, with emphasis on development of public transit and non-polluting forms of transportation of tourists. Electric shuttle buses, for example, can be used in resorts. Proper maintenance of tourist vehicles is important.

(c) Provide open space, parks and suitable landscaping in tourism areas.

(d) Apply environmentally suitable land use and site planning principles, zoning regulations, development standards and architectural design in tourism areas. Control of advertising signs is also important.

(e) Carefully manage visitor flows at tourists attraction features. At fragile sites, the number of visitors may need to be limited or completely prohibited at certain times, or even year-round. For some important sites, the technique of modelling can be used-building a replica of the feature for tourists to visit, with prohibition of tourists at the original site.

(f) Prohibit tourists to cut trees in camping and trekking areas, to collect rare plant and animal species, and to disturb the natural behavioural patterns of wild animals. Hunting and fishing should be allowed only under carefully controlled conditions.

(g) In marine areas, several types of controls are necessary-operations related to ship bulge cleaning and ballast dumping; use of motorised boats in environmentally sensitive areas; collection of live sea shells, coral and endangered sea life; spear fishing; disturbance of nesting turtles; use of boat anchors in coral-bottom bays; and mining of beach, sand and coral for construction purposes. Boat piers should be properly designed so that they do not lead to erosion or other problems.

(h) Maintain environmental health and safety standards for the benefit of both tourists and residents.

There may be other control measures which should be applied in particular tourism areas depending on their characteristics. With respect to visitor use controls, it is important to inform tourists about the controls and why they must be applied. If tourists understand why the controls are necessary, they will more likely abide by them.

Socio-cultural Impacts

Tourism can bring both benefits and problems to the local society and its cultural patterns. Although more difficult to measure than economic or environmental impacts, socio-cultural impacts are major considerations in developing tourism in any place. These impacts can be especially critical in countries that still have strongly traditional societies and economies. Although tourism can generate socio-cultural impacts, it should be kept in mind that any type of new development brings changes. Tourism is only one source of change in a society.

If tourism is well planned, developed and managed in a socially responsible manner, it can bring several types of socio-cultural benefits. These include the following:

(a) Improves the living standards of people and helps pay for improvements to community facilities and services, if the economic benefits of tourism are well distributed.

(b) Conserves the cultural heritage of an area which otherwise might be lost as a result of general development taking place. Conservation of archaeological and historic sites was referred to under environmental impacts. Cultural patterns of music, dance, drama. dress, arts and crafts, customs, ceremonies, life-styles, traditional economic activities and architectural styles are also important attractions for tourists. If these are lost, cultural tourism will not be successful in the area. Tourism helps justify their conservation. In some places, tourism can be the impetus for revitalising cultural patterns which might be disappearing.

(c) Helps develop and maintain museums, theatres and other cultural facilities. Many are, in part, supported by tourism but are also enjoyed by residents. Many major museums and theatres in the world receive much financial support from the admission fees paid by tourists.

(d) Reinforces or even renews a sense of pride by residents in their culture, when they observe tourists appreciating it. This is especially true of some traditional societies which are undergoing rapid change and losing their sense of cultural self-confidence.

(e) Provides the opportunity for cross-cultural exchange between tourists and residents who learn about and come to respect, one another's cultures. This exchange can best be achieved through certain forms of tourism-educational and other types of special interest tours; village tourism; and home visit programmes whereby tourists can arrange to visit local families.

Tourism can generate some socio-cultural problems if not well planned, developed and managed. A common problem is overcrowding by tourists and loss of convenience for residents, which leads to their resentment and sense of hostility toward tourism. If there are too many tourists in an area which can happen particularly at peak season periods attraction and features, and restaurant, shopping and transportation facilities can become so overcrowded by tourists that residents cannot easily use them. If residents are completely prohibited from access to amenity features such as hotel beaches they may become even more resentful. Large numbers of tourists can be especially disruptivé in small rural communities. Resentment particularly arise if residents perceive that they are not receiving many economic benefits from tourism, and that tourism development is controlled by outside interests.

Socio-cultural Problems

Some of the general policies that are applicable to economic and environmental considerations are also appropriate for socio-cultural reasons. An important general policy is to develop tourism on a gradual basis so that the society has time to adapt to it be educated about it and learn how to participate in its benefits. This approach also gives the government sufficient time to monitor the socio-cultural impacts of tourism, and remedy any problems before they become serious. As has been emphasised, residents should be involved in the planning and development process of tourism so that they can influence its decision-making and feel that they are part of tourism. Suitable forms of tourism must be selected that are compatible with the local societies. Also, selective marketing can attract the types of tourists who will respect the local social customs and cultural traditions.

As a policy deliberate use of tourism as a technique of cultural conservation can greatly help in reducing its negative impacts on the culture. At the same time, many societies want to experience some positive change and participate in the benefits of modern development. The approach that they often wish to take is to be culturally selective. They want to keep the best of their traditions that give them a distinctive cultural character, but adopt the best of the changes that will make their lives more comfortable and interesting. Each society must decide on what approach is most suitable for their people when making choices about their tourism development patterns.

Several more specific socio-cultural impact control measures can be applied in tourism areas. These include the following:

(a) Maintain the authenticity of local dance, music, drama, arts, crafts and dress, even though they are somewhat adapted for presentation to tourists. This may require special training programmes being organised and quality controls being applied. However, certain types of ceremonies and rituals such as religious ones should not be modified for tourism, and tourist viewing of them must be carefully controlled.

(b) Preserve existing distinctive local architectural styles and encourage new development, including tourist facilities, to use local architectural motives.

(c) Make certain that residents have convenient access to tourist attractions, amenity features and other facilities, and apply visitor control measures to prevent overcrowding.

(d) If residents cannot afford to use existing commercial tourist facilities, provide inexpensive or subsidized facilities for them to use. It is also common practice to allow residents to pay lower admission fees to attraction features than those paid by foreign tourists.

(e) Educate residents about tourism its concepts, benefits and problems, the local tourism development policy and programme, how they can personally participate in tourism, and the social patterns of tourists visiting the area. Public awareness programmes about tourism can be organised, utilising radio, television, newspapers, magazines and public meetings. Education about tourism should be included in the public and private school system.

(f) Inform tourists about the local society, its customs, dress codes, acceptable behaviour in religious and other places. courtesies to observe in taking photographs, tipping policies, and any local problems such as crime. If tourists understand these matters, they will be more likely to respect them.

(g) Train employees to work in tourism effectively, including language and social sensitivity training where needed. In addition to providing better services this will reduce any possible misunderstandings between tourists and employees.

(h) Apply strict controls on drugs, crime and prostitution if these are considered to be problems in the tourism areas.

Other types of controls may be appropriate in particular tourism areas.

ENVIRONMENTAL IMPACT ASSESSMENT

Application of the environmental planning approach and incorporation of environmental protection measures into the planning process will prevent many environmental problems from arising. However, it is still important that an environmental impact assessment (EIA) be carried out for each specific tourism development project (as well as for all types of major projects). This procedure ensures that specific projects will not generate any serious environmental problems. If it appears that a proposed project will cause problems then it should not be approved unless it is modified to be made acceptable. The EIA procedure is established at the national and regional levels. Many countries have adopted environmental protection legislation and the EIA procedure but others have not yet done so.

The EIA should include all types of impacts—environmental, economic and socio-cultural. Even though a project may generate substantial economic' benefits for example, it may result in unacceptable environmental or social problems. It should not therefore, be approved without modifications.

Tourism has become a high-profile activity in a number of economies. Increasingly, policy-makers and planners are turning to tourism development as a mechanism to restructure economies or to generate jobs. Such policies are found worldwide and are variable in their achievement of objectives. Tourism developments are accompanied by positive and negative effects both economic and environmental. While the procedures for assessing economic costs and benefits are relatively well known the potential environmental .costs and benefits of tourism developments have tended to be left out of the appraisal of tourism projects policies and programmes.

This chapter reviews the previous research concerned with tourism and the environment particularly that relating to environmental impacts. It emphasizes the importance of the environment as a tourism resource before going on to discuss the importance of, and methodological issues raised by the assessment of environmental impacts. The chapter concludes with a discussion of the application of the Delphi technique to environmental impact assessment.

Tourism and the Environment-The literature on Impacts

The growing volume of literature on the environmental impacts of tourism emphasizes the importance of the environment to the encouragement and development of tourist activity (Latimer, 1985). Equally it expresses concern about the potential adverse effects of tourism on the environment (Edington and Edington, 1986) The environment is a key tourism resource and consequently its conservation and management are vital both to the future of the tourism industry and to society as a whole.

Generally, research in this area is still relatively immature. The subject area concerned with the assessment of the environmental effects of development is characterised by a potentially extremely complex set of impact interactions. Mainly because of this complexity and the relative immaturity of the discipline, the research literature is fragmentary. Work has tended to concentrate on the classification of impacts, taking the form of either detailed studies of selected impacts or more general broadly based work (see. for example, Bodowski, 1976; Cohen, 1978; Krol, 1986), Case studies are a common feature of the literature. in which island ecosystems and new tourist areas are the centre of interest (Camhis. 1980; Pluss. 1987). Contributions have originated from a number of disciplinary perspectives including ecological, geographic and socio-environmental but there has been little evidence of the emergence of a true multi-disciplinary perspective.

The literature has concentrated largely on the negative impacts of tourism development and the potentially destructive force which poorly managed tourism developments can create. The improvements and environmental benefits that tourism can bring have largely been ignored (Hall, 1974; Haulot, 1985). This focus on negative impacts is closely linked to the environments that have received the most attention. Studies of environmental impact have been almost exclusively concerned with rural areas and in particular natural or semi-natural ecosystems (Hall, 1974; Cook and Wells, 1983; Dupuy, 1987).

This concern may reflect the fact that the impacts of tourist activity on the natural environment—footpath erosion and fire damage, for example are often easily seen and specific impacts are more easily measured. It may also reflect the greater importance placed on the natural environment its vulnerability and need for protection (Pivert, 1987). Where discusrion is directed to urban areas, it is often superficial and descriptive in nature and frequently avoids the issue of assessment. The urban literature does, however, recognise the potential benefits of tourism (Beioley. 1981; McNulty, 1985). The urban environment, its improvement and maintenance has been the concern of recent work. Tiard (1987), for example, describes the positive impacts of tourism on buildings in Norway.

It is only in the consideration of adverse impacts of tourism in rural areas that serious attention has been given to the methodological issues of conceptualisation and measurement. Much of the work. however, has consisted of detailed measurement of very specific impacts. with little attempt to orientate the results in a form useful to policy-makers (Green *et al.* 1990).

More recently, there has been explicit discussion of the importance of the environment as a tourism resource and the need to consider the sustainability of that resource (Papadopoulas, 1987). These issues have been developed by Romeril (1989), who argues that it is imperative to reconcile the need for an enduring and sustainable environmental tourism resource with a continuing pursuit of social and economic goals. As the tourist becomes more discriminating and has a greater awareness of the impact of tourism in the physical and aesthetic environment, environmental management and careful design will be key attributes of successful projects (McNeely and Thorsell, 1989).

In a discussion of the importance of maintaining a high quality environment in sustaining tourism activity it is appropriate to consider 'thresholds' of tourism activity. A given environmental impact (or combination of impacts) can be tolerated up to a point beyond which the environmental resource (*e.g.* clean bathing water) ceases to be a positive attraction and the tourism activity tnat relies on it has to substitute other resources or decline. Tourism development on the North Sea coast in the UK, for example, places great pressure on sewage treatment infrastructure, with the result that, in some cases, raw (or only slightly treated) sewage is discharged directly into the sea. However, the sea is a significant tourism resource, being used for swimming, paddling, boating and as a source of aesthetic pleasure. Increasing sewage pollution progressively decreases the attraction of the sea to tourists, either through a decline in the sea's aesthetic attraction or through the public's perception of an increased health risk. Ultimately, pollution levels may reach a threshold of acceptability (*e.g.* by contravening water quality standards), access to the sea is withdrawn and the resource is no longer available. What is Meant by Environment?

As noted earlier, recent work on the environmental impact of tourism has been relatively unstructured and unquantitative. It does, however, provide a typology for the 'classification' of environment, which is a necessary precursor for a more systematic and comprehensive assessment of potential impacts. If the maintenance or enhancement of environment quality is to become a major element of tourism impact assessments, such a typology and structure is vital.

The literature suggests that a holistic approach to the definition of environment is necessary for a full appreciation of the complete range of potential impacts that may result from development projects or policies (*e.g.* OECD, 1991). However, for the sake of convenience, and to aid the discussion and understanding of potential impacts, the environment is often conceptualised as being composed of three components: natural, built and cultural environments (OECD, 1981). Although here defined as three discrete elements, the three components are interrelated and there will be cross-component effects associated with tourism developments.

The natural environment is perhaps the best documented and the component on which tourism impact research has concentrated. The natural environment may be seen to include air, land, clear light, climate, flora and fauna. The built environment encompasses the urban fabric, infrastructure, open space and elements of townscape. The cultural environment forms the third element of the typology. It is an area that has received increasing research attention during the 1980s, as the importance of culture as a tourism resource and the impact of tourism developments on culture become recognised (Meyer, 1988; Garrison, 1989). The cultural environment includes the values, beliefs, behaviours, morals, arts, law and history of communities. The cultural environment will include 'high' culture, such as opera and ballet, and popular culture, including elements such as folk, popular, contemporary and native expression, including folk music and craft work (OECD, 1981).

Although this typology is a useful starting point for a structured approach to recognising and assessing potential tourism impacts, it is only a rudimentary initial framework. It is limited to the consideration of potential impacts on the natural and built environments. However, it must be emphasised that the notion of environmental impact is of equal relevance in the cultural environment. Although it is possiby more difficult to isolate in causal terms because of more general influences, such as mass communications, it is important to realise the potential that exists for tourism developments to impact both positively and negatively on the resource of the cultural environment.

❑

10

Role of Hotel Industry

Some hotel industry leaders believe that emphasis should be placed on effective management of demand and capacity. Economists suggest as economists will—that it is principally pricing which will ultimately bring supply and demand into balance. But hotel industry experience indicates otherwise. Accordingly, the predominant philosophy is becoming more and more realistic. Although the end-product of hotels and resorts is undoubtedly different from that of other branches of the travel industry, many authorities believe that their strategies should be similar: focusing on the needs of the customer as key to occupancy, repeat business and profit.

Price is not the main determinant of choice. Price alone does not balance supply and demand. Other crucial factors must be taken into consideration. If a hotel organisation aims to seek out a specific portion of the guest market and to maintain high occupancy levels, then it must pay close attention to modifying the products and services it offers, in order to fulfil the needs of that target group. In this chapter, our primary emphasis will be on the large hotel chains and on marketing consortia. This by no means minimises the importance of small, independent hotels. Rather, it reflects the weight of such international hospitality industry leaders as Hilton, Hyatt, Intercontinental, Marriott and Sheraton companies whose impact on present and future strategies trends is weighted by their enormous investment in the industry, their global positioning and the sheer numbers of hotel professionals they employ. Even among the large hoter groups, there are great differences. Hotels, per se, are by no means homogeneous; the range of accommodations and services they offer varies dramatically. The major city business hotel is different from the resort is different from the conference centre and so on, and infinitum.

The needs, wants, desires and demands of business travellers will change dramatically in coming years. So will the preferences of vacationers, and their expectations of a given destination. Even the destinations of choice can change widely. Today's popular tourist resort may well give way to a very different location ten, or even five, years from now. As guest demand evolves, so must the facilities which a responsive hospitality organisatiod provides. Hence the proliferation of sports and recreation facilities which we are now seeing; hence the addition and upgrading of business centres which provide broad spectrum secretarial and collateral services; hence the abandonment of the once ubiquitous steak house in favour of restaurants which offer the lighter fare—such as poultry and fish which consumers currently favour.

Who Controls the Destiny of the Hotel Industry?

It is a question to which there is not single, simple answer. Some would respond that its customers and shareholders do; others might suggest that the hotel industry must control its own destiny. But both nswers are short-sighted, and neither allows for all of the variables which will come into play in years ahead.

If we see high occupancy as an end-goal of the industry, we fail to take all of the relevant factors into consideration. What is more, we fail to allow for shifts in product, positioning and perception which must anticipate rapidly-changing market demands.

Assessing the Unknowns: In this context, many factors need to be analysed. In the leisure market, these include:

the effect of current events on air travel plans, and on destination choices;

the larger share of disposable income available to childless couples;

the travel patterns of growing families;

and the market potential of an aging population which will include more retired people with the means, and the inclination, to travel.

The business market presents challenges no less complex. For example, the long-term effect of tele-conferencing on corporate travel is still unknown. Considering the continuing importance of 'on-site' meetings, anticipated growth in its use will not sharply affect business travel overall. The opening of new business markets—such as the shift of commercial ties towards the Far East is another factor. The peripheral needs of business travellers for secretarial and related high-tech services that permit instantaneous communication with the 'home office' will also be a growing consideration. The add-on potential of trips for the spouses and children of business travellers may well be another expanding area, particularly as this option relates to special offers for weekends, holidays and other minimum-occupancy periods.

In the area of convention management, there are still more unknowns. With growing sophistication of urban and resort convention centres, and sharpened competition for available business, many hotel industry leaders will be concentrating increasing attention on this valuable business segment, expanding both the variety of services and of location which they offer the meeting planner.

Segmentation the Vital Tool

Soung strategic planning for the hotel industry of the 1990s and beyond requires immediate concentration on several key issues. One of the most important is segmentation analysis of present and potential market demand. Many industry leaders are linking their segmentation plans to carefully-pinpointed target guest groups; others are concentrating on developing products of specific types. But, whatever the means, the interest in exploring segmentation and in pinpointing new products toward the market demands of the future seems universal.

The varieties are endless. The small hotel; the hotel-within-a-hotel idea currently being used in many major urban hotels to accommodate the top-of-the-line business traveller; the family resort; the gaming hotel in all its permutations from high-roller casino operations to the family-type establishments currently being explored. The end-philosophy is constant in this move toward hotel types, which may be easily identified by the consumer, making it relatively simple for him or her to select accommodations which, fit a given need.

Middle Men

The complex role of middle men in the hotel industry of tomorrow will reflect rapidly-changing trends which seem certain to affect the wholesaler in years to come.

Competitive pressures are catalysing new directions. In the decade ahead, the sophisticated wholesaler will base his marketing efforts on the evolving needs, wants and habits of the consumer; those who react to change, rather than anticipate it, may be left by the wayside. In North America, for example, deregulation continues to spawn tremendous shifts. Airlines and hotel chains are beginning to create their own packages. Similarly, travel agents and tour operators must stay ahead of change in order to succeed in the fast-moving hotel marketplace. Current indicators show travel agents themselves to be ambivalent about the directions which they should pursue in order to ensure increased profitability in the decade ahead. In 1960, according to research undertaken by Travel Weekly magazine, business travel arrange ments accounted for just 28 per cent of the North America retail community's overall $5 billion volume. By 1983, more than half of the trade's $43.7 billion in sales came in the form of 'Pure' business and of combined business/pleasure arrangements.

Increasing Productivity

With heavy investments in fixed facilities, equipment and staff, the hotel industry is extremely sensitive to the variations in occupancy which can drastically affect the bottom line. Many chains are attempting to offset this pressure with increased productivity. The current emphasis of many international leaders, variously expressed in their advertising and in their training programmes, is on upgraded service: at once a return expression of the expanding needs, wants and demands of a consumer far more experienced than his antecedent of a generation ago. This trend towards encouraging staff awareness of service leads to another desired strategic objective the creation of a 'chain personality'. Current international hospitality industry studies indicate little in the way of consumer 'brand loyalty'. A customer satisfied with Hilton in one city, for example, may not make a tremendous effort to book at a Hilton in the next stop on his itinerary. To redress this, strong efforts are expected to reinforce brand identification and to create, for each given chain, an easily-identified character which will influence the customer and ensure repeat business.

Managing the Managers

The 1970s was the decade of hotel construction frequently overconstruction—in many world markets; the early 80s have seen the results of the dangerous competitive pressures which the 'edifice complex' created for many leading hospitality groups. The years ahead will witness the inevitable 'shaking down' processes by which industry leaders vie among themselves for industry supremacy. Hotel costs are constantly rising: in most countries they are escalatin more rapidly than inflation. Surging costs, coupled with increased competition and surplus capacity in many areas, have created a new consciousness of the bottom line.

Management contracts must be kept. Sufficient reserves must be created to finance future development, and new partners found.

To realise these aims, the well-trained manager is an essential asset: the professional who combines an understanding of the interlinking roles of marketing, finance and technology with a finely-tuned service attitude. Sensitive, creative management is essential in the fight for increased service and profitability in the face of rapidly-changing market conditions. Creativity comes into play with the need for introducing services which, without increasing costs, encourage guests to spend more money within the hotel. Such services might include franchising space to high cash-generating businesses such as ethnic restaurants, same-day laundry service, chemists, cinemas, sports facilities and the like. Another approach in which creative hotel management is highly desirable, is building a strong, loyal base of local customers in addition to the transient business on which hotels more traditionally depend. Some successful approaches in this direction will revolve around outstanding introduction and clever marketing of 'club' services for locals; special theme parties; outstanding business function facilities. By the same token, to succeed in the competitive marketplace of the future, effective management will be charged, as never before, with responsibility for eliminating costly and unnecessary services, such as complicated menus in restaurants where they are little utilised and making every square metre of the hotel pay. But the most telling demonstration of the new managerial creativity will lie in effective use of staff, in itself a complex art.

Obviously, corporate guidelines will shape the direction of change in the service mentality throughout each property; but in the long run, the effective manager at the hotel level will bear ultimate responsibility for successful implementation of those guidelines in the years ahead. The truly successful managers will be those who can juggle their responsibilities to produce a profit today with the service responsibilities that ensure continuing profits tomorrow.

The Vital Competitive Edge

There is not a more perishable commodity than hotel service. Empty rooms cannot be stored against future demand. Strategic marketing is essential to fill those rooms, either by offering the customer added value, or by reducing prices; some of the most successful strategies combine both! Complicating the question is the dependence of the hotel industry on outside factors: on the airlines, on travel agents, tour operators, wholesalers. Even as the major hotel operators plan continuing, and even intensified, relationships with each of these, they must continue to seek ways of utilising their own resources to achieve the vital leadership edge in an increasingly competitive business.

The hotel trade this year, particularly in Europe, has suffered considerably with the shortfall of US tourists. It has made large chain hotels fall back on more down-to earth marketing techniques and turn to the local markets to generate income. In Brussels, the Sheraton has introduced the Sheraton Club International, an incentive package successfully tested since June 1986 to bring more customers to the group's hotels. Sheraton visitors get bonus points on everything they pay for, including telephone calls, food and drinks and other services. Prizes range from free airline tickets to sports accessories and holiday packages. More than 53,000 Club cards are said to have been issued thoughout the world since June this year.

Expanding reservations technologies constitute one important asset. Increasing utilisation of toll-free telephone reservations systems in parts of the world where they are not yet in common use is one practical example. Recent surveys indicate that, via toll-free phones and Viewdata in Europe, it should be possible for more hotels to set up direct links with corporate customers.

Shaping Strategies

Successful strategy formulation rests with matching the company's strengths and weaknesses to the opportunities and risks within its environment. In manufacturing enterprises, global leadership implies the advantages of economies of scale and consistency of the international product. Among international hotel chains, of course, that is only partially true. For although the product is theoretically standardised, the environment in which they operate presents opportunities and risks that are far from uniform. Standardised operations in virtually identical hotel plants in Europe, the United States and the Far East would obviously be impossible: even though those properties were owned by the same chain, subject to the same ground-rules and staffed by management personnel exposed to hotel operations in many countries.

Individual peculiarities of doing business affect operations in every country: foreign currency laws, inflation rates, laws governing import of needed materials: all of these variables and countless others affect standardised operations. Unpredictable events, such as natural disasters or political upheavals, are further complicating factors. And the question of fashion is a constant one: customer tastes are fickle, and today's favourite tourist site can be deserted tomorrow, as new destinations syphon off customers, leaving lavishly built, expensive properties standing virtually empty.

Obviously, these problems do not apply to principal trading centres' such as London or Chicago, Paris or Tokyo. In such cities, the problem assumes different proportions: how to extend market share for ancillary products, such as conferences, use of leisure facilities, restaurants and bars. Keeping guests on the premises, as we have already mentioned, requires ingenious planning; so does a parallel strategy to widen the hotel's appeal to the local market. The most successful way to achieve these twin goals is segmentation: for from a true understanding of the target market come the products and, services which increase its customer base.

The Role of Research

The role of research in planning and implementing future strategies cannot be overstated, It is the key to marketing success and the means by which changing needs can be pinpointed, analysed and met. As technology helps the industry establish better and better psychographic profiles of its target customers, so skilful interpretation of those profiles will remain an integral marketing function. Here, again, balance is required: between the traditional industry concern with budgeting and return on investment, and the understanding that future success can only be assured by continuing, relevant research and creative implementation of its findings.

Keeping Ahead of the Competition

Understanding the competition the giants already on the field and new teams which will emerge in future years is obviously essential to success in the competitive marketplace. In the battle for marketing supremacy, as in warfare, the key to victory is the element of surprise. Thus it becomes critical to employ a two-part strategy.

1. **Understanding the Present Competition.** With increasing segmentation and the emergence of more definite characters, by which the major hotel chains will be identified, it will become easier for skilled competitors to spot potential advantages and to utilise the established personalities of their own organisations, sound positioning, service advantages, and every other weapon in the marketing arsenal to seek success in each given marketplace.

2. **Conquering the Newcomers.** The probable entry of new competitors requires all of the above, plus some additional skills. One need only analyse the effect of recent newcomers on the airline in ustry to understand how hotel chains could be similarly affected. The airbus industry, for example, was so successful in its head-on clash with Boeing and MacDonnell Douglas that it all but eliminated their presence in Africa, Asia and the Middle East. In the field of tour operation, Intasun's frontal attack on the UK market brought spectacular success and astonishing market position growth.

Potential new entrants to the marketplace may well be companies that already sell other travel-related services. Based on experience in related industries, their tactics usually involve some type of 'flank' attack based on weaknesses in the competitive position of established industry leaders; these weaknesses are then exploited by introduction of innovative services or invasion of new, key geographical locations. The key to success against such tactics is deploying the strength of the established, global organisation against its new competitor, when major hotel chains are structured in such a way as to maximise their worldwide positioning, upon economies of scale and upon a single, consistent s rvice image throughout the corporate network.

Hotels as a concept originated in the 6th century BC in the he form of inns. These were fun by couples and provided sleeping arrangements in big rooms similar to todays dormitories in youth hostels Hotels as is known today emerged in Switzerland and were patronised by aristocracy, In England inns catered to mobility and towerns to common man. Hotel is defined as a "Place where a traveller can receive food & shelter provided he can pay for it". Hotels are classified by the "classification committee" comprising government representatives and trade representatives against set standards necessary, essential and desirable. According to the facilities they are given star rating from 15. They are categorised depending upon their location, number of rooms, type of clientele, length of stay and facilities available.

Hotel industry is also known as the accommodation industry and the hospitality industry. Hotels and Airlines share the name problem *i.e.*, Seasonality.

Hotels can be categorised into the following types

1. **Downtown.** These are also referred to as commercial hotels. They ate situated in the heart of the city and are frequented by businessmen on travel. Owing to their prime location their rates are high.

2. **Suburban Hotels.** These are ideal for study tours and conferences. Rates are moderate.

3. **Resorts.** These are normally located outside cities in sites abounding in scenic beauty, catering to those on holidays. It is ideal for relaxation and recreation. It is divided into beach resorts, winter resorts, hill resorts health resorts and summer resorts. The rates here art normally on American Plan.

4. **Airport Hotel.** Rates are normally on European Plan. These are ideal for transit passengers.

5. **Motels.** These are situated on highways and rooms. These am on European Plan only.

6. **Residential Hotel.** Here the rooms are leased out for a minimum period of one month. The rooms are more or less like a self contained apartment with hotel facilities.

7. **Inns.** These are smaller in size and ideal for people travelling on a small budget.

8. **Flotels.** These are situated on the surface of water-sea, river or lake. O!d luxury ships are converted into hotels and provide a very exotic atmosphere.

Hotels can he classified into 5 Star, 4 Star, 3 Star, 2 Star, 1 Star The 3 bodies decide what star a hotel should be they are:

HCIMÁ: Hotel Catering Institute and Management Association.

Department of Tourism

FHRAl: Federation of Hotel, Resturant Association of India.

1. **Star Hotel.** Location should be in a moderate location with a minimum of 20 rooms, 25% of which should have attached baths and the remaining 75% should have one common bathroom at least for every 3 rooms. Rooms must be well ventilated and furnished. There should be a reception counter with a phone and the hotel should serve the local cuisine. The kitchen should be hygenic and well maintained good equipment should be used. Senior staff should be able to converse in English and have a specific uniform.

2. **Star Hotel.** The location should be better than 1 hotel and so also the decor. Parking facility should be provided and the hotel should have a lawn preferably. The minimum lettable rooms should be about 40 and 50% of these rooms should have attached bathrooms and 25% rooms should be airconditioned. All rooms should have comfortable furnishings. The baths should have running hot arid cold water. All the rooms should have phones. Each floor should have a phone or call bells pantry there should be well equipped pantry. The dining hall should be equipped with good quality crockery cutlery and glassware. The kitchen should be well equipped with a good layout if the hotels are more than 3 storeys it should have a lift facility and also other facilities like laundry, room service. The staff should be well trained and the senior staff should be

from catering colleges. The plan of the hotel should be approved by municipal cooperation of the state.

3. **Star Hotel.** It should be in a good location amid have at least 80 rooms. All the rooms should have attached bathrooms and 50% of them should be airconditioned. Rooms should have a high standard of interior decoration and sanitary Fittings. All the should have a phone, flasks and stationery should be provided the reception counter should he well maintained mid lifts be provided. There should he restaurants serving 2 different cuisines along with a bar era permit room the uniforms should be well designed and all the staff should know English.

4. **Star Hotel.** The hotel must be centrally located in a good environment The parking areas and lawns must be well maintained. The hotels should be centrally air conditioned and have more than 80 lettable rooms. The rooms should have phones, flasks, etc. and the decor of tile rooms must be of high quality and the linens and materials used should be good. High class sanitary fittings should be used with 24 hours running hot and cold arid water along showers. 75% Of the rooms should have colour TV with VCR or VCP. There should he a 24 hours reception counter having the latest systems, swimming pool and a well designed architectural lobby. There should be a restaurant and a coffee shop running 24 hours, banquet halls and a bar with 13 and 15 license for liquors. The kitchen should have modern equipment, qualified staff for each section. The staff in all the sections should be well trained with good uniforms. A sales and marketing office should be available.

5. **Star Hotel.** It should be centrally located with 100 or more lettable rooms, enough parking space. There should be extensive lawns for use of hotel guest and a pool, provision of a tennis court. All the rooms and corridors must he air conditioned. A properly staffed reception counter and

24 hrs. service, provision in public areas for ladies and gents with soaps and towels and also conference and banquet halls. There should be book stalls, post office, bank, shopping centre, satellite TV, multi channel music, efficient staff, fax and telex facilities, secretaries, interpreters, guest luggage room. The furniture should be of excellent standards and beds should be comfortable. All rooms, corridors, staircases should be richly carpeted. The beds, linens should be clean hygenic. There should be a provision for 24 hours room service and food service. Laundry and dry cleaning facility should also he provided.

Youth Hostels

The youth hostels are equipped to accommodate young men and women who travel on foot, by bicycle or other means of locomotion and who, at very little cost, are provided with place to sleep, cat or to make their own meal. The services provided include accommodations, meals and also recreation. The charges for these services are very modest. The hostels are also equipped to enable the users to prepare their own meals if they so desire. The accommodation provided ill the hostels is for limited number of days. The construction of youth hostels is based oil certain norms laid down from time to time all over the world. International requirements for these include provision of separate dormitories for melt and women appropriate and clean toilet wash rooms for both men and women, a kitchen where warden and staff can prepare their own meals, common rooms, living accommodation fur warden and a left luggage room.

There is also a provision of kitchen where warden and staff can prepare meals for supply to hosteliers, separate small rooms for instructors, a dinning room and classroom for school parties and a warden's office. Some youth hostels have playgrounds attached for the use of the hosteliers.

Caravan and Camping Sites. Caravan and camping sites constitute a significant accommodation category ill mails holiday areas. These are very popular in some European countries as also in the United States of America. Theme are also known as open air hostels, tourist camps or camping grounds. Camping originally practised by hikers on foot is increasingly given way to car camping. The sites are usually located within file large cities ill open spaces. Equipped to receive mobile accommodation ill the form of caravans, the camping sites provide facilities for parking, tent-pitching, water electricity, toilet, etc. Though the services, provided generally include restaurants recreation rooms, toilets and at certain places a grocers shop. The type of services often vary front place to place. Some countries have enacted legislation establishing the minimum facilities that must be provided which includes health and sanitation standards and prices to he charged for parking and use of various services and facilities.

Pension. This type of accommodations is very popular ill certain European countries. Particularly in Italy. Austria, Germany and Switzerland these establishments are used extensively by the tourists pension is also described as a private hotel, a guest house or a boarding house. Catering facilities are optional and are usually restricted to the residents. Many of them stay, for a longer and such definite periods as a week or a fortnight.

Bed and Breakfast Establishments. Also known in some countries as apartment hotels and hotel garnis, they represent a growing form of accommodation units catering for holiday as well as business travellers. These establishments provide only accommodation and breakfast and not the principle meals. These are usually located in large towns and cities along commercial and holiday routes and also resorts areas and are used by enroute travellers. Some of theme establishments are very popular with holiday makers.

Tourist Holiday Villages. Tourist villages were established fit sonic European countries after World War II. These villages are situated at warm sea sides and ill the regions which offer certain facilities for the tourist. In certain countries like Italy and Spain, tourist villages are located ill the regions which are economically not developed thereby helping the region economically. The villages are mostly promoted by important clubs. Social organisations and also by tourist organisations.

The village complex is a centre of accommodation providing extensive sports and recreation facilities, riding, swimming, tennis, volleyball, football, sauna, mini-golf, badminton, table tennis and yoga. These provide built board and lodging. The atmosphere ill these villages is kept as informal as possible. Telephones, radios, newspaper and TV are banned unless there is an emergency, Wallets and other valuables are locked away at the beginning if one's stay. Instead of money one uses colourful beads which earl be worn anywhere as bracelets, necklaces, etc. The staff are chiefly educated young people who live oil an equal basis with the holiday makers. The accommodation provided is usually in multiple units and may provide for self catering. The furnishing provided in the rooms is minimal. The easy mixing of guests is encouraged by the banning of advance hooking of tables in the village restaurants so one rarely finds oneself sitting with the same group twice.

The holiday villages are usually based on family units, each providing a convertible living room, bath/shower and sometimes kitchen. The villages are selfsufficient providing almost all necessities required by the residents. There is also available shopping complex where one can buy articles of daily need. The services of a doctor are also available ill the village. The accommodation is sold for a week or a fortnight at an all inclusive price. In Spain and Italy, these are classified into three categories according to the services and amenities provided.

Some of the famous Hotel Chains are the

Taj Group

Welcome Sherton

Oberoi Business Hotel

Ashok Radisson ITDC (Indian Tourism Development Co.)

Holiday Inn-ITC

Leela Kempinski

Centaur

Hyatt Regency

Ramada Hotels

Types of Room Plans

EP	European plan	Accommodation only
CP	Continental plan	Accommodation and breakfast
MAP	Modifie American plan	Accommodation, break-fast and one major meal
AP	American Plan	Accommodation with all 3 meals

General Terms used in Hotel Industry

1. **Check In.** Registration formalities made (on arrival at the hotel. Check in deadline is generally 1800 hrs.

2. **Check Out.** Departure formalities made before leaving the hotel.

3. **Confirmed Reservation.** Oral or written acceptance of the reservation. In cases of late arrivals the hotels should be informed in advance so as to avoid cancellation of the booking at the check in deadline.

4. **Day Rate.** Special rate for the room between 0800 and 1800 hrs.

5. **Guaranteed Payment Reservation.** Whether fire room is used or not Payment is assured.

6. **Service Charge.** 10%-15% of the hotel bill is charged as gratuities for the hotel staff:

Types of Rooms Available

— Single room—Consists of a bed measuring 39" x 81" with good mattress pads, bed linen free of stains and good pillows a writing and an attached bathroom.

— Double room-a bed of 51" x 81" and attractively decorated.

— Twin room-much more cheaper, 2 beds of sizes 39" x 81".

— Triple room-for 3 people, beds of 39" x 81".

— Ouad room-for 4 people with separate 4 beds.

— Cabana: a cottage facing the pool decorated with bamboo. It has its own entrance and is separated from the main building meant for a meant for a single person or a couple.

— Pent house—It is on the top most floor of the hotel. Sometimes part of it is opens to the sky.

— Single Suite—A Single room with a drawing room, bedroom and there may be a dressing room with Colour TV, VCR, STD facility refregirator, fruits and Choclates.

— Double Suite—Room meant for 2 people and the layout being the same as a single suite.

— Studio room-has a bed and a diwan setting.

— Interconecting room—2 adjacent rooms, with a connecting door to each other.

— Recuperating room—Rooms for sick people (adavance notice is given to the hotel).

❐

11

Tourism and Management Strategies

The Growth and development of tourism has been associated with several idealistic notions concerning its contribution to society, but subsequent experience has shown tourism like many other human activities, can have both positive and negative impacts. The industry has frequently been promoted as a force for positive contributions to the social, economic, and natural environments of destination communities. Striving for such benefits through the vehicle of tourism development, however, has made tourism a major agent for change in every society and destination it has touched. Change involves a price, and some communities have been unaware of the costs and difficulties associated with extracting the benefits of tourism.

Evidence of growing antagonism towards visitors is beginning to emerge in the more popular tourist destinations, where some residents feel overwhelmed by the volume of visitors and change in lifestyle. In some areas local nicknames for tourists may be construed as early warning signs of growing tension. In Cornwall tourists are referred to by some as "emmets" (ants), and in parts of southern England as "grockles" (a commercially worthless shellfish. In Banff, Alberta, the term "gorbies" is used to distinguish the awkward and gawking visitors. A sign of the times in Banff is production of a-T-shirt which facetiously records the loss of three tourists to bear attacks one year. In a few regions the hostility is no longer latent with the appearance of anti-tourism graffiti, property destruction and personal violenc. Examples of this include the "Yankee go home" posters in the Europe of the 1960s, the fire-bombing of second homes in North Wales, and reported assaults on Canadian visitors in Hawaii.

The World Council of Churches has examined the issue of tourism-induced social stress and concluded that promotion of human understanding requires more than a simple transfer of people from one region or culture to another. It recommended in its report Leisure-Tourism: Threat And Promise (1970) that the industry acknowledge its social responsibilities by providing more accurate information on the countries to be visited and by arranging informal meetings with local people. It calls for short. pre-trip courses stressing the political, social, and economic issues of destination areas and an extension of "meet the people "'programmes which have been successful in Sweden and Germany.

The flow of tourists and their revenue to peripheral regions has been viewed by some as a counterbalance to the economic pull of our urban-industrial centers. Christaller, the pioneer of central place theory, states:

> There is also a branch of the economy that avoids central places and than agglomeration of industry. This is tourism. Tourism is drawn to the periphery of settlement districts as it searches for a position on the highest mountains, in the most lonely woods along the remotest beaches.

Studies of national economies in underdeveloped countries have shown a considerable amount of generated tourism revenue has returned directly to the tourist-generating countries. In one study it has been estimated as much as 77 per cent of the tourism money returned to these urban-industrial economies (Perez 1974). This return flow is created by payment of loans and dividends on foreign investment the importation of goods and services to supply the tourists, and the salarites of senior personnel who are often temporary residents. It has been given the apt name of "leakage," for a community may heel it is building a prosperous industry but when the final bills and bank charges are paid there is often much. less left in the community account than expected.

Such a situation is not confined to underdeveloped countries; it can and does occur within advanced economies where small and peripheral communities attempt to transform some local resource into a tourist attraction. The development of mountain resorts or the renovation of heritage usually requires capital and manpower in excess of local supplies, consequently these tourism developments rely on investment and labor from distant urban-industrial centers and face the same leakage situation.

The preservation of historic buildings is often supported or financed by tourism-related interests. The renovation of "old town' districts in the older North American cities is frequently founded on a business sector expectation that it will add to the touristic appeal of these cities. Churches which have lost their congregations have at times been saved by changing to a tourist function, such as a museum or "brass-rubbing' center.

The benefits of tourism extend to our cultural environment and daily life because of the diverse nature of its resource base and the intricate way in which it is woven into a community's regular activities. The presence of tourists often adds to the amenities of local areas. Perhaps the most famous example is the live theater of New York and London's West End, which depends on tourist ticket sales to sustain its existence. Of no less importance to other towns and cities are the tourists revenues which support their pageants, sports events, and tradefairs. "Institutions" such as Paris Eiffel Tower, Seattle's Space Needle and Science Center, Munich's Olympic Stadium, and Montreal's "Man and His World Exhibit" on the lle Saint-Helene were created for special events and have remained as prime tourist-resident amenities.

A paradox of tourism, however, is that the industry carries within it the seeds of its own destruction. Successful development of a resource or amenity can lead to the destruction of those very qualities which attracted visitors in the first place.

The development of tourism is occasionally undertaken in such haste and without proper planning that it simply outstrips the local infrastructure and resource base resulting in unexpented costs which further reduce its overall economic benefit to the community. The problem here is tourism's diverse and uncoordinated structure, with numerous individual entrepreneurs striving to make a profit within their own short-term horizons.

> Examples include the construction of hotels on Majorca without proper transport and sewage linkages, the continued construction on both lbiza and Majorca despite clear warnings of insufficient water, and the rapid and heedless construction of hotels on the coast of Keyna, which now struggle to reach 50 per cent occupancy owing to the unforeseen coincidence of the European tourist season and monsoon rains in Keyna.

Elsewhere the tourists themselves are the prime cause of environmental damage, although the destruction is usually unintended because most visitors come to admire a scene or event and the businessman's prosperity depends on an amenity's survival. Sochor (1976) reports more than 300 mountaineering expeditions since 1949 have caused widespread deforestation, pasture destruction, and serious accumulation of litter on the slopes of Mt. Everest and other peaks in the Himalayas. Stonehenge has been placed behind a perimeter fence to protect it from the pressure of countless feet which were compacting the soil around the stores and threatening to tilt and topple the remaining inlets.

It becomes evident from this short review that tourism, as an agent of transformation, can change the social, economic, and physical relationships of communities where it has been adopted. These changes are often slow to emerge or to be appreciated because they can be both desirable and detrimental, so when the net balance is finally determined it is often too late to reverse or redirect the development process. In fact a good simile for the modern tourism industry would be that of a household fire. When the fire is contained and managed within the hearth it offers beauty and comfort to the household. When it runs out of control it can destroy the very household it was designed to support.

Government Involvement

Government interest in tourism stemmed from concern over its economic significance, particularly its sources of revenue. According to Lickorish and Kershaw, as quoted by Middleton, this alone was sufficient reason for government intervention in the development of tourism.

> Justification of such intervention is the tremendous financial stake, taxes paid by various enterprises, indirect taxes paid by visitors and the employment provided in areas where alternative ways of earning a living are pot usually available.

Thus, it comes as no surprise that the governments at national and regional levels have been actively promoting tourism and aiding facility development through the provision of grants and subsidies. Britain's Development of Tourism Act (1969) inaugurated that government's formal involvement with tourism planning in response to a growing travel deficit. Its goals were to provide more effective promotion abroad (British Tourist Authority) and at home (Tourist Boards on a regional basis), to encourage hotel construction and to direct development to economically depressed areas. Likewise, the more recent Travel Industry Development Subsidiary Agreements (TIDSA), signed between the Canadian federal government and various provinces, were conceived as a partial response to Canada's growing travel deficit—a deficit which had reached $1.8 billion by 1978. In all these federal-provincial development plans the prime goal was to develop the attractiveness of a province and make it more appealing to foreigners, especially United States visitors and Canadians alike. The United States government formally joined in the promotion and stimulation of tourism with its 1981 National Tourism Policy Act, although there had been considerable local and state promotion beforehand. The newly created United States Travel and Tourism Administration's basic mission is "to promote US inbound tourism as an export" in an attempt to reduce its traditional travel budget deficit that has become an increasing burden as traditional visible exports have declined.

The most remarkable case of government involvement in tourism for economic development purposes occurred in Spain. Tourism development and promotion was used as the main financing force for the 1964 Spanish Economic and Social Development Plan. By that time tourism was the largest export sector in the country:

> Earnings covered 82 per cent of the commercial balance deficit, financed about 40 per cent of all imports and equalled 93 per cent of the total value of Spanish exports. Little wonder that a prominent banking concern has likened tourism to "manna falling from heaven, impelled by the favourable wings of stabilization".

Using the momentum of mass tourism during the 1960s, Spain invested large amounts of public and private capital in tourism infrastructure and facilities to provide employment and raise living standards in various regions. These included established tourists destinations in the Belearic Islands and Costa Brava and new developments in underutilized areas such as the Costa de la Luz and Canary islands. The timing of this investment programme was perfect. The 1960s and early 1970s were the prime growth period of international tourism, than many northern European holidaymakers ventured from the fickle weather of their traditional home resorts to seek the sun and novelty of package tours in the south. By 1971, 26 million visitors were leaving $2,2 billion in foreign currency in Spain, and the industry was employing 1.4 million people or 11 per cent of the labor force (Parsons 1973).

Spain's example of tourism-induced economic development has been emulated by Yugoslavia on its Adriatic coast. Three five-year economic and social development plans between 1955 and 1970 specified that tourism be treated as "an activity of special importance for the development of the country in general". Accordingly, facilities were developed for tourists along the Adriatic coast at sites with tourism potential and charter links with western Europe encouraged. According to Mihovilovic, by 1980 it was expected that foreign currency earnings from tourism would amount to $1.2 billion (at 1975 prices).

Over time, government involvement with the industry has extended beyond ecomomic concerns and revenue generation because with its growth came increasing evidence of its physical and social ramifications. First among these is the fact that tourism, like any other economic activity, competes for resources. Government agencies needed to accommodate tourism's growing needs with the demands of more traditional resource sectors like fishing, forestry and agriculture. Furthermore, such concerns over resource allocation had to be accommodated in an era of environmental preservation, brought about by a growing awareness of the world's resource limitations and interrelated ecosystem. In North America's western states and provinces conflicting demands for resource exploitation and recreation have become a major issue for government (Hammond and Andrus 1979; Ingram 1981; Newsweek 1983). Federal and state/ provincial governments own considerable tracts of land within the Rocky Mountain chain where increasing user pressures have forced them to consider multiple-use and selfsustaining management strategies. Such government policies are needed if the recreation and tourist demands of a growing urban population for lake and ski resorts can be balanced with increased demands for power (hydro-electric, coal, oil sands), the needs of traditional users (forestry. fisheries) and their respon sibilities to future generations (land reserves, including national and state/provincial parks).

In Europe, the scale of tourism movement and more intensively developed landscape has forced governments to integrate tourism into local land-use patterns and life-styles, or even become directly involved in its development. The British national parks encompass productive farmland and urban areas of considerable size, so their growing popularity as tourist destinations requires careful integration of the leisure industry into an existing economic and social system. In 1974 the Sandford Report of the National Parks Policies Review Committee recommended, and the government accepted, that landscape conservation should take precedence over recreation use. This included a duty to pay heed to the needs of agriculture and forestry, and the socioeconomic well-being of local communities. Subsequent management plans of the ten National Park Authorities attempted to meet these requirements. However, not all successive governments have been wholehearted in their support for a conservation priority and detention of traditional landscapes has come under intense pressure from the growing agribusiness farming methods.

In France the desire to develop a new area of the Mediterranean coast for tourism, to reduce the pressures on the Cote d'Azure and utilize the tourism potential of nearby coastal areas, has led the government to initiate the Languedoc-Roussillon project. Among the multiple purposes of this massive regional development plan (VS$18.5 billion invested by 1979) was the creation of five tourist units. The purpose was to raise the income and employment levels of this depressed area to provide new recreation and amenity facilities for local residents as well as visitors and to provide an increased opportunity for social tourism projects (Willis 1977; Clarke 1981), The early experiences of the Langyuedoc- Roussillon project have not been as positive as first hoped especially in terms of stimulating regional employment and economic growth, and now the French government seems to be adopting the view that it takes time for an underdeveloped region to become an established tourist Mecca.

One problem which the French and other governments have come to appreciate is that a major obstacle to development and planning in tourism is the fragmentation of the industry. For many small businessmen tourism is the last bastion of free enterprise. where with relatively little capital but with good timing and good ideas fortunes can still be made. In this sort of atmosphere, to decide on a public policy is one thing to communicate this goal to all the companies businessmen and communities affected, and coordinate their actions is another. The overall fragmentation of the industry makes it easier for development conflicts to arise and facilitates a situation where the final outcome of individual decisions can place a great strain on the natural and human resources of destination areas. As Gunn sums it up:

> the evidence of fragmentation of tourism development is mounting. As the volume of tourism expands and as

> development increases, many segments of tourism are running on collision courses with growing frequency. These conflicts appear to be expressed in reduced satisfactions to visitors reduced rewards to owner-managers and erosion of basic resource assets.

Acceptance of this fact has compounded government involvement with tourism for it alone possesses the necessary financial resources and legislative power to redirect and coordinate the industry along more desirable courses of action.

Government response to this fragmented growth industry its numerous resource demands and various impacts has been the gradual creation of tourism departments and ministries and an evolution of policy. In most western governments tourism agencies have been linked with trade and commerce ministries, reflecting its business orientation in legislative minds. In a few national and state/provincial governments where tourism has grown into a major economic activity often within the top three activities' in terms of employment or revenue, it has been accorded its own ministry. The initial goal of many agencies was to assist in the creation of an attractive and competitive tourist product. This involved cooperation with the industry and related government departments to stimulate business and supplement facilities through promotion and physical planning. Millions of dollars were spent on the promotion of traditional and new destinations in the belied that the economic return on such "investment" would be justified. New facilities were encouraged through subsidies, tax incentives, or outright grants, especially in areas of high unemployment. This economic and plant inventory emphasis, however has gradually been replaced by a more comprehensive planning approach as the complexity and impacts of the industry have become apparent.

Fragmentation of the industry which has been viewed as a barrier to comprehensive development and maximization of revenue. still retains some merit if it forms the basis for local diversity and character. The joy of travel includes noting regional variations in landscape and culture as reflected in local architecture, customs. and food. Memorable visits can be made by the personal touch of individual owners and operators. Therefore, the problems of fragmentation must not be confused with, or transposed into, the boredom of conformity and mass production.

Mings considers the tourists industry's development prospects are at a crossroads and government involvement will play a major role in its future. As he sees it:

> Rapid growth of any industry requires considerable study and planning in order to maximize its potential assets and minimize its potential liabilities. Commonly, tourism has not received the benefits of sufficient research to enable proper planning. Consequently, development in most plarces falls short of achieving optimum impacts. Simply, too many countries have plunged headlong into an activity with inadequate and, occasionally naive understandings.

Governments, according to Mings, have three options in the face of this situation. First, there is the "no change" option, which consists of ignoring those problems and protests associated with the industry. Such a "hands off" approach is likely to be hazardous for both tourism and the government because the industry depends on local support and no elected government can disregard unpopular and unsuccessful activities for long. Second is the alternative course of action of withdrawing public support for tourism and even attempting to curb private promotion of tourism. In this case a danger exists that government officials under attack may react prematurely, without the benefit of adequate investigations. It may be the case that "whereas at one stage a few years ago officials jumped on to the tourism bandwagon with unwarranted haste, many are now in danger of jumping off in much the same unreasoned fashion". The third option is to pursue rationalization of the industry so as to render it more beneficial. The involves an assessment of the industry's problems and prospects, followed by a plan of action to remedy weaknesses and direct the industry toward long-term goals. Underlying this option, Mings outlines two major issues:

1. Can the Various objectives to tourism be remedied satisfactorily? And if the answer appears to be yes.
2. Will the contributions (economic, social and environmental) of the surviving industry be of a sufficient magnitude to warrant public support?

As Mings notes, none of these three options exist in their pure form, but "most countries have borrowed some characteristics from all three options." The rapid and inadequately planned growth has created a myriad of unexpected and undesirable problems, placing tourism development at a crossroads. Either the industry's shortcomings will be attacked and its potential benefits realized, or the necessary public support will be redirected to other areas of social and economic investment.

Travel Management Strategy

In recent years we have been inundated with advice on how to formulate a strategy. It is something we know we should do, yet sadly we do not do it, preferring to operate *via* the "seats of our pants". We read books on the subject, attend strategic conferences and, in some instances, even propound our own theories. Yet somehow, true strategy never sees the light of day.

When something does emerge then, all too often, at the first setback or sign of retaliation, the strategy is either abandoned or, despite market changes, blindly adhered to. Why do we so often fail to establish a workable strategy? Is it just a question of inertia? Are we the innocent victims of an unpredictable market, or are we terrified about being first with anything new? Do we subconsciously fear the implications of strategy, hindered by too many 'ifs' and 'buts'. Have we any real idea of where we want to be? Is, for example, Hertz just a car hire company or does it knowingly use car hire as a means to earn insurance commissions?

The answer is rarely simple. It usually stems from a mixture of all these questions and the false assumption that the market will keep on growing. The pattern of economic and social life, however.

is changing; calling for newer and more segmented approaches to the market and-perhaps only by the 1990s-will analyssts be able to make a more balanced judgement of where the industry has made mistakes. and where it has got it right.

In this chapter we seek to hightlight the need for strategic focus its elements, potential obstacles and the actual process of strategy formulation. Before embarking on such a major under-staking, it is important to look at the people angle. This should not be viewed in terms of 'customer smiles'. but in terms of how many potential customers for our services that actually are.

The Environment And The Need For Strategic Focus

In Europe, more than in the USA, the age tree is inverting: there are fewer productive people supporting more non-productive people. This definite trend primarily affects health and social security schemes but it also has very significant implications for travel and leisure. Furthermore. the pattern of family life is also changing with the emergence of single parent families, a shorter working week, working mothers and a more sophisticated, experience hungry youth segment.

Since the last war there have been dramatic changes in the economic fortunes of the industries and services making up the world economy. We have seen in manufacturing and industrial companies a disastrously slow response to change; failure to utilise resources effectively and efficiently and an inability in many instances to adjust costs and product offerings. The service industry, particularly in the travel field could so easily fall victim to this malaise unless there is a move to re-think strategies in terms of cost structures and marketing opportunities.

The competitive pressure, no one can doubt, is on. forcing travel companies to tread new paths; challenging old ideas and tearing down traditional boundaries, often for the wrong reasons. In Europe we are beginning to emulate the American preoccupation with change. Change is equated with progress and progress with success. The drive is for the new. As we shall elaborate later, these beliefs originate from new competitors or existing market leaders, and lead to reactions from others, reactions which must be anticipated and evaluated. The inevitability of retaliation is fact for most travel companies are market driven seeking the same solution. Few like to innovate most like, to copy. This is perhaps why we are beginning to see only the enlightened few reassessing their roles and the validity of their strategies in the market. Often this reassessment originates from panic as newcomers poach market share. We cannot stress often enough that companies should identify what they want to be against what they actually are and plan according to their objectives. Managers, according to Peter F. Drucker, live in two time-periodsthat of today and tomorrow. In turbulent times, such as we are facing, no manager can assume that 'tomorrow will be an extension of today'. We must plan. if we are to grasp the advantage.

Those of us who are ready for and accept and exploit, change will be the winners. Throughout this book our common message has rested on the need for five vital characteristics:

- Knowing what you are—leader or fast follower;
- flexibility;
- speed of response;
- assurance of continuity;
- positioning.

We can no longer think in terms of 'the usual' for rapid and abrupt change prevents that. Our strategy as managers must be 'taking advantage of new realities, and to convert turbulence into opportunity'.

Although some of the elements contained in this chapter apply more to the larger firms in the travel industry, small firms will also benefit from this approach. What we are advocating is that all companies no matter what their size, must anticipate or even create environmental change. At the same time the companies need to move forward in a controlled and planned fashion. Unfortunately, the high degree of capital investment required increasingly makes flexibility and speed of response difficult. This automatically gives the newcomers a competitive advantage, particularly when dealing with the latest 'travel fad', or technology.

Who will Create The New Strategies?

The drive should come from within, for nothing can really replace entrepreneurs. Without their vision, drive and skills little can be achieved. However, the challenges which face them are complex. requiring core abilities to analyse the environment, see through its complexities and to induce and pilot the organisation through the process of change. Where these entrepreneurs will come from is difficult to say; all we can ask is they are capable professionals who anticipate and utilise the external and internal potential of a company. Here there must be an understanding of the need to reduce tne dominating role price plays. To avoid reduced margins and potentially damaging price wars, managers should continously strive to differentiate their service offerings so that non-price competitive comparisons will play an increasing role.

What Must The Leader Review?

The company headed by the conductor/manager needs to review the challenges the future holds in terms of:

— changing growth patterns;

— unpredictability;

— demand life cycles;

— technology and delivery systems;

— accountability—to shareholders, employees and customers;

— core business;

— capital requirements.

Having obtained this strategic information, he needs to develop the corporate ability to create and operate a strategy. He needs also to balance the problem of getting weighty systems controlled organisations to move rapidly. He needs, above all to understand his company's corporate capability.

The Concept of Strategic Planning

Potential Traps—People and their Attitudes

Most of us are aware of the hazards and pitfalls out there in the market. A major potential source of concern is the corporate culture, the beliefs and attitudes of the staff. One way to spread new values is to build a team of key opinion leaders, originating from the 'workshop', who can lead and communicate beliefs within their spheres of influence. Because corporate culture and people are difficult to change rapidly the time span of such an activity is inevitably long.

Let us look at the typical response of most employees: they do things their way; whatever gives them the least hassle. We all recognise and know this characteristic. The travel agent will usually recommend the most accessible tour operator where ease of response is evident and efficient. Those tour operators who complicate life or create problems will be avoided. The same applies to recommending insurance, car hire, travellers cheques and any other ancillary services.

The airlines tour operators and hotels have to remember that it is their distributors who initially deal with, customers and wield tremendous power over client choice. Thus, when creating a strategy. the entire concept of service to the customer must be marketed not just to one's own employees but also to those of the distributors. Any supplier who overlooks the key role the distribution partner plays is creating a potential weakness in his own company's activities.

Business rationale and strategy must be clear, avoiding the need for middle managers and staff to read between the lines. Ideally, a shared vision has to be developed enabling everybody to understand why a particular strategy has emerged. By simple illustration, employees can readily see at what stage of development their organisation is at.

Fundamentally. we are talking about making employees understand why times are changing and what options are open.

Corporate Options—The Choice

1. Survival/Divestiture—strengths and weaknesses, life cycle problems;
2. Current Position Maintenance inelastic market/defensive;
3. Expansion—distinctive competence competitive advantage—Successful company strategy;.
4. Diversification—make/buy (often a result of analysis in point 1), within the industry/outside.

Presenting employees with the basic four options companies have, and the actions each demands, helps employees to understand the vital elements concerning strategy. They learn to realise the importance of the match between an organisation's resources and skills and the risks and opportunities present in the environment. It helps them too to understand how the company actually makes its money, not always *via* the core business. It makes for accountability: vision is improved.

Strategies of the Winners

Who are the winners? We hesitate to mention names because of the volatility of the market choosing rather to look at the constituents of a winning strategy.

1. Low cost distribution—understanding the business its development and trends;
2. Concentration on customer group and sales channel-matching them up;
3. Opportunistic use of technology;
4. Differentiating the Services/Products offered: which is done in relation to perceived value to the customers and the cost differentiation in relation to competitors:
   (a) Specialised services—*e.g.* Business Travel A/C Management, free travel to airports, frequent flyer programmes;

(b) Ego products—Golden cards, Concord flights, Orient Express, etc;

(c) Standard products—Package holidays. car hire;

(d) Standard services—Luggage labels, in flight meals. terminal facilities;

5. Understanding the need for both competitor focus and market focus;
6. Avoiding competition on price alone. Constantly looking for competitive differentiation and value added;
7. Consistent management objectives;
8. Measuring performance in wealth creation and cost effective overheads;
9. Constant review of market attractiveness in relation to competitive position;
10. Ongoing search for new products/ markets, understanding the importance of fringe activities;
11. Strong flexible organisation, vision and leadership.

What Must Be Reviewed?

Basically, the 'winners' maintain an ongoing review of the possible directions their strategies can go.

1. The improvement of competitive performance;
2. Changing the method of competing;
3. Establishing new products and markets.

The Losers

Let us now identify the characteristics of the losers—the ones lagging behind in strategic management the ones who need to change to survive. What observations can we make about them?

- Lack of strategic problem solving inflexibility;
- Limited awareness or interest in business trends;
- Too inward-looking;
- Too much emphasis on budgeting planning;
- Lack of strategic focus;
- Unclear cost and service balance:
- No real market position;
- Poor use of marketing techniques;
- Poor use of technology—lack of flexibility in systems;
- Poor leadership;
- Short term management—crisis management;
- Contradictory goals;
- Failure to monitor or evaluate changes.

The losers (or would it be better to say the potential losers) have five options:

1. Improve market position by evaluating profitability of each activity;
2. Exploit synergies;
3. Move into related businesses;
4. Diversify into new markets;
5. Leave the industry.

Each option requires some form of activity and each activity must be viewed against four basic accepted projections about the future.

1. The travel environment is changing;
2. The momentum of change will be rapid;

3. New concepts are needed in relation to products and their life cycles distribution, cash innovation, timing;

4. The age of information and customisation.

Today, with the help of a computer and relevant data a strategy can be formulated. However. danger looms when the strategy needs to be converted into plans and activities. Management is in many companies too thinly stretched, preventing radical and pertinent ideas being carried through.

We see decisions being taken but due to the multiplicity of activities and diversity of client relations. not carried out. It is too often forgotten that a main strategy creates and is dependent on mini-strategies which need to work and develop in harmony if the overall picture is to be achieved. When concentrating on the mini-strategy. sight should not be lost of the overall goals.

To understand this complexity. it helps to create a total framework of the strategy formulation procedure plus a planning and execution chart. The framework should ensure systematic informed decisions are made. programmes for imple-mentation prepared and would make for the measurement of actual results against criteria. A planning and execution chart should also be designed in such a way as to create and maintain commitment to the overall goals. It should clearly show each area of activity and responsibility, demonstrating how the ministrategies interlock. It is important to note the way an organisation structures itself. for strategic decisions may differ from the way it operates in managing daily activities.

Additionally, it will encourage the creation of permanent and 'ad hoc' teams. By this commitment, performance expectations will be huge, with the emphasis on continuous improvements which reflect the requirements of the marketplace. If this commitment is missing, then any new strategy will flounder, leaving a company distinctly more vulnerable than before.

Below is a framework for the formulation of strategy. As a rule, during the early stages of transformation, few immediate changes can occur in the basic structure of the organisation. It is easy to attempt to change too much too soon. How rapid will be the transformation in workforce strategy? Hard facts on this subject are difficult to come by; we have observed the work done is SAS and BA. and although these organisations have adopted a comprehensive version of the commitment approach it is probably true to say that to date only the transitional stage has been reached.

The diagram shows the various stages and variables involved in the process. Each one must be identified and the role it plays understood. It must also be viewed in conjunction with a competitor analysis in order to ascertain an even clearer picture. From all this there would evolve the strategic plan. The strategic plan is the key document which gives guidance and allocates resources. All of us associated with this book believe that not everything in the strategic plan can be based on fact. Certain assumptions about the unknown have to be made.

We have deliberately refrained in this book from discussing the strategic plan in depth because of our belief that the only advice we can extend is that of Drucker who believed it to be a document which will 'organise systematically the effort'. The plan should be designed to be ready for any contingencies should the basic assumptions on which the strategy was built change. or if the strategy fails. After the contingency element has been developed, then a mechanism must be built into the company's monitoring and control system which will bring it into action at the appropriate moment.

What Is The Message?

We think strategy is important. We advocate that its formulation should be managed and not left to chance or overlooked. We need it to identify and develop goals and objectives to recognise strategic issues and to match them to our existing resources.

Each chapter of this book has sought to give in a practical and realistic way. a variety of opinions for the future. Much of what we have written is experience-orientated and attempts to bridge the gap between theory and practice. That is why we offer as a practical methodology. The Strategic Tree highlights a timespan of activities which once set in motion. will ensure the right combination of products services and markets is selected.

We have deliberately omitted the element of capital investment in this chapter, due to the wide differences and needs for fixed assets and equipment etc. All we can stress is that strategy must take into account careful resources. The synergy between needs and capital must be absolute to harness the potential of the company in the market place. Here again each individual company, using sound research and a degree of anticipation, must create its own equation. The worth of each project must be weighed up in relation to net value and calculated risk. What must at all times be remembered is that greater stress needs to be placed on managing financial costs and risks, without crippling entrepreneurship and morale. The only limit to new kinds of financial instruments and techniques seems to be human ingenuity.

There are immense challenges facing us all, for it is a new surprising world, of which nobody is the master. As the travel industry continues to develop and newcomers bring in new dimensions, one thing will remain constant—the need for informed, hands on, heads up management. Really there is nothing else you can rely on!

Tourism Management Strategy

It's known as the "smokeless industry". It's now the world's biggest. And increasingly, tourism claims to offer a sustainable development option to countries short on cash but long on environmental riches. In fact, tourism, even ecotourism, is causing widespread environmental and cultural disruption. In this article, Sue Wheat compares the best of ecotourism with the rest.

"Wanted—an Island to buy or rent" reads an advertisement in the Belize Review, giving an Arizona contact address. Now that Belize has become a mecca for nature lovers-especially from its neighbour the US—such advertisements are commonplace. With its idyllic tropical island cayes, the second largest barrier reef in the world, abundant flora and fauna in spectacular rainforest and ancient Mayan ruin's, this small, Central American state attracts huge interest from both pleasure seekers wanting to get away from it all and keen-eyed investors.

However, Belize is just one of many developing countries which has seen a rapid expansion in its tourist industry. Cheapter flights and increased leisure time have stimulated a dramatic increase in "long-haul" travel in many cases to parts of the world that other industries have never touched. Thirty years ago, few peopole could have imagined the ease with which it is now possible to reach the remotest corners of the world. Today, the search for the exotic destination is on with a vengeance. The combination of palm-fringed islands, adventure, intriguingly different clultures and strong Northern currencies, has meant that international tourist arrivals in developing countries have more than doubled since 1976.

According to the World Travel and Tourism Council (WTIC) tourism is already the world's largest industry and is growing at a phenomental rate-23 per cent faster than the overall world economy. The number of people now travelling for tourism purposes is around 500 million and is expected to rise to 937 million by 2010. For an industry which doesn't have to manufacture anything itself and simply exploits readymade features, these are astounding figures.

But just because the tourism industry does not have factories does not mean that its impact on the world is negligible. In fact, the "smokeless industry", as it has been described, is increasingly being blamed for massive enviornmental cultural and social damage. In a 1992 report entitled "The Tourism Industry and the Environment", the Economist Intelligence Unit (EIU) aruges that a growing number of disasters such as polluted beaches, degraded corel reefs, wildlife parks without wildlife and disappearing indigenous cultures are the result of tourism and are "part of an accelerating pattern".

Growing awareness of these problems and pressure on the tourist industry to become environmentally friendly have prompted a search for alternative froms of tourism". "Ecotourism", "responsible tourism", "sustainable tourism", and "low-impact tourism" are just some of the terms used to describe these new approaches. Ecotourism is one of the most commonly used, referring to a niche market for environmentally aware tourists who are interested in observing nature. But what started off as a small-scale, locally-owned initiative is now succumbing to overdevelopment. Ecotourism has become the fastest expanding seçtor in the industry.

Trickle-down Effect

Belize is Certainly not alone in suffering these problems. The Western desire for the exotic has been identified by many developing country governments as the route to easy wealth and a panacca for various economic ills. However, the proverbial economic trickle-down effect invariably means just that a trickle. While tourism employing more than 127 million people worldwide, in developing countries, the local people normally work in menial, seasonal and low-paid positions, with managerial jobs going mainly to expatriartes working for multinationals.

Transnational corporations (TNCs) , such as airlines, hotel chains and building giants, now dominate the industry and much of the financial benefit. Many of these TNCs have a turnover larger than the gross domestic product of the developing countries in which they operate. According to the World Tourism Organisation (WTO), at least 55 per cent of the foreign exchange earned by tourism leaks back to developed countries through spending on imports for the tourist industry, such as fittings, foodstuffs and labour. In some Caribbean countries, this figure may be as much as 70 per cent. Although the developing world increased its share of international arrivals during the 1980s, its share of tourism revenues actually fell, according to an EIU analysis of WTO figures.

Across the world, the hidden costs of tourism are often severe. On the resort islands of Thailand, much of the indigenous population has been forced to migrate because the price of basic necessities and land is beyond their purchasing power. In many developing countries, children skip school to sell to tourists and traditional livelihoods are abandoned. Local farmers and landowners in tourist destinations are often harassed by developers wanting to build on their property; fishermen are prvented from using public beaches taken over by hotels.

In Tanzania. the Government forced the Masai from their centurie's-old homeland in the Ngorongorn Crater in order to open up the park for tourism. As a result. posing for photographs is one of the only ways they can avoid poverty. The indigenous Berawan in Sarawak are in a legal battle with the Royal Mulu Resort Hote, which is planning to expand and construct a gold course on their ancestral land. The Berawan stress that they welcome tourists but they are concerned that they might loss their Native Customary Rights to land. "Although most of Mulu workers are Berawan they do not hold any position or partake in the development process within Mulu. Is this development for us? Certainly we are left out," says a Berawan statement.

However, many local communities around the developing world have had enough to being exploited by the tourist industry and are trying to garner a better share of the proceeds. The Toedo Ecotourism Association (TEA)—a grassroots organisation of Mayan indigenous people in southern Belize is organising village stays for tourists in settlements built by the Mayans with local materials. Tourists are looked after by the villagers them selves ensuring that all the financial benefits are kept within the community. Special emphasis is put on preserving their ancient culture and fragile environment. Aware of the danger of their tourism business becoming a "monoculture". the TEA members are also developing a firm agricultural base. Their main product is cocoa, which they are selling to a UK company for organic chocolate.

Contemporary Global Tourism Strategy

Increased affluence, leisure time and travel facilities in recent decades have made tourism a new and significant part of human experience. Here we look at what the phenomenon, couched in endless statistics, means to the geographer.

As recently as the 1950 he word 'tourism' was so little used that the average layman might have been forgiven for thinking it was some sort of eastern religion, along with Buddhism or Hinduism! Today tourism is a word on everbody's lips-both in the industralised world and, increasingly, in the Third World. According to the World Tourist Organisation (WTO), tourism has seen a growth of 1,600 per cent over the last 40 years. That is more than 'impressive growth'; it is an explosion.

Tourism has recently been described as a $2 trillion industry, making it the largest single item of world trade. While the validity of that statistic may be questioned, all trends suggest that by the end of the century it will be the most important economic activity in the world. (The WTO's more conservative estimate has tourism accounting for 12 per cent of the world's gross national product, and over five per cent of world trade). Already tourism creates 100 million jobs, which means that it employs more people than any other industry. One in five workers is employed in tourism-related acitvity.

Fundamentally, tourism is a geographic phenomenon concerned with the movement of people from place to place. Geographers study the spatial expression of tourism as a human activity. There are three main geographical components to this movement: *(1)* Generating areas (where tourists come from); *(2)* Tourist destinations; *(3)* Routes travelled between locations. This last point—tourist flows between regions—is fundamental to the geography of tourism.

From a geographical point of view, tourism and tourist flows can be considered on a number of scales, from the global level. through the regional, down to the local level depending on the detail required. Despite the fact that the number of international travellers has increased sixfold since 1960, tourism remains very much a 'first world' phenomenon. Two-thirds of international visitors arrivals are concentrated in just 20 industrialist countries, and 90 per cent of the world travel markets in the developed nations. The United States is the largest single market (21 per cent), followed by Spain, France and the UK. Europe together accounts for per cent of the world travel market.

As lifestyles become more affluent so more and the people are taking holidays abroad. It is predicted international arrivals will have increased from the current level of about 360 million to 600 million by the end of the century.

But while the relative importance of domestic tourist is declining in many countries, it still remains cornerstone of the industry, particularly in the U.S. Probably 90 per cent of the total tourism flows in the world are domestic, though this is difficult to—since even a family day out in the car or a week-end at the 'in-laws' is generally classed as 'tourism'. The encompasses much more than the, two-week packed tour. It also covers business and official (government) travel which itself accounts for one-third of the total industry.

Several questions need to be addressed. Firstly, it has there been such an explosion in tourism general. Secondly, what are the factors which influence tour flows? And thirdly, what is the scope for the future of the tourism industry?

There are several reasons for the extraordinary growth of tourism? The principal determinants of tourism and leisure activities are personal income and availability leisure time. Both have grown at record reates for industrilized nations during the last 25 years. Before 1960's, half the working population of Britain had holiday entitlement of a week or less. By the late 1970 the whole working population of the European countries had paid holiday entitlement of three weeks or more addition to bank holidays and weekends. Never before have so many people had so much leisure time.

Another vital factor accounting for the upsurge of travel especially overseas travel has been technological advances made in the field of transport. Mass air transport in fuel-efficient widebody jets has to a dramatic reduction in airfares, and and increase speed and comfort of travel. Car ownership has increased dramatically. In the UK only one-in-ten of the population had use of a car in 1960; today there is an average of almost one vehicle per family. The mobility the population in the industrialized world has been increased. making travel easier and cheaper than before.

Paradise Lost?

Europe may be our favourite location but long-haul holidays are also popular as high-rise hotels and crowded beaches in Rio prove.

Relative Distance Reduced

Much lower airfares, coupled with increases in the speed and comfort of air travel, have opened up and attractive and fashionable way to spend leisure time. Packages tours bringing Europe within easy reach are now affordable by most people.

UK Training and Career Opportunities in Tourism

In the last few years the numbers of tourism related courses in the UK has mushroomed at all levels. An indicator of the interest in the field is the success of the new GCSE in the Travel and Tourism. This is believed to be the first school-level qualification which has direct indus trey involvement: American Express. British Tourist Authority, Trusthouse Forte. Crest Hotels and the International Leisure Group are all working with Local Concils in a project known as the Travel & Tourism Programme. It is expected that around 120 schools will be offering the new GCSE course in September this year.

Many Colleges of Further Education now offer tourism as part of a business course or in other guises and several Polytechnics and Universities are offering a variety of tourism options an dcourses. Undoubtedly the largest and best-known department is at Surrey University headed by Professor Steve Wanhill. The undergraduate courses here lean towards hotel management. Three graduate courses aimed at managerial level are also popular: Tourism Studies is a more general course, while the planning/ development and marketing courses are aimed at more specific elements of the industry.

Statistics, Tourism Research & Planning

One of the problems which has plagued the tourism industry kis a dearth of credible statistics and information. This has resulted in a general lack of planning and masking of the importance of tourism in the eyes of policy analysts and decision makers. Partly because tourism has been seen as the domain of the private sector, and partly because the industry is so diverse and segmented, development has been largely unstructured and ad hoc. Co-operative data collection efforts and data-sharing agreements are rare in the private sector, despite the potential mutual benefits to be gained when several organizations work together.

There is therefore a pressing need for much more high-quality research in order to generate consistent and credible statistics. Although most countries have data-collection precedures, there is significant variation in the quality of the data collected. The validity of international tourism statistics is notoriously suspect. Despite the efforts of the Would Tourism Organization (WTO) and the Orgainization for Economic Cooperation and Development (OECD) variations in definitions, data-collection methods and accounting still exist between countries.

The WTO's statistics are based on and attempt to collate the record of all arrivals in all countries. They give a useful guide to the total volume of world tourism but at the national and regional level such figures are less than satisfactory, partly due to a failure to distinguish petween short-stay. long-stay, and transit visitors. The lack of standardized procedure and definitions makes comparisons between different countries difficult.

The other main source of tourism statistics in the UK is the International Passenger Survey. (Business Monitor MAC: Overseas Travel and Tourism published annually by HMSO). This is based on sample surveys of visitors on departure and arrival. and is carried out by the Office of Population Censuses and Surveys for the DTI. For detailed national and regional tourism statistics this may show trends more realistically simply because the figures have the consistency of having been obtained by the same standarized procedure for many years.

Much more research also needs to be carried out at tourist destinations on host communities. Methods for estimating the impact of tourism on communities are still in their infancy. A better understanding of this topic would allow the more efficient distribution of resources between competing claims and help to ensure that the environmentally and socially unacceptable side-effects of tourism are minimized in future. "Although research is expanding all the time. there is much more to be done," said Professor Steve Wanhill, of Surrey University. "We want to ensure that host communities will get the best mix of tourists to fit in with their culture."

Quite apart from the lack of hard research results, another continuing source of frustration for tourism planners and analysts is the lack of consistent and universally-accepted definitions. For example, the very words 'tourists' and tourism have been in use since the early 19th century yet there is still no single acceted operational definition for either. Such definitional inconsistency only further confuses any attempts to compare tourist flows and such related phenomena when drawing on data from diverse sources.

❒

12

Environmental and Ecological Parameters of Tourism

The term 'ecology' has been derived from the Greek term Oikos, 'Oikos' means 'home'. By adding 'logy' which stands for 'study'. Thus, we get the meaning study of the home or study of the environment. 'Ecology' is a branch of biology. Biology deals with morphology, physiology, anatomy, behaviour, origin and distribution of animals and plants. Ecology is the scientific study of the relationship between organisms and their environment. Ecological systems powered by solar energy are known as eco-systems. These are basic to support life on the planet-earth.

The world "Pollution" has been derived from a Latin word "Pulluere" which means "to soil" or "to defile". Pollution may be defined as an undesirable change in physical, chemical or biological characteristics of air, land and water which may harmfully affect the human, animal and plant life.

Environment is the surrounding which includes all external conditions and influence affecting the life and development of organisms. It may be broadly divided into two parts-biotic and abiotic-for the sake of ecology. The biotic environment consists of living organisms, which both interact with each other and are inseparably interrelated with their abiotic environment. The abiotic environment considers those physical and non-living chemical aspects which influence living organisms. These are soil water, the atmosphere and the influence of energy from various sources.

Kinds of Pollution

The main kinds of pollution are as follows:

(i) Air pollution

(ii) Water pollution

(iii) Land pollution

(iv) Noise pollution

(v) Radiation pollution.

Green House Effect and Global Warming

The word greenhouse is derived from the phenomenon of the sunrays passing through transparent plastic and glass panes attaching vegetation. In the broad sense of the earth, it means penetration of the sun-rays into the planet and its ecology. A portion of heat received is reflected by the earth in the infrared range of long wavelength. It is trapped by clouds, dust particles, carbon dioxide and water vapour in the lower layers of the atmosphere. This combined and large scale human activity are changing the earth's atmosphere. The increase in the earth's temperature is called global warming. The consequent increase in the melting of glaciers and snow fields could raise the level of oceans by 70 cms per hundred to begin the drowning of most of the sea-ports on the earth. This effect is known as the "Green House Effect".

Impact of Tourism on Environmental Pollution

It is apparent that environmental pollution has taken place on account of march of civilization. Except land pollution, tourists are not responsible either for air pollution, or for water pollution or for noise pollution and pollution due to tourists can be taken care of through regulated and guided tourism. There can surely be arrangements to dispose of the waste materials left by the tourists after visit to particular tourist spots. This should be the basic responsibility of the municipalities.

Tourism promotion, thus, does not adversely affect our environment. In order to attract the tourists the tendency of host countries would be to create a clean and pure environment, clean air, clean water, beautiful surroundings and absence of noise. If we want to achieve a large number of socioeconomic benefits from tourism, a little environmental price in the form of some land pollution would be paid.

Tourism Development at Historical Sites

While developing tourist resorts at historical cities and old villages, native inhabitants are generally distressed to find their narrow streets full with tourist traffic and their market place converted into car parks. Worst towns are those which are cluttered with souvenir stands and the bazars packed with roadside dhabawallas and fastfood restaurants. In our country also damage to our monuments including Taj Mahal, Fatehpur Sikiri, Buddhist temples in Gaya and Varanasi is becoming apparent due to growth of national and international tourism. Thus, it is important to note that the exposure of our historical monument? and sites be carried out with utmost care in order to avoid the damage on account of the rapid growth of tourism.

> The NCT considers that all such damage is not inadvertent. Most of them is caused by petty vandalism of the "new barbarians" the tourist hordes. They furtively chip away pieces of marble to take home as souvenirs. They also steal handicrafts from churches, gouge out mosaics from walls and floors, cut noses of statues. However, this kind of damage cannot be considered as ecological damage. This is damage to our sculpture and cultural heritage. Those assigned to look after our historic sites like the staff of the Archaeological Survey of India are helpless. So tourists continue to threaten our cultural heritage. The protection of our sculpture and cultural heritage is as important as the protection of our eco-system.

Tourism Development in Coastal and Marine Areas

The massive and packaged tourist development has also adversely affected the natural charm of coastal and marine areas. The beach resort facilities of Goa can be cited as an example. They are spread all along the coastline undermining the natural sand dunes eco-system of the area.

The degradation of coastal beaches takes place all along India's extensive coastline. The primary problem is the management of our coastline, which is under the pressure of development of tourism and other economic, industrial, transportation and recreational needs etc. It arises from the fact that beach resources, unless wisely managed, are liable to get dissipated even to the point of extinction.

In addition to beaches, other coastal eco-systems surely affected are mangrove forests, coral reefs and marine waters. Mangrove forests is a product of a complex interplay of sea, coastal land and river deposition. Mangroves also protect our coastline from erosion by the sea. These mangrove forests are being denuded by tourist activities. Apart from it, coral reefs and marine waters are being destroyed by such activities.

Tourism Development in Mountain Areas

Growing incidence of landslides on hill roads is one of the major problems of the mountain areas. Landslide disastrous in the Himalayan region have become endemic due to reckless construction and maintenance of roads to provide access to these resorts. The regions of hills are ecologically frail. Thus, road construction on these hills can create ecological havocs.

Tourism and Urban Ecology

Tourist are the temporary visitors. They do not visit the cities and towns to see the slums areas of these cities. Most of the hotels, specially, star hotels present a pleasing environment for the tourists. It is basically, on account of tourism that the surrounding of such hotels present dream look. However, in spite of the best efforts of the municipalities, administrators and town planners even these hotels do not intend to enlarge such surroundings and beauty. It is the joint responsibility of the Central and State Governments, the local bodies, voluntary organizations, the visitors and citizens to beautify the surroundings and the environment in the cities. Tourists would always be happy to visit these neat and clean places. They should protect the ecology in their own interest. Hence, tourism leads to the protection of urban ecology.

Ecology and Rural Aras

Rural ecology is the study of human eco-system mainly focused on man. Some low order systems are vested within the human eco-system.

Guided and controlled tourism would not have adverse impact on the ecology. Both domestic and foreign tourists may flock to out villages for fresh air and clean water, apart from the beautiful surroundings of the city. In most of the developed countries, workers working in the cities move to the rural areas during holidays far getting a fresh lease of life.

The concept of "folk villages" has been developed in a few countries. In South Korea at a plilce near Seoul, there is a beautiful "folk Village". It is a place for tourist attraction. It is maintained by the South Korean authorities. It encourages tourists to visit the village for enjoyment. The harm to ecology is from permanent dwellers and not from the temporary visitors. If concrete steps are taken, the dangers to ecology may be minimised from the permanent settlers in the country.

Island Ecology and Tourism

In order to study island ecology and tourism a case study of one of the tourism products of India-Andman and Nicobar Islands have been taken up. First we may examine the meaning of Island. Island means a land mass surrounded by water. They are of three types-continental, oceanic and coral.

The Andman and Nicobar forests have been taken into account as the most efficient bio-converter of solar energy. Its metabolic processes help in maintaining atmospheric balance, control run-offs, conserve surface water and prevent soil balance.

Tourism Prcmotion Scheme in Andman and Nicobar Islands

Based on the guidelines issued by the Island Development Authority, a number of steps have been taken by the Andman and Nicobar Administration to the tourist sector.

(i) Provision of subsidy for preparation of feasibility projects reports;

(ii) Investment subsidy as applicable under orders issued from time to time;

(iii) Provision for incentives for training to local manpower;

(iv) Augmenting availability of funds from State Financial Corporation;

(v) Allowing concession in electricity and water charges;

(vi) Allocation of land at concessional rate;

(vii) Provision for exemption from building tax levied by the Municipal Corporation; and

(viii) Provision for concessions under the Development Schemes of the Central Government, *i.e.*, Interest subsidy, Transport subsidy etc.

The above concessions can be granted to a cross-section of the tourist industry specially to the following categories of institutions:

(i) Classified Hotel 1-5 star;

(ii) Restaurants, approved by the Classification Committee of the Government of India;

(iii) Purchase of luxury cars, coaches, boats, etc. by tour operators approved by the Government of India and by the Department of Tourism;

(iv) Building up structures like Auditorium, etc., by School/ institutions teaching traditional art forms of the Andman and Nicobar Islands;

(v) Recreation centres and amusement parks, approved by the Union Territory Administration or by the Government of India;

(vi) Building of traditional House boats;

(vii) Ropeways at Tourist Centres; and

(viii) Institutions teaching surfing, gliding, trekking etc., which will promote tourism.

The island tourism has its own peculiarity and it gives a new direction in tourism promotion.

The ecology and environment of these fragile islands should be given protection. The Ministry of Tourism, Government of India, has to be the nodal agency for all tourism schemes/projects. Moreover, other Ministries, Departments and agencies have to accelerate clearance of projects and must provide sufficient funds for the schemes which fall under their purview.

Wildlife Ecology and Tourism

Wildlife takes into account all flora and fauna available in the biosphere uninterrupted by human beings. In a narrow sense, wildlife includes any animal that lives in a free condition in an environment that provides a habitat. Such wildlife can be microscopic. It includes insects, spiders, reptiles, fish, amphibians, birds and mammals.

In the present age tourism is going to be another factor for disturbance for the wildlife. Is this really an established fact? What are the adverse effects of tourism on wildlife? What are the advantages of tourism to the preservation and management of wildlife?

As a matter of fact wildlife tourism has contributed significantly to the foreign exchange earnings of a number of developing countries of Africa, Kenya, for example, depends heavily on its wildlife tourism. Out country offers a large number of wild animals.

Wildlife tourism must always be planned. While planning tourism projects we must consider that comforts and pleasures to the tourists must not be arranged at the cost of nature and wildlife.

A Case Study of Delhi

Delhi, the capital city of many old kingdoms—the mythical Pandavas, Pathans, Mughals and British—and now it is the capital of free India includes lavish museums and galleries. Red Fort, Jama Masjid, Lutyen's Complex of imperial Delhi, the reputed shopping centres of Janpath, Connaught Place, Chandni Chowk, Trade Fair and Exhibition Centre at Pragati Maidan, Qutab Minar, Purana Qila, Lodhi Gardens, Mughul Gardens, Budha Jayanti Park, Bahai Temple, Indira Gandhi International Airport, Palika Bazar, etc.

Delhi is facing an unprecedented rise in the number of vehicles and thereby escalation in the levels of pollution which affects tourism activities. Total number of 19.671akh vehiclas have been registered with the State Transport Authority (STA) of Union Territory Delhi till the end of March, 1992. The number of vehicles might have crossed 20 lakh till date. One Lakh vehicles, on an average, are added to the number of four wheelers, three wheelers and two wheelers every year. A total of 10,300 applicants were awaiting draw of lots for the 3000 buses under the STA of Delhi in the year 1992. Total number of buses and two wheelers are 14 and 12-13 lakhs respectively as on March 31, 1992. As far as fatal accidents are concerned, six lives are lost on average per day in the metropolis. Unfortunately, out of a population of 93.7 lakh of the city, 58.71 lakh commuters are expected to make use of the public transport every day Officials of the Union Ministry of Surface Transport with the help of the experts of Delhi Administration are studying a ban on plying of cars and two wheelers including odd or even number plates on Saturdays and Sundays, alternatively. All this will ultimately affect the tourist activities in this Union Territory of Delhi.

❐

13

Destination Planning and Economic Development

It is no coincidence that this destination zone concept agrees with contemporary views of urban development. At one time, apparently in response to urban congestion, the principle of dispersion was put forward. Many conservation proponents still adhere to this principle. But, dispersion can reduce the indigenous value of both community and hinterland whereas combining a central city with its periphery into a single unit allows each to function in a symbiotic relationship. Grades and Stern called this a "regiopolis." The regiopolis combined the advantage of social, human, and economic development within and around communities. Likewise, the tourism destination concept allows retention of community identity but also recognizes the important interdependency of the surrounding area.

It is the intent of this chapter to put forward the fundamental of place for planning at the destination scale and offer models. concepts, and processes for planning tourism at this level.

The Imperative of Place

The greatest imperative for all of tourism is place. Throughout history, place has played a dominant role in society. Sovereignty of place continues to foster strong land protection, and even to stimulate wars. For many peoples of the earth, the qualities of place mean survival or death. In spite of man's gargantuan efforts to reshape the earth possesses its own peculiar characteristics both as result of natural physical forces and acts of man.

As the topic of tourism planning shifts from the macro (the region) to the micro (destinations and sites), the importance of place dominates every concern. As tourism developers and promoters tend toward homogenizing the world with sameness, the opportunities for extracting the unique qualities of place so important to the traveller are being missed.

Characteristics of Place

Place, as defined by Motloch, "is the mental construct of the temporal-spatial experience that occurs as the individual ascribes meaning to settings through environmental perception and congestion." Explicit in this definition are important meanings for tourism. All travellers must have a place to go. Simple as this may be, it is not well understood. Place qualities are absolute for all developers of services, facilities, transportation, information, and promotion—the components of supply.

Temporal aspects of place are critical to tourism planning. Visitor impressions and experiences very greatly with time a place is visited. When visitors report they have already visited a location and see no point in visiting it again they may miss an entirely different experience at a different time. Weather conditions brilliant midday sun cloudy sunset time, snowclad winter, cold, heat, stillness, or wind-can give places quite different meanings. Places seen at night may be in absolute contrast when viewed in daylight. Not only will the landscape differ but also will the patterns and colours of activities and users be quite different. For example, a dramatically different experience results from visiting the French Quarter of New Orleans in the day as compared to night. Places of a singular year-round climate have different appeals to travellers as compared to places with seasonalchange—spring flowers, summer green, autumn foliage colours, and a white landscape of winter. The new market surge of nature tourism selects places as much on the time of viewing wildlife as on their habitat location. Animal migrations are critical to viewing wildlife.

An equally important dimension of place is its age—ancient to new. Generally the older the place the greater its amenities. An author of the southern region of the United States has stated. "Older places have accumulated more meaning but they also very often are more tied to a specific setting or are simply more humane in scale or character and thereby more engaging than new places". Viewing the ruins of Delphi on the wooded slopes of Mount Parnassus cannot help but evoke dramatically different images for the visitor than visiting the more recently planned cities of Canberra or Brazilia. Even within a lifetime. "the special places of childhood are not sacred but the memory of them is necessary for attaching sacredness to place." An enlarging travel segment seeks the experiences of visiting historic sites and places of prehistory. Planning for visitor use of these sites creates challenges never before faced by designers and managers-maintaining the integrity and patina of age at the same time providing for mass visitor use. For example, the removal of ancient skeletons from grave sites for display in museums is opposed by many native populations.

Spatial distribution of places around the earth has deep meaning for tourism and its planning. Each place has its own unique relationship to all other places, far or near. Analysis of geographic content described in the last chapter for regional planning are attempts to identify spatial characteristics of importance. In modern context with changing air fares and access spatial distribution of destinations takes on new meaning.

Another important characteristic of a place is its name. "Landscapes without place names are disorienting; without categorical forms. awful". Place names call up fantasy and imagery. The names of places from northern Michigan to the Arkansas River in the United States—Wisconsin. Peoria. Des Moines, Missouri, Osage, Omaha, Kansas, Iowa, Wabash, and Arkansas stimulate recollection of French Jesuit explorers. Louis Joliet and Jacques Marquett's trip through this land in 1673. For settlers of Taxas, religious themes dominated place names; San Antonio, San Jacinto, San Saba, Corpus Christi, and the Brazos River. Deeper analysis of market characteristics would probably prove that few travellers seek out places with unfamiliar or no names.

In spite of today's great mobility and migration of peoples. certain landscapes retain people-place qualities. A travel writer stated, "I believe you could exterminate the French at a blow and resettle the country with Tartars and within two generations discover to your astonishment that the national characteristics were back at norm". Thus is the dominance of the landscape as place. Landscapes have special values even when some cultural labels are the same. Durrell points out that the spirit of place has modified Catholicism to the extent that it is different in Ireland. Italy, Spain, and Argentina. The theology and practices result from modification due to place. Although these subtleties are not always readily available to travellers, with some time and introspection they become real.

Of course, place can be described by technical and scientific facts. For example, Mount Everest is five-and-onehalf miles (8.9 kilometres) above sea level is located in the Himalaya range, and was named for a British. Surveyor General of India. Sir George Everest. Madrid is located at latitude 40° 20' 30" North and longitude 0° 14'45" West and occupies about 550 square kilometres. In resource analysis as has been cited in the discussion of regional planning the quantities of natural and cultural resource facts are listed: arrest of forest land, sizes of lakes, lengths of streams, numbers and species of wildlife, and so on. Often, this is called inventory.

Human Attribution of Place

Although such inventorying is necessary in describing place it is of little value unless interpreted and given meaning. Human attribution of resource facts is essential. "Neither the environment as such nor parts or features of the environment per se are resources; they become resources only if, when, and insofar as they are, or considered to be capable of serving man's needs. In other words, the word 'resource' is an expression of appraisal and, hence a purely subjective concept". Resources are not; they become. For tourism and travellers. "The environment is encountered in a way in which self and place are related". Statistics of resources are of value to the planner only as anticipated visitor contact can be assessed.

An excellent example of place attribution is the concept of scenery, No such thing existed until after the Middle Ages. Forests were filled with demons and were of no value until felled for agriculture. Not until the painters and writers of the nineteenth century romanticized nature did vistas of landscapes become scenery, The terrible away of God was made into an aesthetic or, if you prefer, the forests and mountains of the earth came to be revered with religious intensity. The enjoyment of primeval wilderness had not been possible before".

Another aspect of human relationship to place is social. Cheek and Burch's (1976) early work emphasized the many social dimensions of leisure and place relations, There may be activities, such as picnicking, where the social group has higher priority than the location of place, as long as the needed amenities are present. Wilderness buffs often subscribe to Thoreau's tenet of seeking such places to find one's self. Certainly, the social context—solitude, friend, family, and lover can evoke different visitor meanings even from the same place.

Perhaps the greates lesson from this brief examination of place is the understanding of its powerful and almost inexplicable necessity for tourism. And, if its power and necessity are accepted, planning and design action must follow-placemaking. Areas that seek to become destinations for tourism have no choice but to become involved in placemaking, But, this process is not to be interpreted as artificially contrived. Quite the opposite. The challenge before the designer is to have sufficient understanding of both physical and human dimensions of place in order to design. Again, from Motloch, "placemaking should include the effective management of order and spontaneity for understanding and exploration."

Destination Planning Issues

Opportunities

Although much marketing of tourism is done at the regional (national, state, and provincial) scale, for most travellers this is to generalized. That size of geography is often too large to comprehend as being able to satisfy travel objective. It may be open to question as to whether travellers really seek their rewards in the United States', Canada, and Australia, or in destinations such as in and around New York, Montreal, or Sydney. Communities and their environs-destinations-more frequently carry with them images of appeal for both business and pleasure travel.

At this period in the history of tourism, it would appear that so many destinations have already been developed that there are few opportunities left. This is a half-truth because of the dynamics of both the market and supply sides of tourism. Changes in markets-demographics, economics, lifestyles, fads, and interests are constantly opening up new areas for development. Change in transportation, attractions, information, services, and promotion are introducing new areas as having potential.

Issues and Coustraints

If opportunities for destination development are so abundant, why haven't more destinations occurred? One might glibly answer that this is due to lack of planning, but that is too simple because destination tourism planning is complicated. Because communities are the focal points for tourism destination, it appears that there are several constraints for community action toward tourism development.

Blank (1989) outlines several salient limitations.

- Lack of comparative advantage (location, quality of potential).
- Carrying capacity limitations.
- Lack of community's acceptance of change-preference for status quo.
- Power structure's preference for other development. Myopic view of tourism.
- Fear of tourism—erosive Characteristics.
- Environmentalist resistance to any development.
- Narrow and inflexible policies on public lands.

Canada has experimented with much planning for tourism, most of which has stimulated valuable development. Yet, in working with destination planning a few researchers have observed some important constraints at the local level. Go et al. (1992) analyzed imlementation of tourism strategies there and derived the following resistances:

- Tourism involves such a diversity of actors that clear mandates for development are lacking.
- Lack of local guidance and will.
- Mandates are unclear or in conflict.
- Local jurisdictions seek a quick fix and fail to provide financial and human resources to do the job.
- Lack of monitoring system to measure success.

A consequence of the geographic reality of a destination zone is that it transcends political jurisdictional boundaries. This fact complicates planning and development. Tourism leadership and political decisionmaking such as for promotion, taxation and development of amenities also usually stops at such boundaries. Within the several small towns, rural areas and focal cities there may be different population characteristics and different traditional, attitudes, customs, and even conflict or animosity.

If tourism is to be developed these barriers against cooperation must be removed or at least ameliorated. Tourism leaders and constituencies of all jurisdictions within a zone must be equally committed to tourism development or it will not take place. Conversely. tourism may be the catalyst to bring peoples of these separate parts of the zone together for a common cause.

Destination Planning Guide

In recent years, governments and other organizations have prepared guideline manuals for public use at the local level. Often these are titled community planning manuals but in the context of definitions used in this book, they generally include an entire destination zone. The guides offer step-by-step processes that can be of great value to leaders and local population constituencies in their search for better tourism development.

Alberta Manual. An excellent example is the Community Tourism Action Plan Manual (Alberta Tourism 1988) developed by the provincial tourism agency of Alberta, Canada. It was prepared over several years of study by staff, outside consultants, and representatives of the private sector. It was prepared over several years of study by staff, outside consultants, and representatives of the private sector. It contains five main sections.

Book 1. Introduction. This section begins by defining tourism to include attractions, promotion, infrastructure, hospitality and services. It emphasizes that deficiencies in any of these components can limits tourism. The content includes answers to questions such as, Where do we fit in? Who benefits? Who doesn't benefit? And Is it for us?

Book 2. Organization. This chapter opens with emphasizing the need for organization but only after full commitment to tourism. There must be first a strong desire for tourism by residents. business and the municipal council. The first step following expression of commitment is to create a tourism policy and Tourism Action Committee.

Book 3. Process. The suggested flow of twenty four action steps to develop a tourism plan at the local level. Step 1 is market analysis. Step 2 is gaining input from organizations and agencies. Steps 3- 7 involve study of the area to determine assets and concerns. Step 8-10 include identification of goals, objectives and strategies for reaching objectives. Steps 11-18 involve completion of the plan, obtaining input from several public and gaining official approval. The final steps 19-24 consist of action implementation and reporting to the city council.

Book 4. Appendices. This book contains sources of assistance. such as private and governmental sources of grants as well as individuals and agencies that can offer technical and educational assistance.

Book 5. Workbook. The manual includes outlines for use in detailing the results of the several steps in the planning process.

As of September 1. 1990, approximately 250 of 429 eligible Alberta communities had developed tourism action plans. Based on the Alberta experience. Go et al. (1992) have identified five conditions for destination tourism development:

- A clustering of communities each supporting the other.
- Avoiding duplication.
- Key players who are ready, willing, and able to cooperate.
- Resident cooperation.
- Finance for start-up is available.

Wight (1992), as a member of the provincial tourism agency. further emphasizes the need for local stakeholders to integrate their ideas with governmental agency initiatives. When communities waver in their involvement, progress bogs down. In recent years, developers have seen the new regulations of the Alberta Environmental Protection and Enhancement Act (AEPEA) and the Natural Resources Conservation Board (NRCB) as red-tape hurdles that are costly in both time and money.

A plan for the Calgary-Canmore destination zone (Pannell Kerr Forster 1985) identified many opportunities for tourism. Table 1 lists these together with potential impacts and funding support. Wight (1992) expands on the analysis and information required for public and private tourism development decisions, summarized as

- Tourism projects inventory
- Muncipal financial impacts
- Transportation analysis
- Service and utility needs

- Private sectors EIAs and NRCB
- Tourism market demand study
- Visual impact assessment
- Assessment of natural areas
- Needs of expanded public services
- Water quality evaluation of Bow River
- Analysis of environmental issues
- Environmentally significant areas
- Quality of tourism/recreation experience
- Baseline information summary
- Municipal operative workshops
- Annexation proposals
- Employee housing issues
- Rock industry study
- Recreation trails study
- Updates of general muncipal plans
- Rock Mt. utilization study
- Sustainable wildlife study

Rural Tourism Guide. Based upon general decline in the U.S. rural economy. Congress in 1988 directed the Travel and Tourism Administration to sponsor a study of tourism potential in rural areas. The National Policy Study on Rural Tourism and Small Business Development (Economic Research Associates) was issued in 1989. Another product was the preparation of a planning and Commerce. U.S. Travel and Tourism Administration, and the U.S. Economic Development Administration requested the University of Missouri togather information and produce a manual. The first edition was published in 1978 and the second in 1986 and revised and updated third edition in 1991 (Weaver 1991). The following discussion summarizes the contents of this guide.

TABLE 1

Tourism Development Opportunities in Alberta, Canada

Opportunities	*Capital or Operations Emphasis*	*Social*	*Potential Economic*	*Impacts Environment*	*Cost*	*Primary Action or Funding Emphasis*
(1)	*(2)*	*(3)*	*(4)*	*(5)*	*(6)*	*(7)*
General						
Attract world class sports events before and after the Olympics	0	2	2	-1	C	Pr
Develop an annual winter festival	0	2	2	1	C	Pr
Develop a western heritage theme	0	2	2	0	C	Pr
Promote the scenery by making highways "visitor friendly"	C	2	1	0	D	P
Capitalize on linkages to attractions outside the zone	0	1	2	0	A	Pr
Prepare circle and exploration tour publications	C/O	1	1	0	B	Pr/P
Develop and promote major attractions in locations outside of Calgry	C/O	2	2	-1	X	Pr
Provide tax incentives and concessions for tourism developments	C/O	1	2	0	X	P/M
Develop and promote tourist of Olympic facilities	0	1	1	1	B	Pr

(1)	*(2)*	*(3)*	*(4)*	*(5)*	*(6)*	*(7)*
Expand the variety of fixed roof accommodation available	C	1	2	-1	X	Pr
Improve and develop recreational vehicle (RV) parks	C	1	1	-2	B	Pr
Develop transportation services to destinations in Rural Zone 10	0	1	2	0	C	Pr
Adjust zone boundaries to include Cochrane. Highway lA, and Stoney Indian Reserve	0	0	1	0	A	Pr

Appraising Tourism Potential. This section of the guide provides information on how tourism can benefit communities with incomes, jobs, and tax revenues, especially as an aid to a diversified economic base. It also identifies costs of development: transportation. roads, parking, signs, water, sewage, restrooms, safety, health, and welfare. Included is the relationship of the community to attractions, services, and markets.

Planning for Tourism. Included here is the recommendation for leadership and organization. The need to coordinate the many components of tourism is addressed. The following planning steps are suggested:

1. Inventory and describe the social, political, physical, and economic development.
2. Forecast or project trends for future development.
3. Set goals and objectives.
4. Study alternative plans of action to reach goals and objectives.
5. Select preferred alternative(s) to serve as a guide for recommending action strategies.

6. Develop an implementation strategy.

7. Implement the plan.

8. Evaluate the plan.

It is recommended that all segments of the community participate in all steps.

Assessing Product and Market. This chapter of the guide offers methods of market analysis characteristics of visitors. expenditures, and activity preferences. Ways of inventorying and evaluating the match between market preference and attractions are presented. Forms for inventorying other elements of the supply side are included.

Marketing Tourism. Development of a promotional plan, target market advertising !ocal advertising and promotion public and community relations, cooperative promotion and souvenirs and promotional mementos are the main topics of discussion in this chapter of the guide.

Visitor Services. Visitor services are defined as all the normal city services together with those needed for hospitality. Recommendations on anticipating and planning service needs, coordination of visitor services, training for visitor services, hospitality training, public awareness, establishing tourist information centres, and evaluating visitor services are offered.

Source of Assistance. Suggested help sources from federal, state, and local agencies as well as private consultant aid are recommended in this section. Examples of tourist organizational structures and tax legislation are included in the Appendix of the guide.

Community Tourism Guide. Another helpful guide for planning tourism development at the destination scale is *The Community Tourism Industry Imperative: The Necessity, the Opportunities, Its Potential* authored by Uel Blank (1989). This book is organized into twelve chapters and is directed to local individuals and organizations interested in development of tourism. Although all chapters provide basic guidance, of special value in planning are the following final three chapters of the book.

Getting It Together—The Matrix of Decision Making, includes important topics, such as the process of decisionmaking, how to assess opportunities, the importance of longterm planning, and how to move from knowledge to action.

Getting it Together—Tourism Development Policy, emphasizes and relationship to state and federal tourism policy. The section on planning cities the need for several agencies, organizations, and individuals to exercise planning roles. Planning guidance must include:

- Attraction development
- Hospitality services
- Activities
- Promotion/ advertising
- Transportation Systems
- Community ambience aesthetics
- Local information, direction, and interpretive system
- Community ambience aesthetics
- Local information, direction, and interpretive system
- Community infrastructures
- Financing of development
- Resource quality and management
- Agency responsibility and coordination
- Special market thrusts
- Seasonality
- Residents' living quality

Getting it Together—From Policies to Plans to Actions, provides guidance on preconditoning for action, brining out the genius of the community, and the following action steps:

1. Initiative—recognition of need.
2. Set goals and objectives.
3. Collect needed information
4. Analyze information.
5. Develop concepts for future development.
6. Develop specific strategies.
7. Carry out the plan.
8. Monitor and evalutate on regular basic.

Local Govemment Tourism Policy. As an aid to destination zone planning and development for tourism, the Western Australian Tourism Commission has created a model policy statement to be implemented by the city council. Because of its value, it is quoted here in its entirety (Western Australian Tourism n.d.)

Objectives. In establishing a tourism policy, the council has as its major objectives:

1. To recognize tourism as a social and economic force and as a major or potential major employer within the Council area.
2. To foster and create a community awareness of the benefits of tourism within Council's area.
3. To ensure that Council will guide and influence the development of tourism in the Council area.
4. To provide the basic facilities and infrastructure sufficient to encourage development.
5. To ensure that facilities within the area are adequate to cater for visitors and residents.

Policy Document Guidelines. The following policy guidelines provide a basis for consideration and adoption by council to guide and direct the development of tourism throughout the Council area, and to ensure a consistent approach to this development.

1. Council will liaise with the Western Australian Tourism Commission and other relevant Tourism and Government Departments and members of the public in all aspects of tourist development.

2. Council will establish an Advisory Committee which will address Tourism issues.

3. Council will endeavour to provide an adequate budget allocation for tourism expenditure.

4. In the formulation of its planning regulations and preparation of by laws and other regulations. Council will have regard to the requirements of tourism development.

5. Council will endeavour to assist (financially and by other means) tourist organizations or events which have the potential to develop tourism in the region.

6. Council will seek representation on Local tourist associations.

7. Council, in its review of planning instruments, *i.e.* Strategic Plans. Town Plans and Development Control Plans, will take into consideration policies on tourism and other leisure related issues.

8. In the preparation of by-laws and regulations, Council will have regard to their impact on tourism and the balanced development of the Council's area.

9. Council will encourage a high standard of design and aesthetics in all forms of tourist development.

10. Council will encourage tourism product development and investment through out the area and will facilitate the development application process.

11. Council will ensure the welfare of the whole community when supporting tourism development and the provision of facilities.

12. Council will ensure that where sensitive environmental, historic or cultural areas exist, these areas will be adequately protected in relation to development or usage.

13. When considering tourism developments, Council will consider the social, cultural, economic, and environmental impact of the proposal within the area.

14. Council will initiate the provision of facilities sufficient to cater for destination and day trip visitors to appropriate areas within its boundaries.

15. Council will encourage the landscaping of residental and commercial centres within Council's area.

16. Council will seek financial involvement form other sources wherever possible in the provision of tourist facilities.

17. Council will, where practicable, support the establishment of National Parks, enhancement of specific natural features. conservation areas of outstanding beauty, and recognize items of heritage significance.

DESTINATION PLANNING MODEL

The engine that powers the destination for travellers is composed of the attraction complexes. These are geographic places, rooted in resources that have been developed to provide for visitor activities. These attractions serve two functions-drawing people to the places and fulfilling their expectation from a visits. The term complex is used to imply that there is value in clustering compatible attractions together, either physically or by tour. Attraction complexes may be within the focal city, nearby, or reasonably remote, such as a national park. (A national park is usually a complex unto itself because of the great number of compatible attractions it contains.)

Several other components of a destination zone function as facilitators. The linkage corridors between the key city and attraction complexes are important planning elements, requiring careful design consideration in order to provide a visual prelude to the attraction objective. For rural and remote attractions, self-guided and guided tours should provide the visitor with interesting explorations of the background and characteristics of the landscape being traversed. Key to planning these corridors are elements such as signage, maps, and other way finding information. Long linkages may require travel stops for rest rooms and food services, and interpretation of the travel corridor. Often, these are located along designated scenic highways. Again, the principle of adapting to the land resources and development as well as visitor desires and needs is paramount.

Related Policies

Tourist information services and distribution	Proposals for specific areas of land
Licensing of seasonal entertainment and attractions	Traffic flows and generation Levels of environmental impacts
Scenic routes and lookouts Use of old building for tourism purposes	Protection of areas of out standing scenic beauty

For all destination zones, one or more cities (communities) are essential. They provide several critical functions. All travel modes lead to terminals at cities. Terminals—train depots, airports, bus terminals, and highway exits-perform an entering function important to travellers. The quality of physical planning, development, and management can set the psychological setting for further visitor activities. Cities offer the preferred location for most travel services-hotels, restaurants, car services, travel agencies, tour companies, shops, and ancillary services such as post office, drug stores, health services and communications. Cities are preferred settings because they offer greatest financial feasibility, catering to both resident and traveller markets. Cities contain a basic infrastructure that would be costly to devclop at remote locations-water supply, waste disposal, police protection, fire protection, and power. Cities have an organized management structure providing public services and amenities important to tourism. Cities often contain existing and potential attraction complexes entertainment, parks, exhibits, festivals, historic sites, sports arenas, convention centres, trade centres, industries, institutions (midical, religious, and organizational), and homes of friends and relatives.

Many destination zones will be served by a major city surrounded by several small towns in rural areas. Many advantages to both small and larger cities can be derived through cooperation tour efficiency, increased mass of attractions, and greater promotional impact.

Another important component of a destination zone is access from markets. Too often, communities internalize their tourism planning to the extent that cooperation and assistance are not provided to developers and managers of transportation systems. Many transportation agencies focus policies primarily on resident or nearly markets, thereby developing routes and signage not easily mastered by outside visitors. For example, the main places of transport route penetration of a destination zone and city deserve special planning attention for visitors. It is at these sites that directional information is critical. A major information centre at the gateway that provides maps, brochures, and personal guidance is essential.

Although the actual configuration of destination zones will vary around the world, these same components and relationships will require planning and integration for best service to the traveller. All components must function in concert, each depending on the successful rendition by the other.

DESTINATION ZONE PLANNING PROCESS

As was recommended for regions, two approach to destination planning are equally valid—project planning and continuous planning.

Destination Planning Project

A project should include the follow basic steps:

1. Identify sponsorship and leadership.
2. Set goals.
3. Investigate strengths and weaknesses.
4. Develop recommendations.
5. Identify objectives and strategies.
6. Assign priorities and responsibilities.
7. Monitor feedback.

1. Identify Sponsorship and Leadership. Because the focus of the destination zone will be on the principal community, it may provide the best organization and leadership. Although a chamber of commerce, convention and visitor bureau, or industrial development agency or organization may initiate destination tourism planning, a new ad hoc or permanent council or commission may be needed. The organization and leader should be drawn from a wide cross-section of the community and surrounding region. Again, it is important to have representation from the greatest diversity of constituencies possible, not only the primary tourism business. Commitment to tourism and the desire to collaborate on planning are more important than expertise in tourism.

2. Set Goals. The same goals as were stated for regions apply to destination planning—enhanced visitor satisfactions, protected natural and cultural resources,. improved economy and integration into the life and economy of the entire destination area.

3. Investigate Strengths and Weaknesses. Local people, with perhaps input from a tourism specialist or consultant should gain a good understanding of the area's strengths and weaknesses. Each destination will pose different problems but an objective study of the following in the entire zone would be useful:

- Natural resources: location, kind, quantities, qualities, problems, issues, viability for attractions.
- Cultural resources: location, kinds, quantities, qualities, problems, issues, viability for attractions.
- Potential environmental impact.
- Transportation and access: capacities, access, quality, deficiencies.
- Service business: quality, suitability to all markets, problems, issues.
- Information about area for tourists: quality of maps, guidebooks, descriptions, hospitality.
- Promotion: effectiveness of advertising, publicity, public relations, incentives.
- Organizations: sectors, organizations, agencies best suited to take leadership and implement development.
- Present commitment of public and private sectors-resident attitude toward tourism growth.

4. Develop Recommendations. From the above investigation, those performing it will be able to conceive of how the positive factors can be enhanced and the negative issues can be ameliorated or corrected. Specific recommendations should be expressed on the same list of topic included in the investigation:

- Natural and cultural resource potential
- Transportation improvement
- Service business improvement
- Information improvement
- Promotion improvement
- Key organizations to take action
- How to improve commitment

5. Identify Objectives and Strategies. The step is a refinement and expansion of the last step. It should identify specific objectives and how to reach them for each of the recommendation above.

6. Assign Priorities and Responsibilities. The entire list of objectives and strategies should be reviewed for assignment of priorities. Short-range objectives are critical and deserve highest priority. They should be of small enough size and cost to demonstrate immediate improvement. But, long range objective need to be kept in mind so that each increment of shorter range accomplishment will build toward a wellplanned overall destination zone. At this stage, it is important to assign responsibilities for action-who and what organizations are most logically the ones to get the job done?

7. Stimulate and Guide Development. With the identification of specific project development needed derived from steps 1 through 6, these opportunities should be publicized for action by business, non-profit organizations and governments. It is their responsibility to develop feasibilities plan and design, build and manage the needed development within the destination zone.

8. Monitor Feedback. Regularly, all implementation of action should be monitored. Enthusiasm and commitment may wane if it appears that no one is concerned about whether the objectives and strategies are working. Each increment of development, whether it be a newly built project or a new programme will change overall relationships and demonstrate new market-supply experience. Part of this feedback is to check on the relationship between this and other destinations and regional plans. Especially for touring circuit markets who visit the destination en route, it is important to know about planning and action in the zones that come ahead and after in the touring sequence. Also, the relationship between zone and regional promotion should be understood. Related to this feed back step may be the need for new research and education-seminars, workshops. conferences and hospitality training.

Destination Continuous Planning

Although a destination planning project for tourism development can stimulate specific action, accomplishment is likely to lag if a continuing planning function is not in place. The destination zone planning document can provide guidelines for development, but every change needs to be monitored for its impact. For example, the destination plan may have called for first creating new parks and historic sites but, because sponsorship for an interesting outdoor recreation parks became available first, it was established first. In the recreation park's first year of operation, it demonstrated that there was a strong travel market interested in natural resource-based activities. Thus the potential was suggested for expanding existing parks, developing adventure travel, nature trails, camping, and natural resource interpretation.

However, unless there is a permanent body charged with tourism leadership and continuous planning, new opportunities may be missed. Such a body would represent a diversity of interests within the destination zone and also be capable of carrying out specific functions on a regular basis.

As was done in Alberta a Tourism Action Committee may be the best organization for continuous planning at the destination level. This committee should have representation from all governing bodies within the destination area: major city, satellite towns, countries, and regional government. Committee members should also represent important constituencies such as developer, businesses, nonprofit organizations and residents.

Among the duties of such a committee would be the following:

- Foster the renewal of a Destination Zone Planning Project every five years.
- Monitor each increment of supply development to determine how well it is succeeding, resolve issues that impede its success, and examine its integration with, other tourism development.
- Promote new and expanded attraction development based on the special natural and cultural resources of the area.

- Promote the establishment of needed service business to meet needs of travellers.
- Encourage resource protection not only by tourism supply development but other threats to the environment.
- Integrate tourism planning with city, county, and regional plans.
- Integrate all plans for information services and promotion.
- Monitor changes in market trends in order to determine new supply needs.
- Gain cooperation and integration of tourism development by all three sectors-governments, non-profit organizations, commercial enterprise.
- Cooperate with regional tourism planners, managers, and policy makers to assure a continuing viable role for the destination.

Evaluation

Planning action at the destination level need regular evaluation. Communities and their surrounding regions are involved daily in a great many public and private actions other than tourism-services, education, sanitation, land use, and policing. Whatever is done to plan tourism will need to be evaluated frequently in context with all other planning and development. If the destination area has a tourism plan in place, it will need monitoring and frequent assessment. Go et al. have developed a taxonomy for implementation of a community tourism action plan.

Integration with Community Planning

Because communities play such a critical tourism role in destinations, all plans and planning processes at this level need to be integrated.

Official community plans traditionally focus on physical public needs especially for updating and enlarging public structures and systems. These needs are often for resident transportation, water supply (potable and industrial), sewage disposal (solid and liquid waste), electrical and gas) fire protection and policies and public safety. Regulations for land use and structures, such as zoning ordinances and building codes are included in most city plans. Also included are concerns over housing, education, trade, amenities (zone, parks, and recreation areas), and industry.

Unfortunately, in most communities, these traditional plans do not include issues of tourism and visitors even though their decisions affect tourism and vice versa. Too often, planning for the five components of the supply side of tourism-attractions, services, transportation, information, and promotion are not seen as responsibilities of city officials and city plans.

Dredge and Moore examined this issue as found in Queensland, Australia. They cited several inhibitors to the integration of tourism planning into traditional community plans. Much of tourism involves private sector facilities and services, often outside the perceived role of local planning. Local understanding of the complicated multi-owner supply side of tourism is not helped much by their perception of industry involving only a few physical plants. The overlap between the needs of visitors and residents as well as their differences, is not well understood. The dynamics and interdependence of the components of the tourism functional system are foreign to their day-to-day decisions relating to residents. Finally. the training and education of planners and designers have not encompassed tourism as a curriculum topic.

The conclusion of Dredge and Moore, equally applicable elsewhere in the world, is that town planners have not only great opportunities but responsibilities to incorporate vision, guidelines, and specific plans for tourism into their traditional local roles.

Special Destination Needs

Scenic Highways

Driving for pleasure, implying the use of scenic roadways. continues to be one of the top travel market activities. Although some

TABLE

Taxonomy for Implementation of Community Tourism Action Plan

Lever of	Activity and Qestions			
Analysis	Interacting	Allocating	Monitoring	Organizing
Actions	How can community leaders and residents be encouraged to see their destinations through the eyes of a tourist?	How can communities best acheive their tourism action plan objectives?	How are community resource persons best evaluated by community tourism action members?	How can the local community become involved in the tourism action plan and get a feeling of ownership of the process?
Programmes	How can the level of service and hospitality be developed to sustain and enhance the image of community; specifically, the existing attractions, facilities, and infrastructure?	How should communities selected for the funding of their tourism action plan?	How is research into present and potential tourism target markets best conducted by the tourism action committee?	How can sound local tourism strategies be built into a regional strategy?
System	How should the community promote attractions and facilities to travellers and tour Operators?	How should a provincial government ensure that the local council is directly involved in plan development proceedings?	How is quality of tourism action plan evaluated?	How should the community organize its own unique tourism strategy?
Policies	How should the tourism action plan be managed on the community level to coincide with existing master plan and economic development strategy on the provincial level?	How should dollar and manpower resources be allocated to ensure that a community covers all important steps toward plan preparation?	How does a community regularly check the effects of tourism on its social structure?	How should the industry be restructured so that it will have a broader base, making it more representative of and responsible to the community?

Source: Bonoma, Thomas V. 1984. Go et. al. 1992

scenic highways are major regional access routes, most lie within, the context of a destination zone.

Many areas have designated scenic highway segments of travel routes. But, in creating such roads, their planners have discovered that what appeared to be a simple task became very complicated. Their dual function transportation and scenic appreciation poses a great challenge to policy makers and designers.

A report of the U.S. Department of Transportation (Federal Highway Administration 1991) pertaining to "scenic byways" identifies some of the key issues of design and designation for these special places:

Ambiguity of Definition. Although there may be common public opinion of what a scenic road is, the issue of defining it in order to plan, build, and protect its assets becomes very difficult. Generally accepted is the principle that it embraces both the visual countryside as well as the roadway. But there is no accepted definition of design standards visual depth beyond the roadway roadside maintenance, vertical and horizontal curvature, and vehicle speed and capacity. Each case needs its own definition and standards.

Corridor Protection. Because the entire highway corridor is involved, the protection of the natural and cultural resources that caused it to be identified becomes an issue. Owners of adjacent lands have property rights that sometimes conflict with the scenic highway concept. Special land use planning that is acceptable to adjacent owners must be employed.

Traffic Issues. When high-speed commuters and truckers are mexed with slower-speed, roadside-viewing tourists there may be increased conflict and accidents. Roadway design standards for these two types of users may need to be different, even requiring entirely new roadways.

Signing and Classifying. At present there is conside rable proliferation and diversity of policies on how scenic highways are to be classified and signed. Travellers are confused over the policy rules and identification of attractions and driving hazards. These need to be integrated and clarified.

Community Acceptance. Because many scenic highway designations have been put forward by others, local people may not agree that the rewards (tourist revenues) are worth the added traffic and land use restrictions.

Bicycle Conflict. Because both bicyclists and automobile tourist may enjoy the same qualities of scenic highways, their use is often in conflict. More automobile traffic creates hazards for the safety of slower bicylclists.

Funding and Management. Because scenic highways traverse many political jurisdictions and a multicity of properties with different owners, questions of who will fund and manage these special routes are not easily answered.

Even though the issues just described are widespread the movement toward establishing more scenic road designation continues. For example, by 1990 there were 51.518 miles of designated and potential scenic byways in the United States. Virgin Islands and Puerto Rico. All but seven states have some kind of scenic highway programme. Germany has more than 70 scenic highway, including the Castle Route Fairy Tale Route. and Route of Emperors and Kings.

Although the criteria for designating scenic routes vary. most are similar to those adopted by the North Carolina Board of Transportation in 1990.

The development along the byway should not detract from the scenic character and visual quality.

There should be significant visible natural or cultural features along its borders. These include agricultural lands, historic sites, vistas of marshes, shoreline, forests with mature trees or other areas of significant vegetation or notable geologic or other natural features.

There should be preference for roads that are protected by land use controls.

There should be provisions for de-designation should the character of the road change over time.

Smardon (1987) describes a survey process used in analysis of scenic highway potential for the 450-mile Seaway Trail located along the Lake Ontario and St. Lawrence River waterfront in northern New York. Investigative panels of 50 college students and 45 area residents, guided by professional planners, documented and evaluated the entire corridor. Positive and negative attributes, listed by priority, included the following:

In order to provide guidance for the designation and maintenance of scenic roads, the state of New York has developed a manual Preserving New York State Scenic Roads (n.d.). The manual recommended a five step process.

1. From a Nominating Group. A community nominates at least three members who then notify the Department of Environmental Conservation (DEC) of their intent. They are then given forms and further guidance.

2. Select Candidate Roads. The nominating committee tours roads for visual inspection needed to nominate potential scenic reads. The search should encompass the landscape characteristics that typify the scenery.

3. Prepare Narrative Description. Each candidate road is to be described in terms of topography, water, vegetation, sky, human or animal activities, structures, and patterns or rhythms. Cultural as well as natural resource features should be included in this description.

4. Evaluate Candidate Roads. The nominating committee, accompanied by special interests if needed, travel the roads again but with more detailed examination. This step usually climates some candidates and the team must describe its reasoning for the selections, noting the components that contribute most to its scenic quality. The list is then evaluated, using the form illustrated in Figure 2. This form serves two purposes—a checklist of uniform criteria and an organized cataloging for future reference. Both negative and positive characteristics must be identified. Designating team member roles will assist in the process. The driver identifies odometer readings as a front seat passenger appraises the scenery. Visual scanning should cover both sides of the highway. A recorder checks the characteristics as they are identified by the team. In order to expedite the process, a team of volunteers may be assigned to evaluate each candidate road.

Negative Attributes	*Positive Attributes*
1. Utilities	1. Views/presence of water
2. Trailer parks	2. Vegetation
3. Screening development	3. Natural landscape
4. Signage	4. Rural image
5. Excessive vegetation	5. Water features
6. Flat topography	6. Views of opposite edge
7. General clutter	7. Unique landscapes
8. Boats, docks	8. Edge variety
9. Poor field maintenance	9. Superior view
10. Fences	10. Nearness of water

5. Nominate Roads. The recommendations are then refined by team consensus. Further evaluation before nomination may include the length of the highway segment; relationship of road to other development, and implications for protection and future maintenance. The team's recommendations are submitted to the local government for approval. The evaluation forms and resolution of government support are then submitted to the DEC staff.

Historic Scenic Roads Advisory Committee (PHSRAC) for final apprival import by the Arizona Department of Transportation (ADOT). This advisory committee is made up of eleven members, including six citizen appointees by the governor, and each from ADOT, Arizona State Parks Board, Arizona Historical Society, Arizona Office of Tourism, and Tourism Advisory Council.

The PHSRAC reviews, prioritizes, and evaluates the requests from individuals and organizations for designation.

Documentation of an inventory process is included in each request and application for approval. Historic road application emphasize cultural resources, and scenic road applications emphasize natural and visual resources. A list of the features for which information is to be determined and described follows.

Natural Resources

Geology	Biota
Hydrology	Topographic
Climate	

Cultural Resources

Architectural	Archeological
Historical	Cultural

Visual Resources

Visual Quality Assessment Procedures

- Landscape Classification Process

  Identify on map proposed highway segments.

  Identify biotic community.

  Identify transition zones.

  Describe vegetative cover.

- Landscape Inventory (a Visual Assessment Inventory and a Viewpoint Rating).

Criteria used by the PHSRAC for evaluating parkways and historic and scenic roads include the following:

Parkways

One mile distance between access roads.

Meet criteria for historic or scenic roads.

Interpretive area space is available.

Controlled access and property rights obtained.

Historic Roads

Impact of route- importance within national, state, or local framework.

The Arizona Parkway, Historic and scenic roads designation process

Impact of area-contribution to exploration, settlement, or development.

Proximity—physical and/or visual access to historical place.

Uniqueness—relative scarcity or abundance.

Scenic Raods

Vividness—memorability of visual impression.

Intactness—integrity, freedom from encroachment.

Unity—harmonious composite.

Important criteria and standards of operation include protection of vegetation, freedom from negative impacts, and compatible development (if any) along all designated routes. Recommended are local and county protective zoning and design review overlay along all designated highways in order to protect, maintain, and enhance the quality of the highway corridor environment. Special emphasis is placed on the establishment of pullouts for interpretation. Normal highway standards of design and construction may be amended in order to protect and enhance special features or unique resources important to such designated highways. Final approval lies with the Arizona Transportation Board.

This examination of scenic highways, their importance, and planning issues, demonstrates the need for close collaboration among decisionmakers; local people, and designers/ planners. It seems that the answer to better planning lies within each situation rather than a set of rigid standards and policies.

❒

14

Tourism Marketing

The problems of marketing in tourism are somewhat different from the problems of traditional product marketing. The differences are the result of the characteristics of tourism supply and demand. Tourism first of all is a service. An intangible experience is being sold. not a physical good that can be inspected prior to purchase. Because it is a service production and consumption take place at the same time. In manufacturing, goods are produced, stored and sold. The inventory process serves as a way of linking these stages of production and consumption. Tourism supply cannot be stored. Unlike a can of food which. if it is not sold one day can be sold the next, airline seats, hotel rooms or restaurant seats not sold today lose that particular sale forever. Although the inventory cannot be stored and adjusted to changes in demand the capacity to produce these tourism services must be developed ahead of time. This puts a great deal of pressure on producers to effectively plan the proper amounts of facilities and having developed those facilities to keep them as fully used as possible. This in itself creates another kind of problem for tourism supply is relatively fixed. The resources and infrastructure of a destination cannot change as quickly as can tourist demand.

A second important factor that makes tourism different from other industries is that the service provided a vacation is in fact an amalgam of several products and services. A vacation has a transportation component a lodging component a food and beverag, component an attractions component. an activities component. and so on. These components are usually offered by different firms. and they may be marketed directly to the tourist or combined into a package in which they are offered as one vacation but the services are supplied by different firms. This lack of control over the entire vacation means that a great deal of interdependence results. A satisfied tourist results from many independent businesses, each providing a satisfying part of the total vacation. The marketing efforts of each of the parts are thus affected by the efforts of the others providing a part of the vacation. The satisfaction provided is also a function of the human element providing the service. This also is very difficult to control in terms of the consistent quality of service provided.

A third factor that makes tourism different from other industries concerns the role of travel intermediaries. Because most tourist services are located at distances far from their potential customers, speciaused intermediaries organisations that operate between the producer and the tourist are often necessary to bridge the gap. Also. the fact that many tourism producers are relatively small means that they cannot afford to set up their own retail outlets. Thus, while in most industries. the producer exerts much control over every stage in the development and delivery of the product in tourism the travel intermediaries can influence if not determine which services should be offered to whom when and at what price.

The last factor that makes tourism different from other industries relates to demand. Tourism demand is highly elastic. seasonal in nature and subject to subjective factors such as taste and fashion as well as the more objective factors of demand such as price. In many cases. the "product" sought can be satisfied be any number of destinations wilh particular emphasis on no one in particular.

"Marketing is a management philosophy which, in light of tourist demand makes it possible thtough research forecasting and selection to place tourism products on the market most in line with the organisation's purpose for the greatest benefit." This definition suggests several things. First it indicates that marketing is a way of thinking about a situation that balances the needs of the tourist (as indicated through tourist demand) with the needs of the organisation or destination. This can be explained by an examination of the development of an appropriate orientation. Second, the definition stresses tourist research that culminates in the selection of tourist demand. The concept of market segmentation is useful here. Third, the concepts of the product life cycle and positioning are useful to underscore the proper placement of tourism products on the market and to suggest the appropriate marketing policy and strategies resulting from that decision.

Orientation

Before embarking on a programmes to market tourism in general or a specific tourism product or service in particular, it is necessary to develop a philosophy or orientation that will guide one's marketing efforts. Such a philosophy will set the tone for every subsequent decision made as part of the overall marketing effort. Although several different orientations are possible, experience has shown that they are not all equally effective.

Some destination areas have marketing efforts that are guided by a product orientation. A product orientation suggests that the emphasis be placed upon the products or services available. A destination area has many physical, historical and cultural resources. for example. The extent to which "our" resources are better than those of the competition will determine how many tourists visit our destination. This orientation has been used by the local authorities of a town on the south coast of England who decided in the late 1960s to print brochures only in English. When it was pointed out that a major potential market was the French residents across the English Channel the reply was given that if the French wanted to visit. then they would be interested enough to learn to read English in order to understand what was available. Although it cannot be denied that the quality of resources is important, a total emphasis on tourism supply fails to take the wishes of the potential tourist into account. A product orientation may in fact be successful if there is a surplus of demand over supply. In this case the destination or company that offers the best product will get the tourist. The old adage that reflected this said "build a better mousetrap, and the world will beat a path to your door."

When there is more supply than demand, however, the problems becomes "How can I sell all these mousetraps?" The number of destinations actively seeking tourism has increased as has the number of places throughout the world with easy accessibility. The entry into the market-place of more professional tour packagers has increased competition for the tourist dollar and has meant that destination areas can no longer sit back and wait for tourists to come to them. It has become increasingly necessary to sell tourists on the benefits of visiting a particular destination or of purchasing a particular product or service. The orientation for many has moved from one of emphasising product to one of emphasising selling. The accent has been placed on promotion of what is available for sale. Yet, this selling orientation focusses on the needs of the seller-to sell the product—rather than the needs of the buyer—What will satisfy me? The attempt here is to convince the potential tourist that what is available will please.

A further development in orientation is one in which the needs and wants of the tourist are placed foremost in the mind of the marketer. This is a marketing orientation philosophy that begins with the needs and wants of the tourist and seeks to provide a product or service that will satisfy those needs and wants. It involves being open when the tourist wants us to be: serving breakfast when the tourist wants it rather than when it is convenient for management: providing the kind of experiences that tourists want rather than what we feel they "should" want. It is realising that from the example used above an individual does not want to buy a mousetrap: rather she wants to kill mice. If and when a better way is developed of satisfying a need, people will use it.

The uniqueness of tourism suggests that a philosophy that concentrates solely on the needs of the market is not the best orientation even for the market itself. Tourism supply is oriented toward the resources of a community. To become totally marketing oriented all aspects of the community would have to be oriented toward satisfying the needs and wants of the tourist. The risk for the community as well as for the tourist ultimately would have to be oriented toward satisfying the needs and wants of the tourist. The risk for the community as well as for the tourist ultimately is that by orienting strictly and totally for the tourist's needs, the needs and integrity of the community may be abused. Consider the situations that have adapted to the needs of the tourist and have, in the process, lost their uniqueness, their heritage and their natural resources while getting a relatively poor economic return on their natural resources while getting a relatively poor economic return on their investment. Destination areas that have attempted to adapt their resources to satisfy tourist needs may have lost the very thing that has made them attractive and unique in the first place. The tourist is the ultimate loser as more and more destinations take on an increasingly similar and familiar appearance.

A solution to the problem is to develop a marketing approach that focusses on the satisfaction of tourist needs and wants while respecting the long-term interests of the community. This orientation is often referred to as a societal marketing approach. Such a philosophy will provide for planning, development. and marketing activities that will focus on the needs of the tourist, but it will also enable one to equally consider the effects of such action on the long-term interest of the community before the action is taken.

All marketing activities will be guided by the philosophy of those responsible for the marketing campaign. It is essential that any marketing effort have an agreed-upon philosophy to guide the further development and marketing efforts of any property, company, or destination.

Segmentation

The second aspect of our definition of marketing refers to selection of tourism demand. Market segmentation is a recognised and universally accepted way of analysing. demand. Market segmentation refers to the process by which people with similar needs and wants are grouped together for the purpose of better focussing on and serving the market.

Segmentation is based on four assumptions. First. the market for a product or service, for example a vacation is made up of particular segments the members of which have distinctive needs and preferences relative to the product or service being marketed. Second, these potential tourists can be grouped into segments the members of which each have similar and identifiable characteristics. Third a single product offering. such as a Caribbean cruise, will appeal to some segments of the market more than others. Fourth, firms and organisations can improve their overall marketing effort by developing specific product offerings to reach specific segments of the market. A cruise package will be suitable for one part of the market, but an historical tour may be more suitable for another.

The process of segmenting a market can lead to many strategic management decisions. Market segmentation can be more than a statistical technique used to analyse demand. It can be utilised as a management tool that leads to specific marketing decisions. The development of such a strategy begins with the identification of profiles of segments of the market. At one extreme, a firm or destination may maximise its marketing orientation by developing a unique product offering for every potential tourist. Limitations of time and money prevent this. At the other extreme, the firm or destination may save time and money by offering one basic option to everyone. Although that one option will undoubtedly appeal to some potential tourists it will not to others. The compromise is to assemble potential tourists into segments each segment having similar preference characteristics. and produce offerings geared to the needs of these segments.

To determine the compromise point between developing a product for everyone and offering one product for all, it is necessary to examine the criteria a segment must meet to determine its viability. A segment must be:

1. **Measurable.** Can we determine how many potential tourists are in this segment?

2. **Accessible.** Can these tourists be reached through promotion and through existing or potential methods of distribution? How easy will this be?

3. **Substantial.** Are there sufficient numbers of tourists in this segments to support a marketing effort aimed specifically at them?

4. **Defensible.** Are the tourist characteristics unique enough to justify a separate programme targeted at them? Is such a programme immune to the mass marketing approach of competitors?

5. **Durable.** As the market develops, will this segment maintain its differences or will these differences disappear?

6. **Competitive.** Do we have a relative advantage over the competition in our attempts to serve this market segment?

Many criteria have been developed by which a market segment can be constructed. Four general categories have been developed.

(1) Social. Early segmentation studies used socio-economic criteria as the basis for forming market segments. These criteria remain the most commonly used today. This is probably due to the relative ease of collecting data, the comparability of such information through census as well as media data and the fact that such data is easy to understand and apply. Age and income have in fact been very successful predictors of recreation participation. However, the use of only socio-economic criteria to segment markets has come under attack. It has been argued that the rapidly changing nature of society makes it impossible to rely solely on demographic data as a means of plotting marketing strategy. Just because a segment of people are within a particular age or income group does not necessarily mean they will have similar vacation preferences. Also socioe-conomic information does not give the marketer sufficient information about likes and dislikes to properly position the product in the marketplace. Positioning refers to the decision to serve a particular segment of the market with a product offering that is specifically aimed at satisfying its needs and wants.

Greater success has been found in using demographic criteria that are multivariate. Status for example, includes dimensions of income, education and occupation and family life cycle is a composite of marital status, age and the numbers and ages of children at home. Life-cycle segmentation has proven to be an effective way of segmenting in a number of tourism and recreation cases.

It is unlikely that segmentation on the basis of socio-economic criteria will cease to be used. Although other segmentation methods provide substantial information useful for strategic decisions on what to offer, it is still necessary to reach the market segment so described. For all its shortcomings, demographic segmentation offers the best way to determine the accessibility of the market.

(2) Product Related. A major advantage of segmenting by means of product related criteria is that the information gained is directly related to the particular product in question. Indeed, a major flaw in some studies is that information is sought from the potential tourist that deals with general benefits sought or, in the case of psychographic segmentation, general attitudes about types of products/ services rather than with specific products and services. Some attempts have been made in recreation and tourism to use heavy-half segmentatior. Heavy-half segmentation refers to the idea of segmenting a market on the basis of quantity purchased or consumed. As with other types of products, however, heavy-half segmentation has been found lacking. A major problem is that, in many cases, the characteristics of the heavy half (the major purchasers) have been found to be similar to those of the light half. In a study of down hill skiers, it has been found that preferences and use patterns of both heavy and light skiers are similar except for such volume-related characteristics as level of skill, incidence of ski vacations, ownership of equipment, and quality of slopes. Similar difficulties have been found when one tries to segment on the basis of brand loyalty.

Benefit or attribute segmentation is fast becoming a very popular segmentation method to use in recreation and tourism. This method involves segmenting a market according to the relative importance assigned to benefits that consumers expect to realise after purchasing the product. The method entails determining the relative importance of specific product benefits to prospective consumers. Clusters are then formed of people who attache similar degree of importance to the same product benefits. Although results can have important ramifications for the development of new products and the determination of advertising messages it is necessary to develop demographic profiles of those identified in the clusters in order to reach the market segments.

(3) Psychographic. Much has been made of this relatively new tool. This technique of segmentation, although expensive to use and difficult to cany out has been useful for describing segments. It can probably be best used in highly specialised and extensively developed markets to supplement the information gained from simpler analyses. Demographic data may be likened to the bones of a skeleton, and psychographic data may be likened to the flesh. The bones form the basis of the structure but it is only by covering the form with flesh that the features become recognisable. Information about an individual's attitudes interests and opinions give a much closer picture of the segment being described.

(4) Geographic. Geographic considerations are very important to tourism. Much of the attractiveness of a tourist destination is based on contrast-contrasting cultures, climates, or scenery, for example. This implies there being a certain distance between origin and destination. Also, we have already seen the crucial role that accessibility of tourists to a destination plays in tourism. To date, destinations have used geographically based studies solely to identify primary, secondary and in some cases, tertiary markets. State and national tourist offices tend to use geographic segmentation for the purposes of determining the extent of their promotional efforts.

Once market segments have been identified and profiles drawn up, it is necessary to select which segment(s) the firm or destination will seek to attract and serve. This decision can be made only in light of an analysis of which market segments will bring most benefit to the firm or destination. Such an analysis involves four concerns:

Sales Potential. What is the current, and future potential for revenue from this segment? Revenue is a combination of thc number of current and potential tourists and their current and potential per-person spending.

Competition. To what extent does competition exist for the segment(s) in question? How strong is our advantage compared to the competitors?

Cost. How much investment is required to develop products to attract this segment?

Serviceability. Do we have the financial and managerial capability to design, promote and distribute the appropriate products and satisfactorily serve the market segments attracted by the External Forces products produced?

The segments chosen become the tanget market. The process of selection and the corresponding decisions to develop a marketing programme suitable to meet the needs of those segments is known as "positioning."

Market Planning

Market planning implies a future orientation. It involves identifying suitable marketing objectives as well as determining appropriate marketing strategies to achieve those objectives.

External Forces

Marketing objectives can be set only after an analysis of the interactions of five factors-product, market, competition, overal development of objectives of the firm or destination, and the external forces within which the destination or firm in question must the destination or firm in question must act.

Planning must be accomplished within the framework of the external environment over which the marketing manager may have little or no control. The first of these factors concerns the legal environment. Certain countries in the past have placed legal restrictions on their residents that have hampered the flow of tourism. Residents may be restricted from travelling, or they may be unable to take more than a certain sum of money out of the country. Political factors must also be considered. Tensions or hostilities between country of origin and a country of destination will affect the marketing function. On the cultural level, it is important to consider the educational background of the countries being considered for tourism purposes. More international travel is generated from countries, exhibiting higher educational standards from societies regarded as more cultured. and from countries having a higher degree of industrialisation. An important factor is the technical consideration. The destination must be accessible to tourists from the generating countries being considered. A final factor is economic. It is obviously important that there exist in a country of origin sufficient numbers of people that can afford to travel.

The marketing plan should be part of the overall business goal of the firm or the development plan of the destination. Tourism is one and only one. strategy for development. As it was noted in previous chapters, tourism can be used, as a political social and economic force. Yet other alternatives are available. The overall plan for tourism must be consistent with the overall plan for the destination area.

Market/Product/Competitor Analysis

The overall objective of the market/ product/ competitor analysis is to determine where our product presently stands compared to the competition in the eyes of the market. Competition is defined as any firm or destination seeking to serve the same market as ourselves. This objective is accomplished by analysing product, market and competition. The product and competitor analysis consists of a comparative evaluation of the following factors:

1. Natural tourist resources such as climate and topography.
2. Cultural and historical resources such as historical monuments, museum, traditional events, ways of life.
3. Infrastructure such as fresh water supply, road network, and communications.

4. Means of access and internal transportation facilities such as airports, railroads, and bus companies.

5. Attractions and facllities such as sporting events, hotels, and restaurants.

The culmination of such a comparison between a product and its major competitors is a determination of comparative strengths and weaknesses. What do we have that is better than our competition? This information is important by itself but in keeping with the marketing orientation stated above, it is necessary to place such intelligence in the context of the existing and potential market. Although marketing is not a science and has no scientific laws to guide its actions, there are several useful principles that "guide its actions. For a firm or destination developing a marketing plan for the first time, one such principle may be: Attract people similar to those you already serve. This implies defining our existing market and seeking to develop more people with characteristics similar to those already attracted. An analysis of people in the market seeks to answer:

> Who are they? How many of them are there? What are their socio-economic and psychographic characteristics?
>
> When do they vacation and for how long? When is the decision made?
>
> Why do they vacation? What are their important motivations?
>
> Where do they come from and travel to?
>
> How do they make plans, travel to and within the destination?

The crucial task is to determine a picture of the actual tourist, then project that picture into the future by considering trends in the country of origin. A second task is to discover potential markets by compiling a picture of the present tourist and seeking to find other markets that meet that profile. For example. if most people in the existing market come from within a 500-mile radius, potential markets may be discovered from areas within 500 miles from which visitors do not yet come.

From a consideration of the above five elements, a picture will emerge of problem areas and areas of opportunity. This will enable planners to set marketing objectives, to determine where they are. where they want to be. If one recognises the guidelines of overall business or development objectives, is aware of the constraints of the external environment and is cognizant of the strengths and weaknesses of product compared to competition in light of market demand, objectives can be set.

Marketing Mix

Once the target markets of a property or destination have been determined, an appropriate marketing mix can be developed. The marketing mix is comprised of four elements-product, price, promotion and distribution. All four elements are provided in accordance with the needs of the target markets.

Product

It has already been noted that a action consists of a number of different parts or products—from transportation and lodging to sightseeing and souvenirs. It is clear that a variety of providers will offer one or more of these products or services. Each provider is thus interdependent with the others to offer an attractive and satisfying overall vacation experience. The philosophy of a marketing orientation suggests that products be developed to satisfy the needs and wants of those in the market. Also market segmentation indicates that properties or destination areas cannot possibly provide products that will satisfy everyone. It is necessary to select a target market and then provide a variety of products and services that will satisfy its needs. The balance between providing narrow customised products to appeal to a particular market segment and providing sufficient variety to appeal to aprovide diversity of tastes is a difficult one for management.

Crissy has suggested several important criteria that should be met in the decision to provide a product or service. First, there should be a relatively heavy demand for the product or service from at least one important market segment with the possibility of additional business from other segments of the market. It may be that the product can expect to break even on the basis of business from the major market segment and produce profit from business from the rest of the market. There may, of course, be a period of time before sales for a new attraction or service reach the break-even point.

Second, new products and services should fit in with the general image of the property or destination area and complement existing offerings. This does not mean that a destination area must appeal to only one segment of the market and that all products must meet the needs of that market segment. A great deal obviously depends upon the size of the destination area. One part of a destination area may appeal to the jetset, while another part may be appealing to senior citizens. Within each of these parts, however, it is important that separate products and services be oriented around the one theme and market segment.

Third, any new offerings should be proposed in keeping with the available supply of manpower, money and natural resources. Although new products and services should exploit an advantage that a property or destination area has, it is important that new offerings be within the ability of the destination area or the management to satisfactorily provide them. A destination area may have magnificent mountain terrain suitable for skiing but may lack management knowledge in ski-area operations. Experienced management may have to be hired on a permanent or temporary basis before a ski area can be proposed.

Finally, it is necessary that any product or service added contribute to the profit and/or growth of the entire property or destination. In some cases the new offering may bring in no profit itself, but its provision may contribute to growth. The hotel pool for example, may cost the operation money while bringing in no direct revenue from admission for swimming. However, the provision of a pool may bring in additional room business and its elimination may drive existing room business elsewhere. Similarly a destination may institute its own airline not as a revenue-producing venture but as a necessary means to bring visitors in to spend money.

Price

Several factors influence the pricing policy set as part of the marketing mix. The price charged in any situation is unique to that situation and is affected by the combination of the factors to be discussed. Nevertheless, some guidelines can be suggested to assist in the pricing decision.

In purely economic terms, price is a result of supply and demand. When supply exceeds demand, price will tend to decrease. The reverse is true also. Of greater importance is the extent to which demand changes (as measured by the amount purchased) as price changes. This refers to the elasticity involved. A five percent reduction in price may result in a corresponding ten percent increase in the number of buyers and a subsequent increase in total sales revenue. Demand in this case is elastic. General products aimed at the luxury end of the customer scale are less susceptible to changes in price and consequently tend to be price inelastic. For destinations or properties that are open only part of the year, supply is limited and prices will have to be correspondingly higher (everything else being equal) than destinations open year round. Because demand is not often uniform throughout the year. it Is common to charge higher prices during the peak season and lower prices when demand slackens. The expected length of an the product's place in the previously discussed product life cycle is also relevant here. A "fad" item with an expected short life cycle will have to charge sufficiently high prices to recoup the investment in a relatively short period of time. A product that expects a long life can be priced lower.

The price charged is influenced by the competition. If our offerings are essentially the same as those of our competitors, our prices must be similar to theirs. The extent to which we are unique reflects the extent to which we can charge more than the competition. Related to the influence of competition is the management policy regarding market share. If a decision is made to increase market share, prices will probably be lower than if a decision to skim a small number of tourists from several market segments is made.

Pricing policy is obviously related to the needs of the market segment that is served. If a destination or property is seen as serving the needs and wants of the market and if those needs and wants are perceived as being important to the members of the market segment, those members will be willing to pay a higher price for the destination or property. The price charged must also be perceived by the market as less than or at least equal to the value received. In certain situations the influence of the market seems to go against economic principles. With certain luxury items, demand may increase as price increases. This phenomenon reflects a certain amount of snobbishness on the part of the market. The feeling may be that the higher the price the greater the perceived value and the greater the demand. But the actual value in the minds of the buyers must still equal or exceed the price paid.

The effect of each of these variables cannot be determined exactly in quantitative terms. The effect of their interaction is more difficult to determine. However, the general guidelines stated above can give guidance on pricing decisions for particular destinations or properties.

Planning and Marketing Destination

Even though the end products of regional tourism planning should include stimulation of tourism awareness, new interagency governmental cooperation, greater public-private collaboration, and identification of zones of greatest potential, seldom does this process immediately results in new brick-and-mortar tourism development. This can only take place at the destination and site scales and as follow-up to regional planning. It is in and around communities that tourism development can and will succeed. The vision, the policies, and the integration at the regional scale provide the blueprint for a systems planning approach, essential to the elimination of many obstacles and the determination of desirable directions. But, eventually.

commitment and land use decisions at the destination and site scales are necessary in order to translate these guidelines into reality. It is at these levels that economies may be strengthened and visitors may be enriched.

The concept of designation community, attractions, and traveller access is used here for several reasons. It regionalizes the significant role of community in traveller flow, providing the majority of service needs. Communities also contain many of the attractions sought by travellers. All transportation modes lead to communities contains. But, in addition to these factors the area around communities contains a great many resources and outlaying attractions upon which the community travel services also depend. Using the concept of destination allows these important rural areas to be included in planning framework and principles.

It is no coincidence that this destination zone concept agrees with contemporary views of urban development. At one time, apparently in response to urban congestion the principle of dispersion was put forward. Many conservation proponents still adhere to this principle. But, dispersion can reduce the indigenous value of both community and hinterland whereas combining a central city with its periphery into a single unit allows each to function in a symbiotic relationship. The regiopolis combined the advantage of social, human, and economic development within and around communities. Likewise, the tourism destination concept allows retention of community identity but also recognizes the important interde-pendency of the surrounding area.

MARKET-SUPPLY MATCH

Travel Markets

At any manufacturer knows, the best product to manufacture is one preferred by the market. This is equally true with tourism. People in the travel market are those who have the interest and ability to travel. Because the majority of travel markets live in areas of population concentration in industrialized nations, the cities become primary sources of travellers. But, such populations have a great diversity of ability and interest in travel. Some segments cannot afford even the minimal costs and some prefer to spend discretionary incomes on purchases other than travel. Even more complicated are the divergent preferences of those who are able to travel. Therefore, a major topic of planning concern is the understanding of travel market-their location, preferences, purposes and ability to travel.

In recent years many studies and models have been put forth to identify travel market characteristics. Sources. such as Travel Tourism and Hospitality Research—A Handbook for Managers and Researchers and journals, such as Annals of Tourism Research. Journal of Travel Research and tourism Management, should be reviewed for current information on markets.

Chadwick classifies travel market studies into three groups. Household surveys are made at places of travel origin and often cover non travellers as well as travellers. A statistically random sampling process can reveal information about the entire population within reasonable limits of accuracy. Data on frequency of travel volume such as personal trips party trips and vacation trips are popularly obtained. Travel expenditures, on or before trips are important economic data obtained by household surveys.

Location surveys are made at sites on trips such as in-flight surveys, exit surveys, entry surveys and highway counts. These surveys cover one visit and may relate to the entire trip or only to the site experience. Data may be obtained on expenditures activity participation opinions and attitudes, as well as socio-economic status of travellers.

Business surveys approach travel from the other side the supply side. Surveys of travellers in hotels and at theme parks can reveal many important facts about such visitors. Sources of travellers, extent of visits, size of parties, place of residence socio-economic characteristics and modes of travel are often measured.

One of the most popular forms of traveller research has been measures of economics. Nations states and communities often wish to distinguish between expenditures of foreign and domestic travellers. This is based on the concept of tourism as an export creating economic impact only from new dollars coming from outside. Direct observation of expenditures is often used as a method but it is combersome and costly. Secondary effects are difficult to measure in thIs way. Estimation by a simulation model of key relationships is set up in equations and data are collected for basic impact. An elaborate equation has been established by the U.S. Travel Data Centre for measuring economic importance of tourism in all states of the country. Frechtling identifies the following criteria for evaluating economic studies-relevance. coverage, efficiency, accuracy and applicability.

Forecasting of travel demand is desired by the planner but is one of the most difficult to accomplish. Forecasting is defined as the art of predicting the occurrence of events before they actually take place. As the uncertainties of travel increase—taste, policies, international currency exchange and diversity of destinationsprojections become less reliable. Because of planners, developers and promoters are in constant need for forecasting. the concept continues to occupy an important place in market evaluation. Although scientific research methods are used increasingly, forecasting as defined remains an art based on experience and judgment.

Uysal and Crompton have provided helpful descriptions of qualitative and quantitative approaches to tourism forecasting of demand. Under qualitative approaches, three methods used by experts are described. Traditional approaches include review of survey reports to observe consistent trends and changes. Sometimes surveys within originating market sources are made to obtain the past history of travel as well as opinions of future trends. The Delphi method is an iterative type of research inquiry using opinion of knowledgable experts. It consists of several iterations by a panel that responds to specific questions about trends. Each panel member is anonymous to one another. Of course this method relies heavily on the extent of expertise of the panel members and the influence of the director. But, it is a useful tool, especially when used alongside other measures of prediction. A judgment-aided model (JAM) uses a panel in face-to-face contact and debate to gain consensus on several scenarios of the future. Each scenario is based on a different set of assumption, such as political factors, economic tourism development, promotion and transportation. Among quantitative approaches, Usual and Crompton describe three kinds. Time series studies are often statistical measures repeated year after year. Here it is assumed that all variables are working equally over time. In order to reflect changes in influential variables, transfer function models have been developed but involve complex mathematical and statistical techniques. Gravity and trip generation models assume that the number of visits from each origin is influenced by factors impinging upon those origins. The primary factors are distance and population. Some researchers criticize gravity models on the basis of not reflecting price not accounting for shrinking of distance perception by new modes of transportation, and other difficult variables. Multivariate regression models allow the use of many variables in predicting travel. Income, population, travel cost, international context and other variables can be introduced.

This brief discussion is offered only to suggest that much experimentation of methods for forecasting demand is taking place. Some quantitative and statistical approaches can provide clues to future tourist flows. Although professional market nalysis may be required for major planning projects, less complicated study by local people can be productive.

Market Segmentation

Until recently any tourist was considered like all other tourists and all planning and management strategies treated tourists as a homogeneous whole. As has been found in marketing other products, there is much merit to dividing the totality of tourist into groups with similarities.

Market segmentation has been defined by Pride as "the process of dividing a total clientele into groups consisting of people who have relatively similar service needs." Generally, marketers, suggest three basic conditions which should be met for segmentation. First, there must be great enough numbers in each segment to warrant special attention. Second, there must be sufficient similarity of characteristics within each group to give them distinction. Third, the subsets must be viable-worthy of attention. When planning for physical development, as well as assessing social, economic and environmental impact, it should be very helpful to have segmented refinements of potential tourist groups who might travel to the area.

Earlier segmentation was directed toward grouping tourists by demographic characteristics—age, sex, income, ethnicity, stage in life cycle, and occupation. It has been found that grouping according to these characteristics has not been as useful as anticipated. While some extensive foreign vacations are relatively costly and require higher income markets, income is more of a limitation than a determinant. Many people with a wide diversity of incomes are found at tourism destinations.

Ages of travellers have a bearing on what is developed. Ryan points out that children constitute a significant segment of travellers. They influence the design of exhibits and educational programmes and play an important role in adult satisfactions. One bracket that has increased in importance in the United States is the 50-plus traveller. Norvell found that convention travel is just as popular with 50-plus travellers are more likely to travel for entertainment, sightseeing, theatre, historical sites, and shopping than for outdoor recreation. Regarding regional destination preference, there was little difference from other travellers. Older travellers tended to spend more time on trips but stay less frequently with friends and relatives than younger travellers. Although the use of recreational vehicles (RVs) was greater among the 50-plus group. this use declined in favour of package tours over the age of 65. In 1984, the 50-plus traveller accounted for 30 per cent of all domestic travel, 30 per cent of all air trips, 32 per cent of all hotel/motel nights, and 72 per cent of all RV trips. Continuing research on age segmentation will be of value in planning destination and site development.

Anthropologist V.L. Smith (1992) has put forth a possible function.

TABLE 1

Travel Market Segments

(1)	*(2)*
1. Purpose of Trip/Use Segmentation Pleasure travel Personal business Other business Conventions/meetings Tournaments/sports groups	* This is usually the most effective segmentation approach because the target market is actively seeking a specific kind of product.
2. Channel of Distribution Segmentation Direct customer sales Travel agents Tour operators Tour wholesalers Airlines Government marketing Regional/local tourism associations	* This approach is effective in further afield markets that cannot be reached directly at reasonable cost or where travel trade companies have a market that is closely matched.
3. Socio-economic or Demographic Segmentation Age — Family life cycle Sex — Social class Education — Home ownership Income — Second home ownership Family size — Race or ethnic group Occupation	* This is a commonly used segmentation approach, since these segments are often easy to reach and information on them is usually available.
4. Product-related Segmentation Recreation activity Equipment Brand loyalty Benefit expectations Length of stay Transportation mode Experience preference Participation patterns	* These are difficult segments to reach, but they are well matched to the use of specific products
5. Psychographic Segmentation Personality traits Lifestyle Attitudes, interests and opinions Motivations	* In tourism, this can be an effective segmentation approach, since tourism product use is extensive among certain psychographic groups. Also, many advertising media are segmented this way.

(1)	*(2)*
6. Geographic Segmentation Country State, province. and country Region Urban, suburban and rural City size Population density	* This is the most common segmentation approach because these markets are clearly defined and accessible. It is often not an efficent approach, however, unless it is used in combination with other approaches.
7. Use Frequency/Seasonality Segmentation Heavy users Moderate users Infrequent users	* Data should be readily available on these customers so this method is likely to be cost-effective.

Source: Marketing Management, 1986

between the pilgrim and the tourist. Pilgrimages, travel with primary religious motivations, have become especially significant worldwide in recent years. Nolan and Nolan (1989) described pilgrimages in three categories: centres of interest for religious tourism; shrines and events related to religion, folklore or ethnicity. Other scholars have documented the many form of travel pilgrimages today and throughout histoxy. However, Smith points out that secular tourist travel has become increasingly diffused with pilgrimage travel.

A generalized market segmentation especially important to physical tourism planning is by activities dependent upon development using natural or cultural resources. It has been the foundation for geographic assessment of destinations with tourism potential. Forbes and Forbes emphasize special interest travel. such as adventure travel and ecotravel as a growing segment. They characterize these travellers as interactive, highly involved and interested in quality experiences, focusing on in-depth activities within destinations.

Planners and developers—public and private—must have current information on travel market characteristics in order to understand why, where and what development is most appropriate.

Matching Supply with the Market

In order to satisfy this market demand, a nation, region, or community must be able to provide a variety of development and services—the supply side. How well this supply side matches the market is the key to reaching the ultimate in correct tourism development (Figure 4). Taylor called this the market-plant match and his model is illustrated in Figure 5. He based the model on his observations in Canada that "the characteristics of tourism demand are changing rapidly and these changes outstrip the present ability of the plant to adjust and that a measurment system can be devised that will permit the plant to adapt to changing demands in a rational manner." Although the search for such a measurement system continues, there is fundamental logic in always striving for a balance between demand and supply. An Australian tourism research guide recommends steps for a gap analysis, determining the differences between what travel markets seek and what is provided for them in the region.

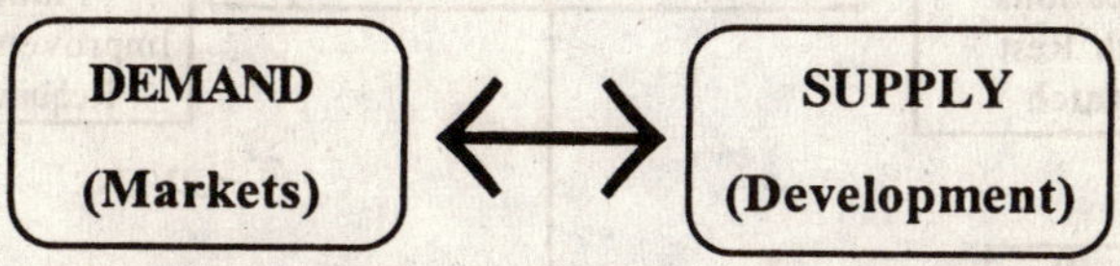

Figure: Demand-Supply Balance. The Planning of tourism should strive for a balance between demand (market) and supply (development). This requires an understanding of market characteristics and trends as well as the process of planning development to meet market needs.

Plant-Market Match Model. This macro-micro systems model of planning is directed toward matching appropriate supply development with market segment demand.

THE FUNCTIONING SYSTEM

One can take this demand-supply balance one step further by identifying components of the supply side and their relationship to demand as illustrated Figure. Although others may use different terms this relationship is now described much the same as identified in Gunn. Leiper (1979) described the system in a similar manner with tourist generating regions" connected to "tourist destination regions" by means of "transit routes." Boniface and Cooper (1987) called this a system of generating areas connected to destinations by routes travelled between these two sets of locations. No matter how it is labelled or described, tourism is not only made up of hotel, airlines,

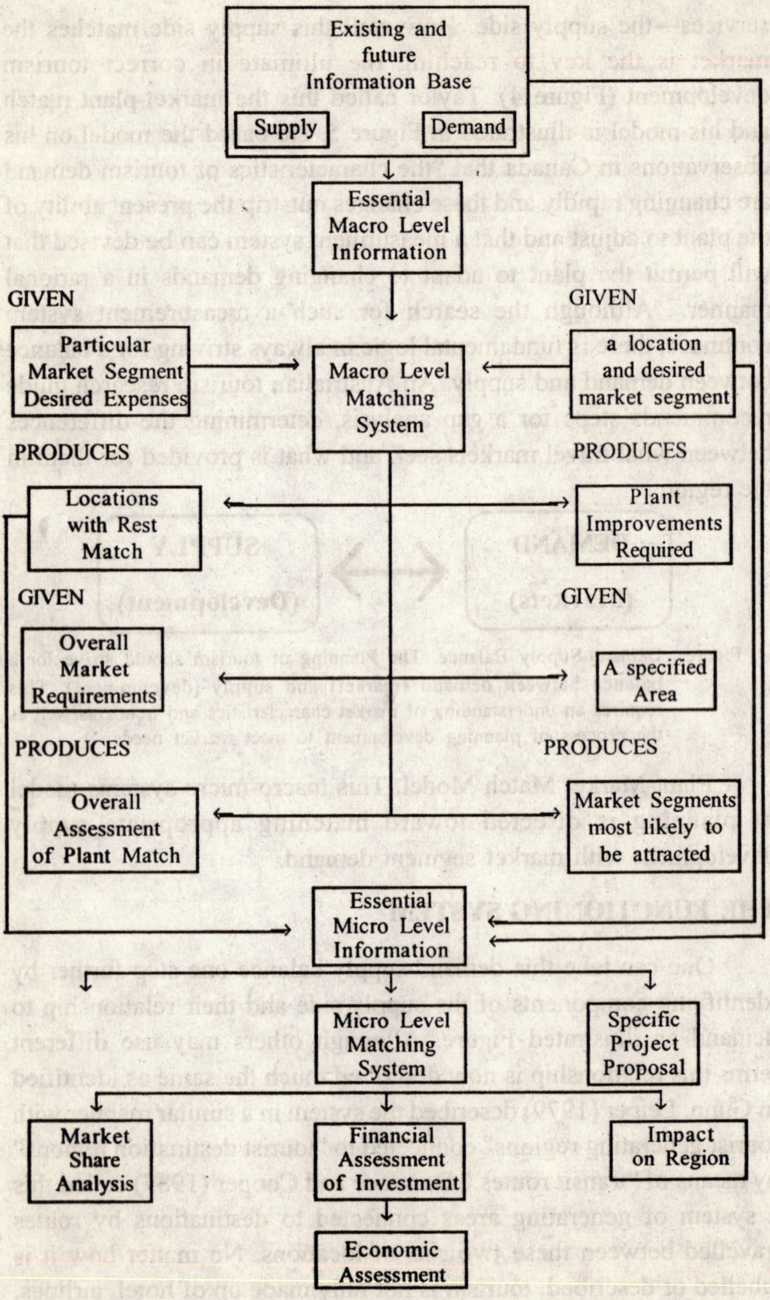
Existing and future Information Base
Supply
Demand
Essential Macro Level Information
GIVEN
Particular Market Segment Desired Expenses
Macro Level Matching System
GIVEN
a location and desired market segment
PRODUCES
Locations with Rest Match
PRODUCES
Plant Improvements Required
GIVEN
Overall Market Requirements
GIVEN
A specified Area
PRODUCES
Overall Assessment of Plant Match
PRODUCES
Market Segments most likely to be attracted
Essential Micro Level Information
Micro Level Matching System
Specific Project Proposal
Market Share Analysis
Financial Assessment of Investment
Impact on Region
Economic Assessment

Figure: Plant-Market Match Model. This macro-micro systems model of planning is directed toward matching appropriate supply development with market segment demand. Such a process can reveal needed development projects.

or the so-called tourist industry but rather a system of major components linked together in an intimate and interdependent relationship. This model is one way of describing the functioning tourism system.

The Supply Side

The supply side includes all those programmes and land uses that are designed and managed to provide for receiving visitors. Again, these are under the control of all three sectors-private enterprise, nonprofit organizations and governments. For purposes of planning. the supply side could be described as including five major components. as shown in Figure. Although others have described these with different labels. it is generally agreed that these represent the supply side of tourism.

Figure: Functioning Components of Supply Side. Planning should strive to interrelate development of all components of the supply side of tourism. Developers and managers within each component include all three sectors-commercial enterprise, nonprofit organization and governments. This model emphasizes the dynamaic relationship requiring regular monitoring. Change in any component influences all the others.

Jafari refers to these as the "market basket of goods" and services, including accommodations, food service, transpiration, travel agencies. recreation and entertainment. and other travel trane services." Murphy also includes similar components of the supply side. Mill and Morrison combine attractions and services into a destination component.

Focusing on community tourism, Blank (1986,6) combines transportation, communications, attractors, services, and other community components for the supply side.

Implications

For all three decisionmaking sectors, there are several important implications when these supply components are understood as operating in a system. First, all components are interdependent. For example, a hotelier—a member of the services component is dependent upon planning decisions made in all other components. Transportation is critical. Airline price changes or bankruptcy, highway rerouting, and changes in fuel price can dramatically influences hotel success. Equally influential is the addition or demise of a major attraction. A river impoundment that creates new opportunity for outdoor recreation, a major new museum, or a new convention centre could greatly increase the volume of visitors needing lodging. The accessibility and quality of informational literature—attraction location, admission fees, open hours could greatly influence whether visitors come to the area near the hotel. Finally, the effectiveness of promotion as compared to other destination promotions could greatly impact hotel success. The same interdependency can be traced for each of the other components and all development within each. Promotion, for example, cannot be productive if the attractions or services are inadequate.

Second, the tourism system is very dynamic. This is an important dimension or interdependency. Changes are continually taking place not only within each component but also between supply and demand. Perhaps this is the greatest factor making tourism planning so difficult. Few planners, developers or managers today are monitoring changes in each component or maintaining data on trends.

Third, the system is difficult to manage. It is owned, developed, and managed by thousands of separate actors within the three developer sectors. In the United States, over 50 federal agencies and hundreds of state agencies own and manage parks, reserves and cultural areas of significance in attracting tourists. Hundreds of nonprofit organizations own and develop land important to tourism. Add to this the great number of businesses involved in tourism and it becomes clear that the tourism system is not under single management control. It should not be implied here that such a control would be desirable; quite the contrary.

Fourth, each component, and every actor within it is dependent upon the characteristics of the market. Tourism markets are much more capricious than local retail markets. Tourists are much more mobile and have a much greater deversity of destination opportunities. For example, for a traveller located in New York, a small price differential could cause a switch in travel plans from the western United States to Europe. Conversely, internal conflict or war in a destination could remove it from consideration, bringing another one at an entirely different part of the world into equal competition.

These and other implications of the tourism system must be taken into consideration when tourism plan are laid.

External Factors

Such a core of functioning components is greatly influenced by many external factors. Planning cannot be concerned solely with the core only because all sectors may be as subject to outside influences as those inside their own control. Several factors can have great influence on how tourism is developed. A brief examination of these may help in understanding the complicated reality of tourism, critical to planning the proper functioning of the tourism system.

Natural Resources

The popular emphasis on tourism economics and business tends to divert attention from very important foundations for tourism development. Again, the causes or travel to a destination are grounded in the destination's resources, natural and cultural, and the attractions that relate to them. Even destinations such as Walt Disney World that seemingly are contrived and unrelated to the resource base, in fact benefit greatly from it. Nearby Orlando and its rounding area have many complementing attractions art museums, a science centre, a

72 building historic district, Lake Eola, wildfowl (ducks, geese, herons, anhingas, cormorants, and moorhens), Leu Botanical Gardens, Florida Audubon Society Centre for Birds of Prey, Bok Tower Gardens, and Wekiwa Springs State Park (Whitman 1992). Natural and cultural resources identify the uniqueness of place, very important to travellers and their objectives. Even a cursory review of publicity and advertising

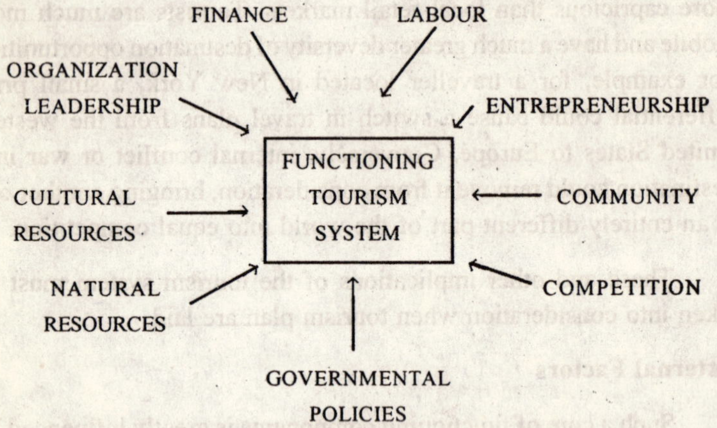

Figure: External Influences on Tourism System. The core of functioning tourism components is influenced greately by several external factors: organization, leadership, finance, labour. entrepreneurship, community, competition, governmental policies, natural resources, and cultural resources.

of travel today demonstrates the high'value that promoters place on attractions related to natural resources. Generally, the term natural resources, refers to five basic natural features: water, topographic changes, vegetation, wildlife, and climate.

Outdoor recreation has been a major travel purpose for many years. Although promoted primarily for its health and social values, outdoor recreation is very important to tourism economics. For example, a study in Taxes revealed that Texas travellers spend approximately $9 billion annually on only 20 outdoor recreation activities. Critical, then, for future tourism developmental is the location and quality of the natural resources that support these activities sought by travel markets.

Probably the most popularly developed natural resource for tourism is water. Surface water is magnetic and has appealed to travellers for many years, stimulating many kinds of waterfront development. Ancient fresco paintings of the Egyptian dynasties include generous illustrations of water's attractiveness.

Reflection pools, ponds, fountains, rivers, lakes waterfalls, and the seas continue to provide appeals that have no substitute. The appeal of water to both residents and visitors is bound up in cultures throughout the world. "We still like to go beachcombing, returning to primitive act and mood. When all the lands will be filled with people and machines, perhaps the last need and observance of man will be, as it was at the beginning, to come down and experience the sea"

TABLE 2

Tourism Development Related to Natural Resources

Resources	*Typical Development*
Water	Resorts, campgrounds, parks, fishing sites, marians, boat cruises, river float trips, picnic areas, water scenic areas, shell collecting areas, water festival sites, waterfront areas, scuba diving sites, water photographic sites.
Topography	Mountain resorts, winter sports areas, mountain climbing, hang gliding areas, parks, scenic sites, glacier sites, plains, ranch resorts, scenic drives, vista photography.
Vegetation	Parks, campgrounds, wildflower sites, autumn foliage areas, scenic overlooks, scenic drives, vacation homes, scenic photography sites, habitate for wildlife.
Wildlife	Nature centers, nature interpretive centers, hunting, wildlife observation, wildlife photographic sites, hunting resorts.
Climate	Sites suited to sunbathing, beach use, summer and winter resorts, sites with temperature and precipitation suited to specific activity development.

It is for its great value to tourism that water quality and its protection must be seen by all sectors as absolutely essential to tourism's success economically as well as socially and environmentally.

Historically, and even today, topography hills, mountains, and valleys provides the physical setting for much of tourism. Land relief is an essential ingredient in contemporary culture's assessment of landscape scenery, now heightened by the boundless popularity of photography.Hillsides and mountaintops offer spectacular vistas, near and far. Mountain resorts, winter and summer, retain their appeal for contemporary travel market segments. Related to topography soils are of significance to tourism development—construction stability, landscape modification, and erodability. Because some mountainsides and slopes are highly erodible, resource protection must be part of the catechims of tourism development.

For many kinds of tourism development, from the tundra of the north to the rainforests of the tropics, vegetative cover is an important natural resource for tourism development. While deserts may have some appeal to tourists, much more popular are verdant landscapes. Forests create appealing scenic vistas, support wildlife, offer dramatic panoramas of colour in autumn, and aid greatly in preventing soil erosion. Often special plant areas (redwoods, the Big Thicket, silverswords in Hawaii, Michigan jack pine for Kirtland warbler) are singularly important in travel destinations for some market segments. Wildflowers are spectacularly attractive in forests in the North and over open fields in the South in springtime. But, forested and vegetated regions are extensive and are subject to varying policies by owners and managers. Some timber harvest practices, such as clearcutting, destroy landscape scenery and stimulate soil erosion. Vegetation is dynamic; trees sprout, grow, and die, and may be damaged by disease and fire.

One primarily of interest only to travel segments interested in game hunting, wildlife today is even of greater importance for non-consumptive tourist markets. Viewing and photographing wildlife have grown significantly in recent years. It is estimated that about $18 billion was spent by travellers on wildlife watching in the United

States in 1991. Photo safaris are far more important today in Africa than hunting ever was. Colour slides and videos are becoming important tourist trophies. Animal habitat management is necessary if the resource is to continue for tourism. Some wildlife is extremely sensitive to human intrusions, requiring special design and management techniques if visitors are to be enriched by this resources.

Climate and weather are qualities of place that greatly influence the planning and development of tourism. Travellers generally prefer sunny weather even in winter sports areas and certainly for beach activities. For example, for many of the national parks of the United States, peak visitation occurs during sunniest weather. Some northern countries, such as Canada, do not try to promote travellers seeking sunny and warm beaches but other attractions more appropriate to their climate. Without doubt, climate plays an important role for the popularity of the Hawaiian and Caribbean islands. There is little evidence to suggest that storm hazards-lightning, tornadoes, and hurricanes have more than a temporary impact on travel. In fact, some fishing in the Guif of Mexico is stimulated during periods of hurricanes. Related to climate are conditions of air quality. Although air quality controls are lessening air pollution in some parts of the world, travellers object to areas where door, manufacturing gases, and automobile pollution are prevalent.

Cultural Resources

In recent years, several travel market segments have increasingly sought destination with abundant cultural resources. This category of resource base includes prehistoric sites; historic sites; places of ethnicity, lore, and education; industries, trade centres, and professional centres; place for performing arts, museums, and galleries; and sites important for entertainment, health, sports, and religion. Examples of development related to cultural resources are shown in Table 7.

Peterson's research categorized cultural travellers as aficionados (sophisticated, professional), casual visitors (urban backyard visitors), event visitors (activities at sites), and travel tourists (historic site visitors). She cited three reasons for visiting cultural sites: experience a different time or place, learning, and sharing knowledge with others. A major international conference on cultural and heritage tourism concluded that in spite of the surge of interest within the travel market, there are major gaps in planning and operation of such attractions. Also stressed was the need for greater public private cooperation.

The travel market interest in prehistory, such as archaeology, has stimulated development of these resources for visitors. Locations where scientists are discovering structures and artifacts of ancient peoples are of increasing interest among travellers. Nautical, archaeology (discovery and analysis of ancient ship transport and ways of life) is becoming as important as terrestrial archaeological digs. But, because of their rarity, these sites must be under rigid control to prevent their destruction by visitors. Archaeologists emphasize the fact that the context (relationship to setting and other artifacts) is more important than the artifact. Documentation of what these clues suggest for ancient peoples—dates, foods, and customs—is more important than collecting.

Popular literature and films have heightened traveller interest in historic areas. Even though every place has a history, places of local significance are of less interest to visitors than those of state, provincial, national, or world importance. Generally governmental

TABLE 3

Tourism Development Related to Cultural Resources

Resource	*Typical Development*
(1)	*(2)*
Prehistory, Archaeology	Visitor interpretive centres, archaeological digs, prehistory parks and preserves, nautical archaeological sites, festival sites related to prehistory, exhibits and customs related to prehistory.

(1)	*(2)*
History	Historic sites, historic architecture. historic shrines, museums depicting eras of human history, cultural centres, historic pageants, festivals, landmarks, historic parks.
Ethnicity, Lore, Education	Places important to legends and lore, places of ethnic importance (customs, art, foods, dress, beliefs), ethnic and national cultural centres, pageants, festivals dude ranches, gardens elderhostels, universities.
Industry. Trade Professionalism	Manufacturing and processing plants, retail and wholesale business, conference centres, educational and research institutions, convention centres, performing arts, museums, galleries.
Entertainment. Health, Religion.	Sports Spas, health centers, fitness resorts, health specialty restaurants, religious meccas, shrines. sports arenas, night clubs, gaming, casions, theaters, museums (history, art, natural history. applied science, children's folk), art gallerlies

agencies and nonprofit organizations have been to leaders in preserving, restoring and developing sites important to history. The topic of history deals with the documented past. For tourism, sites, structures, and events related to places are the foundations for historic attractions. As with archaeological sites historic sites require very special control. design and management so that the resource is protected at the same time visitors gain historic appreciation and enriching experiences. It is important for tourist businesses to support the development and maintenance of historic sites because they stimulate the market for services.

For discussion purposes, places important for ethnicity, lore, and education have been grouped together as a category of cultural resource foundations for tourism development. Travel interest in the exotic and special customs, food, costumes, arts and entertainment of ethnic groups continues to rise. As an example 42 per cent of the visitors to South Dakota want to see Indians (Mills 1991). Because native resources are rooted in the past they are prone to disappear because of the social and economic desire of localities to progress and modernize. Many cultural organizations have established programmes to protect early cultural elements and special design and management is required to develop such places for tourism. For example, Barry Parker, executive director. First Nations Tourism Association of Canada has identified goals objectives for organization.

Goals

To position native tourism business as a major player in the Canadian tourism industry.

To preserve, protect and promote cultural uniqueness in the tourism industry.

To facilitate growth in the Canadian native tourism industry.

Communications to enhance image/perception by establishing a data base and networking system.

Human resource development to coordinate national level training to ensure cultural integrity through standards, quality, certification.

Advocacy to influence policy development at the federal, provincial and territorial levels.

Marketing to develop a national marketing strategy.

Close cooperation with ethnic groups is essential in order to avoid misinterpretation that may demean a past society. Often legends and lore are as important to visitors as true ethnic culture. Universities, colleges, technical institutions and research centres are of interest to many travellers but require special access, exhibits, and tour guidance for tourism.

Travel objectives of industry, trade, and professionalism continue to be very important for several travel segments, and are often combined with pleasure. Manufacturing and processing plants are not only of interests to business travellers but also to pleasure travellers if the site provide tours, falsities and services for visitors. Trade and business centres are important cultural sites for many travellers. Places that establish meeting services and convention centres are attracting many travellers for professional and technical seminars, meetings, and conventions. Many areas are major tourist objectives because of the diversity of shops. Shopping is a very important activity for many travellers.

Finally cultural resources also include places that provide for entertainment, health, sports, and religion. Health spas, centres for physical fitness, weight reduction, and special medical treatment become travel objectives for many travellers. Sports arenas throughout the world attract millions of visitors to special events such as the Olympic Games. Some communities are known as centres for certain religious groups. Other attract many visitors because of their cultural resources such as gaming casinos, music halls, opera houses, and night clubs.

Entrepreneurship

Because tourism is dynamic, enrepreneurs are needed who visualize opportunities for new developments and creative ways of managing existing developments. The ability to see an opportunity to obtain needed financing to obtain the proper location and sites. to engage designers to crater physical settings and to gather the human resources needed to manage the physical plant and services is important for travel development. For industrialized nations. entrepreneurship is a part of the culture. It is known that the lack of this factor in many underdeveloped countries is a major handicap that increases the difficulty of creating and expanding tourism.

Finance. Certainly, capital is required for the development of tourism. But the ease of obtaining the financial backing for tourism varies greatly. Public and private lenders are often skeptical and have a negative image of the financial stability of tourism. Because so much of the tourism physical plant is small business and has attracted many inexperienced developers some of this reputation is justified. However, recent trends have demanded much greater business sophisticated and higher capital investment. Tourism takes considerably more capital than is popularly believed. Investors are more likely to support projects that demonstrate sound feasibility. Financial backing is an important factor for both public and private tourism development.

Labour. The availability of adequately trained workers in an area can have considerable influence on tourism development. As markets demand higher levels of service well-trained and competent people are in greater need. The popular view that the untrained can perform all tasks needed in the diversity of tourism development is false. When the economic base of any area shifts those taken out of employment may be retrainable but are not truly available for tourism jobs unless such training is provided. Remote locations become more costly for development because employees must be housed on site. The labour capacity of an area has much to do with tourism development.

Competition. The freedom to compete is a postulate of the free enterprise system. If a business can develop and offer a better product it should be allowed to do so in order to satisfy market demand. However, before an area begins tourism expansion it must research the competition what other areas can provide the same opportunities with less cost and with greater ease? Is there evidence that tourism plant has already saturated a market segment? Certainly, competition is an important influence upon the tourism system.

Community. A much more important factor influencing tourism development than has been considered in the past is the attitude toward tourism by the several community sectors. While the business sector may favour greater growth of tourism, other groups of the local citizenry may oppose it on the grounds of increased social, environmental and economic for resources and other negative impacts. Political, environmental, religious, cultural, ethnic and other groups in an area can make or break the proper functioning of the tourism system.

Governmental Policies. From federal to local governing levels, statutory requirements may foster or hinder tourism development. How the laws and regulations are administered loosely or rigidly can influence the amount and quality of tourism development. Policies on infrastructure by public agencies may favour one area over another. The policies of the many departments and bureaus can have a great bearing on how human, physical, and cultural resources are utilized.

Organization and Leadership. Only recently being recongnized is the great need for leadership and organization in tourism development. All planning is subject to implementation by many sectors. Many areas have hired consultants to plan for tourism opportunities by frequently such plans for development have not materialized for lack of organization and leadership.

Without doubt as tourism development research and experience broadens, more influential factors will be found. Any planning for tourism in the future must take into account the core of the tourism functional system and the many factors influencing it.

Conclusions

Every stakeholder of tourism will gain, not lose by making plans in the context of tourism as a system. Governmental agencies can gain because their plans and decisions on parks, highways, infrastructure and promotion will be more supportive of development by the other sectors. As capitalistic and market economies grow privatization can be integrated to a higher degree with public agency activities. Nonprofit organization development of tourism can fulfil goals and objectives more successfully it is designed and managed in the context of the overall tourism system. Certainly, the business sector of tourism will benefit greatly when it takes advantage of the complementary action by the other two sectors. And, finally, the tourist and the travel experience, the true product and purpose of all tourism development, will gain because the system is working in greater harmony. Travellers benefit when all parts of all supply side components make their travels easier, more comfortable and more rewarding. Difficult and challenging as system planning for tourism may be, it holds promise of the greatest for everyone. All parts depend upon one another for smoothest functioning. By considering tourism functions as a system, several conclusions can be drawn.

Market, as well as Supply, Drive Tourism Development. Critical to all tourism development and its planning are the many characteristics of travellers' tourism demands. All physical development and programmes must meet the interests and needs of travellers. If not, economic rewards may not be obtained the environment may be eroded, and local conflict may ensure. Planning for visitor interests can ameliorate or prevent these negative impacts. All sectors seeking improved tourism must be fully congnizant of market characteristics and trends.

Supply Development Must Balance Demand. All sectors involved in the devolvement of the supply side of tourism should strive two ward meeting the desires and needs of the travel market. Whenever demand and supply are out of balance, planning and development should be directed towards improving the supply-demand match.

Only through analysis of both demand and supply can a region destination or site know how to plan. All supply side components-attractions, transportation, services information and promotion must be planned and developed to meet the needs of markets.

Supply Side Components are Owned and Managed by all Three Sectors. Supply side development is not exclusively under control of the business sector. All five major components of supply-attractions, transportations, services, information and promotion are created and managed by governments and nonprofit organizations as well as business. This means that for tourism to function properly, planning should integrate policies and actions by all three sectors.

Supply Side Components are Interdependent and Dynamic. Successful development within any component is dependent on action within all other components. Because changes in demand and supply continue to take place the system is dynamic not static, Therefore, constant monitoring of demand and all five components of supply is essential to planning successful tourism. Every developer must be aware of this dynamic relationship.

The Tourism System Requires Integrated Planning. Even though private and independent decision making are cherished by most enterprises in all tourism sectors each will gain by better understanding the trends and plans by others. The public sector can plan for better highways. water supply, waste disposal, parks and other amenities when private sector plans for attractions and services are known. Conversely, the private sector can plan and develop more effectively when public sector plans are known.

External Factors Impinge on the Functioning of the Tourism System. The tourism system does not operate in an isolated manner. Several factors need to be analyzed and worked into plans for best future operation of the system. These external factors include: natural resources, cultural resources, entrepreneurship, finance, labour, competition, community, governmental policies and organization and leadership.

Business Success Depends on Resources and Their Protection. Tourist business enterprises are as dependent upon natural and cultural resources as internal management. Good business practice is not the only cause of travel. Equally important are the attractions nearby that in turn, depend primarily on basic natural assets. Without protection, restoration and visitor development of these assets, business cannot thrive.

Tourist Business Location Depends upon two Markets. All tourist businesses gain revenues from sales of products and services to local as well as travel market. Therefore, their business operation, and especially site locations, must be planned to serve both markets. It is important for all community planning to recognize this fundamental for best economic input.

❑

15

Redevelopment of Tourism

To talk of tourism in the year 2000, in the recessionary United States of Europe is to talk of a completely different reality from the postwar economic climate which first gave rise to the phenomenon. For a start, tourism can hardly be looked upon as the well-deserved reward for work well done in a world where unemployment is the general tonic or affliction. For much the same reasons, neither can tourism be considered any longer an inevitable province of the young; in earlier days youth was equated with active employment and this, unfortunately, is very rarely the case nowadays. With the 21st, century just round the corner, the world belongs more significantly to the 'babyboomers', to the generation born in the postwar baby boom, who grew up with tourism as a normal component of their existence and who have effectively changed every aspect of everyday life oil which they have impacted up until now (hippies, flower power, the Pill, women's liberation, yuppies, test-tube babies, genetic engineering etc.). We have only to look at Europe (and for the purposes of this paper we will consider Europe as being composed of the present European Union plus the countries of EFTA) to see how different the demographic profile is nowadays from when the first international tourists of 'mass tourism' embarked on voyages abroad in the 1960s. At the time of writing this paper, the population over 55 years old is already far more numerous to the population with ages ranging between 13 and 19. By the year 2000, it is estimated that the imbalance will be even greater with an adult population in Europe of over 300 million, 100 million of whom will be over 55 years old.

It is not only the economic recession but also growing concern for the ecological 'climate' and environmental matters in general-everything 'green' in the widest sense of the adjective which has forced upon us a need to reformulate theories and reappraise ideas. The mass tourism of the 1960s and 1970s was largely composed of sunseekers: the classic shopfloor worker in search of the three, or usually four, 'S's booked up a package holiday which afforded him just that with the minimum of problems and surprises. The major mass resorts of the 1960s such as Torremolinos and Benidorm in Spain and, now to a lesser extent thanks to a whole policy of rethinking and restructuring in time, Majorca, stand as testimony to the havoc wreaked by the mass tourists in the pursuit of their pleasures. The tour operators, in an attempt to eliminate perceived problems for the ordinary British or German 'man-in-the-street' unwittingly triggered off a process of standardisation of the product on offer with one common denominator, *i.e.* guaranteed sunshine. The result of packing them in to these resorts, apart from profits for the tour operators and the land speculators, was to wipe out differentiating features which may have attracted the discriminating tourist to the resort in the first place, with the result that a holiday to Torremolinos, Benidorm or Majorca in the 1970s was considered almost tantamount, from the point of view of exotic experiences and' 'difference', to Bognor Regis with sunshine. Global warming, the depletion of the ozone layer, the greenhouse effect and the increased danger of skin cancer are all realities of our times which, logically, impact on the decision-making process of any potential tourist. The standard, and now largely standardized, resorts of the past are now faced with the grim reality that what represented their main pull in days gone by, *i.e.* their guaranteed sunshine, no longer is guaranteed, nor is it attractive for many potential tourists.

To some extent, it could be argued that the reformulation of past values and definitions has already begun in tourism, as can be witnessed in the upsurge in the last few years of literature relating to 'sustainable tourism' formulas or 'alternative tourism' recipes. The panacea for all our evils, if we are to believe everything we read, lies in 'quality not quantity'. In other words, 'mass tourism' is evil, no matter what form it takes, whether mass, green tourism or mass rural tourism. Whatever form it takes, it would seem, if it is 'mass', it is not resort-friendly.

The question which begs to be asked is what happens to the resorts of the past which grew up around mass tourism and which, although very clearly on the downward slope of their life cycles and reflecting varying levels of unsustainability due to the effects of mass tourism, depend almost exclusively on the income and employment afforded by this sector? On the one hand, they can hardly restrict quantity without losing revenue. On the other, they can hardly offer quality in their present state: neither from the point of view of exclusive accommodation and services, nor from the perspective of quality seen as a different and exotic cultural experience. Nor can it be 'quality' from the perspective of 'quality of life' for the host population who can scarcely benefit in its present precarious situation of employment from a major fall-off in tourism numbers.

The other great issue which has been addressed recurrently in the tourism literature of the last decade has been the need to break the deadlock of seasonality. This problem does not affect the Canary Islands, which is perhaps the only region within Europe, particularly in the sun and sand sector, that is not influenced economically by the changing of the seasons. The grossly misnamed 'third age' tourism has been considered to be the solution to the problem, in this case. Which sector of society has free time all the time? Obviously, those who are retired from active fulltime employment and can take their holidays whenever they please, *i.e.* mature tourists. Noone has ever bothered to consider whether, in fact, these resorts which are unattractive to every other sector of the population outside their peak seasons, basically because they lack the organised entertainment, full service and climatic conditions which usually complement the physical draw of the resort, should be found appealing by our older generations. This lack of consideration for the needs of the mature tourist is intimately linked to the idea of economic usefulness' of the person in our consumer society. Once a person fails to produce, he is no longer useful and therefore must make do with what society sees fit to bestow upon him. The changing demographic profile of Europe, Japan, Canada and the United States of America, however, render this conception of society debatable. The mainstream tourism of the future will be mature. To look upon mature tourism as a stopgap remedy for breaking the deadlock of seasonality is grossly shortsighted.

The changing demographic picture in the world, demands that we redefine tourism and the tourist. The young have time to travel but no money. The adult population in active employment has the money but not the time. The mature population has both. It is time to tap this market which even back in 1985, Scott Supernaw, then the President of Olson Travelworld, described as: 'The gray market, it's been such a mystery to us for so many years... I don't know of a bigger, more lucrative, more misunderstood, more confused market that everybody in the US covets at this time.

The Malta Conference of 1991, cofinanced by the European Commission together with American Express and Tourism Canada (both of whom, plus the Hilton chain of hotels, have carried out important research programmes into the needs and wants of mature tourists)' revealed that mature tourism accounted for over 20016 of the total tourism in Europe in 1990-142 million domestic trips and 41 million international. In the USA, the population over 55 years of age in 1990 accounted for some 21% of the total population. This 21% accounted for 28% of all the international trips taken by Americans in 1992. Even more revealing is the fact that, should the age be brought down to fifty, then mature tourism represented 49% of all international trips taken by Americans. Some seven million American tourists visited Europe in 1990, two million of whom were mature, over 55 years old. It is estimated that this figure will go up 78% by the year 2000, thereby representing some 3.5 million mature American tourists. In the same period, 1990, some 400 000 mature Canadian tourists chose Europe as their holiday destination with clear preferences being shown for the UK, France, Germany and Italy. It is calculated that this figure will double by the year 2000, a fact of greater importance when we consider that the Canadians spend approximately double the amount the Americans do per capita.

This gradual ageing of the populations in the developed countries has several repercussions, all of which will necessarily be reflected in future trends in tourism. First and foremost, the growing social costs of an inactive population in times of recession and rampant unemployment will prove to be an excessive burden for any of the developed countries' governments to bear. Instead of early retirement programmes, the age of retirement will probably rise, as it already has in Japan. The accrued experience of a lifetime's work will no longer. be blown out with the candles on the 65th birthday cake but will be used by companies who will place their senior members in consultancy and executive posts. A prolonged working life, though not necessarily fulltime or office-bound, will provide extra income over a longer time for a generation which, in any case in most of the developed countries, had subscribed to equity and pension schemes to see them through their old age in comfort. The mature citizen has less family commitments, usually owns his residence and is not, therefore, burdened by a mortgage and, in this day and age, is a market-conscious and aware person. The scarce economic resources and fragile states of health, accountable between them in survey for over 62% of the mature tourists who did not travel in 1990 are part and parcel of the profile of old age and senior citizens which has predominated up until now but is hardly applicable to the 'babyboomers'.

The 'babyboomers' are people like Jane Fonda, Richard Gere and the Billary duo (Bill and Hillary Clinton) who have enjoyed a greater awareness of the need to work and play hard. These are the people who first investigated yoga, aerobics, alternative medicine and macrobiotic food. It is the generation of women who expect to work outside the home owing to improved educational circumstances,and who have had greater economic independence than their forefathers (or foremothers). It is the generation with a greater cultural baggage than any before it, thanks to the massive introduction of computers in all walks of life and a much expanded media system. The generation which radically changed lifestyles in the 'swinging sixties' will hardly do less when they swing into their sixties. Wayne Haeffer, the Director of the American Association of Retired People said in the Mogan conference on Mature Tourism in 1993, 'Shattering stereotypes about ageing will mean better trips for mature travellers and better business results for all of you'.

Current trends in tourism have indicated an evergreater segmentation of the market in general. This is also the case in the demands of mature tourists. Whereas in the past the industry tended to segment tourists by age, the demographic, sociopolitical and economic pointers would seem to indicate that from now on it will have to segment the sector of mature tourism (and tourism in general) by lifestyles and attitudes. By the year 2025 in Western Europe alone, the people between 40 and 59 years of age will account for 26% of the total population and the people over 60 for another 26%. Therefore any attempt which is made to cater for this sector's needs, apart from meaning good healthy tourism practice, will also make good economic sense. Here we are dealing with the occasional mature traveller as opposed to that sector of the market known as 'retirement tourism' and second home owners, already dealt with more than capably by other authors. According to the data of ETIC (European Travel Intelligence Centre), most mature tourists travel for purely recreational and leisure motives: 80% in the cases of the UK, Germany, The Netherlands and Finland but slightly less than 60% in the cases of Spain, Greece and Portugal (all of which are countries with high indices of domestic tourism). The average percentage of business travel is 8016 though there is a tendency for this figure to vary widely with age, from over 13% for people between 55 and 59 years of age falling to 3% for the over 75s. For leisure travel abroad, the three/four 'S's variant is the most popular, accounting for 31%, followed by touring holidays (29%) and city breaks (11%), with sporting and other holidays lagging a long way behind (1 % and 5 %). Therefore, if the present trends persist, this would represent a new lease of life for the traditional resorts, a fact borne out by recent market surveys and research carried out in the island of Gran Canaria, Spain.

The mature tourist represents a boon for the travel industry in that the large majority of this sector opt for all-inclusive package tours, with transport either by plane or by coach contracted through their local travel agency. Even when travelling by private car, that mature tourist will still have recourse to the agency to reserve hotel accommodation. Because they have more time at their disposal to do so, and also owing to the fact that they are highly value-conscious, the mature tourists will use the travel agency's brochures and staff to much greater effect than other sectors of the population. They also tend to stay longer in anyone place than other tourists: the average stay for long overseas trips is 12.12 nights and for short trips, 2.1 nights. Eighty per cent of mature international tourists make trips of over four days' duration whilst a substantial 14% stay for longer than two weeks in anyone destination. The mature tourists prefer hotel accommodation on their trips abroad (64%) and 83% of the tourists who opt for hotels, stay in four-or five-star establishments. Four and five-star hotels are much more labour-intensive, which bodes well for employment figures in resorts which specialise in this kind of tourism. Since many mature tourists travel alone, the four and five-star hotels that specialise in conference tourism (perhaps the most lucrative form of tourism and most certainly of shortest duration) can more than cover costs on single room accommodation without economic penalty to the mature tourist who opts for the same.

All told then, the prospects for the traditional resorts could hardly be brighter—if, indeed, the host population has been made aware of the longterm advantages of accommodating mature tourism and can revitalise its characteristic hospitality patterns. To achieve a healthy sociocultural balance in the resort, the tourism authorities should strive to accommodate all sectors of the tourist demand to a greater or lesser extent. The tourists who are known to seek merely sun, sand, cheap booze and holiday romances, *i.e.* the real consumer tourists, can be accommodated in areas which cater for their needs, always allowing, nevertheless, for variation, above all in spending power of this sector. Enough surveys have been carried out for us to know that the package tourist will spend directly proportionately to the amount s/he originally laid out on the holiday abroad, with the Germans spending most, in the case of the Canary Islands (they also pay most for their package), and the Irish and the Finns spending least. Incentive tourism should also be encouraged since, although a low consumer power area, this type ot tourism is positive in that the tourists participate actively in making the longsought trip a success and are anxious to investigate the resort to the full without being disrespectful of local customs and countryside. Conference tourism, as we have already mentioned, which can be highly controlled, has little environmental impact on the resort and economically contributes greatly (this sector represents the greatest source of souvenir, as in craft, buying). However, as has been proved in resorts such as Majorca, the change from the traditional formulas of 'S' tourism and unsustainability as the result of too much of the same is not untraumatic and demands firm commitment on the part of both public and private sectors of the industry. Also, care must be taken not to throw the baby out with the bathwater; in other words, the standard 'S' tourism and all the progress made up until now in the development of 'alternative tourism' variants are totally valid for the mature tourists of the future as long as the common denominator of quality and value service for money are borne in mind. If the public authorities make road traffic signals easier to read and comprehend, they must see that they are contributing towards a better quality tourism for all age groups, not only the mature. By making minibus travel more available for groups of six to eight people in car-hire firms-in order to avoid the problems of car insurance for mature tourists and yet ensure safety levels whilst allowing for a certain margin of independence-exclusively tailored to their needs and wants, not only are we contributing towards improving employment figures plus reducing road congestion and pollution, but also we are providing a more personalised attention to the guest.

The 'global village' and a United Europe demand of us that we view all of our activities in a much wider geographical context than the merely local or national level upon which we worked before. The consumer society and the system of mass production which underpinned all the definitions and concepts of the 1960s are far removed from the highly automated, workforce reductive 1990s. As such, it is no longer valid to consider all activities and component factors of our everyday existence in terms merely of their economic relevance. Just as the European Economic Community of the 1970s evolved in time from a principally economic necessity to the European Community, where socio-cultural and ethnic values took the forefront to the European Union, so tourism (the play component of the balance of work and play, vital for a healthy existence) must now be viewed not as just an economic tool, but rather as a service sector which brings a community together in pursuit of an improved wellbeing in the future and a greater defence of its characteristic past.

❐

16

Tourism and Govt. Administrative Systems

This chapter deals with the importance of human resources development and the corresponding GTA role. It goes on to describe the steps taken in seeking to establish internationally agreed minimum working conditions.

Importance of Human Resources

The need to develop human capital is the starting point for all development. Nothing is possible without trained and skilled people. A human resources development policy can be split into two parts:

(a) To offer competitive employment conditions and career opportunities to ensure the adequate recruitment of all levels of personnel.

(b) To provide educational and training opportunities for all occupations and specializations, at agreed and specified levels of skill wherever necessary in the country.

The responsibility for human resources development at the GTA is normally assigned to a separate department. This department should coordinate all aspects of a national tourism human resources development strategy.

Developed countries tend to have more money to spend on training initiatives. However, they often spend money on expensive training at the tertiary level; training which might be provided more cheaply in secondary schools or throughon-the-job/work based training schemes.

They may also develop adult training schemes which only seem to Compensate for inadequacies in earlier education and training, or are merely a response to high rates of unemployment. Governments may also assume other training responsibilities, which are best left to the private sector.

The relative roles of the public and private sectors do differ from country to country. Much will depend on the stage of development of the. private sector, and its capacity and willingness to tackle training effectively. This, in turn, may depend on the level of organization of the professional and trade associations.

Human Resources Development Strategy

The human resources development strategy can also be published as a short document. It should cover the following main areas:

— The relationship of the tourism development policies to human resources.

— The current tourism product and the existing labour force this will summarize characteristics such as numbers of staff, geographical distribution, age, gender, educational level, staff turnover, length of employment, seasonal employment, training background and experience, occupation, and levels of skill. It will also assess the level of technology, operational standards, and occupational skill standards.

— The expected development of tourism and future workforce and training needs indicating the expansion in the number and category of hotels and other tourism enterprises.

— The current situation in the development of all training and education for tourism both for pre-employment and post employment levels. This will assess the adequacy of existing courses and programmes, location, capacity and output. As a result it will existing and future training gaps.

— The future development of all levels and types of education and training, located where it is needed and including the establishment any new public and/or private sector tourism training institutions. It may also propose measures to encourage the development of other new private sector training initiatives.

Tourism has developed steadily but conditions of work, worldwide, have not kept up. Workers, in many countries, have been "forced to tolerate poor conditions. This has been mainly true. of hotels, catering and similar establishments. The International Labour Organization's (ILO) Hotel, Catering and Tourism Committee is of fairly recent origin. The first meeting was held at the ILO in Geneva in December, 1989. A convention concerning working conditions in hotels, restaurants and similar establishments, ILO Convention 172, was not adopted until 1991. This convention applies to hotels and similar establishments which provide lodging, and restaurants and similar establishments providing food, beverages or both.

The convention, which is rather general in content, states that workers should be entitled to reasonable working hours, overtime provisions, and daily and weekly rest periods, according to national law and practice. They should also be given sufficient advanced notice of work schedules. Workers should be compensated in time or pay, if they work on public holidays, as determined by collective bargaining or in accordance with national law or practice. They should also receive annual leave with pay also as determined by collective bargaining or in accordance with national law or practice.

Regardless of any tips, the workers concerned should receive a basic remuneration that is paid at regular intervals, The sale and purchase of employment are prohibited. Although this is all the convention covers it, represents a step forward, However, such a belated and limited starting point gives an idea of the backward nature of the sector on a worldwide basis. Many of the more developed countries have already legislated far more comprehensive conditions for their tourism workers.

At the same time as the convention, the ILO also adopted a recommendation which goes further but lacks the teeth of a convention.

It states that measures fixing hours of work and overtime should be the subject of consultations between the employer and workers or their representatives. Overtime work should be compensated by a higher rate of pay than normal. Working hours and overtime should be properly recorded, and each worker should have access to the records. Split shifts should be progressively eliminated.

The number and length of meal breaks should accord with local customs and traditions, and with whether the meal is taken in the establishment itself or elsewhere. Weekly rest should be not less than 36 hours which, wherever practicable, should be an uninterrupted period. The average daily rest period should be 10 consecutive hours. If the length of paid annual holidays is not four weeks for one year of service, it should be brought progressively to this level. Programmes of vocational education and training, and management development, should exist. They should be aimed at improving skills and the quality of job performance; and enhancing career prospects.

A GTA should encourage consultations between workers and employers to arrive at sound, fair and mutually acceptable working conditions. These are fundamental to the successful development of the sector.

Education and Training

There are various definitions of the terms education and training. Education is about teaching ideas and knowledge; it's about understanding the world better. Training teaches specific skills; it's about how to do a job effectively.

In most cases students need some of both. 'This is particularly true when studying vocational subjects at an advanced level, for example, medicine, engineering, business, tourism and hotel management. The exact mix and balance between skill and educationally slanted subjects are questions of judgement.

The dividing line between education and training is often very fuzzy. The usage of each term also tends to differ from country to country. To avoid such difficulties, it is often best to link the two terms together education and training. Sometimes there is an aspect of elitism in the rejection of training. Superficial values often judge education as superior. As a result students are taught too few skills, and may be poorly qualified to take up many jobs.

A National Council for Tourism Education and Training

The GTA will look for ways to achieve the best possible coordination between the various agencies and organizations involved in human resources development. It is possible to establish either a national committee or council for tourism education and training.

This committee or council can be advisory and consultative, aimed at bringing together all the various interests: the government agencies responsible for tourism, tabour and education; the worker's organizations; and the profession at and trade associations. Also the association of the country's hotel and tourism schools, if it or a similar organization exists.

The committee or council provides for the active participation of the tourism sector itself, in setting standards and reviewing policies, objectives and results. It also monitors educational and training activities, watching for adjustments and improvements as they become necessary. The committee or council will be required to:

(a) Monitor, tabour market conditions, and all related trends.

(b) Keep under review the existing and future needs for management, supervisory, skilled and unskilled staff.

(c) Keep under review the existing education arid training institutions and centres, arid their relevance to the identified needs, Liaise closely with the appropriate authorities and recommend any changes or modifications as considered appropriate.

(d) Recommend, based on the above, the development of any new centres or programmes listing their proposed objectives and programmes.

(e) Liaise with the university system so as to promote the development of appropriate programmes and activities.

(f) Encourage the private sector to take initiatives in the provision of training facilities and programmes, and to recommend any tax and fiscal incentives.

(g) Advise, in particular, and encourage the sector in the development of inservice training programmes, establishing guidelines and organizing workshops.

(h) Keep under review a current database on the numbers and backgrounds of lecturers, instructors and trainers needed to meet existing and future needs.

(i) Set out guidelines as to the career development of vocational educators and trainers, and their recommended participation in intermediate and advanced programmes of further study.

(j) Promote the organization of seminars and workshops in management and supervisory techniques, and teaching and training techniques for trainers (train the trainers).

(k) Liaise with the relevant authorities in the development of occupational skill standards, and the testing and certification for agreed occupations.

(l) Enhance the image of the sector as an employer, and improve recruitment.

(m) Promote the effective teaching of foreign languages for tourism.

(n) Undertake all other activities which will assist in the development of education and training for the sector, and the general improvement of standards.

Linking Types and Levels of Training

Training should last a lifetime. One should build on what has gone before, adjust training to changing demands, and develop and upgrade People's skills. 'The links should exist between various stages and types of training. Each successive type of training should open up a further stage of personal advancement. These links are important. Training and education should not be categorized, and then sealed off within tight compartments. People should be able to transfer between different levels and types of course. The chef, for example, should be free to study management. The university graduate in management should be free to study cooking.

Surveys of the Workforce

The first step in formulating a human resources development strategy is the study of the workforce. If aqequate data do not already exist, surveys of the personnel currently employed in the tourism sector should be carried out. These will identify their characteristics, and training needs. They will also assess the level of technology, operational standards, and review the development of occupational skill standards for the sector.

Surveys start by "identifying the number of hotels, tourist facilities and services in the country by size, category and geographical distribution. The methodology used to collect and analyse data should be discussed and agreed with the private sector itself.

Estimates of Future Workforce Needs

The various employment ratios from the Survey, adjusting for trends, can be applied to the expected development of tourism to estimate future workforce requirements by occupation and level of skill.

The expected development of the tourism sector will cover growth of tourism traffic, number and location of new hotels and tourist facilities, and other future perspectives. These requirements for new staff should be reconciled against labour market conditions and the sector's current recruitment and selection policies.

The Adequacy of Existing Education and Training

The current situation in the development of all training and education for tourism both for pre-employment and post-employment levels, also needs to be surveyed. As a result the adequacy of existing courses and programmes, location, quality, capacity and output, should be evaluated.

All educational institutions, centres, and training programmes should be identified and their curriculum, training materials and standards assessed for their current relevance and' effectiveness. Post-employment training, including all in-service training, and train-the-trainer courses should also be assessed.

Future Training Needs

Future workforce needs should be translated into future training needs. These can be compared to the capacity of the existing educational and training facilities and programmes. As a result, shortfalls in this capacity to meet future needs can be identified. These are termed training gaps. They are gaps which will need to be filled.

One should develop a strategy to respond to all future training needs. It has to be developed according to all levels, all specializations and all parts of the country. It should cover as appropriate, universities, tertiary level vocational training institutions, and secondary schools. It will also cover a framework of minimum standards, inservice training, supervisory and management short course programmes; and foreign language training.

It will also recommend, if justified, the establishment of any new public and/or private sector tourism training institutions to interrelate appropriately with the national educational and vocational training framework. And it may also propose measures to encourage the development of other new private sector training initiatives.

Human Resources Information System

The human resources information system will form a part of the GTA's MIS, normally coordinated through the research department. It will monitor trends in employment, the profile of the labour force and labour market, the continuing trends in sectoral growth and development, future manpower and training needs and the capacity of existing education and training systems to respond to them.

To do this, it should input the results of the surveys described above. As a requirement in the annual licensing of hotels and other tourism enterprises, applicants may be asked to supply specific human resources data.

From time to time, other special surveys may be conducted to complement the information system. These may cover certain sections of the sector, or particular questions, or specific locations and provinces.

A Framework of Minimum Standards

Occupational skill standards, trade testing and certification Occupational skill standards are the minimum standards of knowledge and skills that a worker in a particular occupation, at a particular level, should possess. These are minimum acceptable standards staff can do better than the standards but nobody should fall short of them.

The emphasis of these standards is on employable skills. There is also a certain amount of knowledge needed with each skill. Standards for different occupations are agreed, and trade testing and certification are developed according to basic, intermediate and final levels of skill. Corresponding curriculum development and skills testing follow on. There are three steps:

(a) The standard specifies what people have to be able to do, where, when, how and under what conditions. It indicates both the skills and knowledge they should possess.

(b) Curriculum and teaching material which reflect the standard enable the trainee to reach the correct level of performance.

(c) The test validates that the trainee can reach satisfactorily this level of performance.

Skill standards help support sector-wide quality targets. They also assist employers in performance appraisal, career planning, recruitment and selection, and the development of training plans and targets. They create a basis for intercompany comparison, and they enable skills development to be monitored for the whole sector. National certification enables the quick recognition of levels of skill as well as the outputs of training institutions. Through the system of testing, all personnel can gain recognition for their level of skill.

Where classification schemes exist for hotels and other tourism enterprises, minimum training requirements may also be included.

At first glance, it may seem that industry-wide occupational skill standards are very production oriented rather than market oriented. One starts by asking—what do workers do? One then asks what skills and knowledge they should possess to be able to do it. A marketing approach would start with what staff should be doing to meet the needs of the customers. Skill standards, however, are usually influenced by the major hotels, and tourism enterprises, many of which are operated by multinational companies, Usually these enterprises have already attuned their product to the mainstream market demands.

Regardless of which government agency is authorized to approve and license training institutions, minimum standards should also be established. Applications and submissions should include:

(a) A plan covering a period of at least five years. It will describe the needs and justification for the courses offered, and give details of student recruitment and links with the hotels and other tourism enterprises.

(b) Standards and curriculum describing their interrelationship with the relevant national skill standards and curriculum.

(c) The number of instructors and teachers, their qualifications and experience, and teacher/student ratios.

(d) The numbers of students enrolled or targeted, and the capacity of the programmes and their annual outputs.

(e) The financial structure including capitalization, projected operating results and sources of funds; government or any other grants and any proposed student fees.

(f) The facilities: land area, floor area ratio, range of facilities, planning ratios, classrooms, offices, laboratories, library, student facilities, and other are as.

(g) The organization and the administrative staffing and systems.

(h) The employment expected to be obtained by students, on the completion of their education and training.

Pre-employment Education and Training

Vocational Secondary Schools

Some, secondary schools may have, or should have, courses specializing in hotel, catering and travel subjects. This will keep this type of basic pre-employment course at the secondary level of education, leaving the tertiary level to concentrate on higher level courses. These basic courses will prepare school leavers for careers in the sector.

Tertiary level institutions of this kind are usuallt costly to build and equip and expensive to operate. Some countries have attempted to leave this level of training to the private sector. However, the private sector may not be sufficiently well developed to make this feasible. In such cases, the public sector will need to play a catalytic role setting up one or two key institutions to:

(a) Teach and develop management and supervisory level courses and programmes.

(b) Conduct research on employment trends, manpower and training needs, acting as a resource for the GTA, and assisting in the upkeep of the human resources section of the MIS.

(c) Maintain well-developed libraries, centres of documentation, and possibly computer Internet access.

(d) Act as a key resource in the development of national vocational skills standards and curriculum, and a system of trade testing and certification.

(e) Develop training material for all levels of tourism education and training.

(f) Train future vocational teachers for the country's secondary schools, as well as for private tertiary level hotel and tourism schools.

(g) Act as a major resource in the development of government tourism officials in tourism management and tourism development planning.

(h) Act as resource centres in certain specialized areas of tourism development, for example, in acting as custodian of the culinary heritage, or in acting as a resource centre in the promotion of small enterprise development in tourism.

In developed countries, without limitations of resources, there may be numerous tertiary level institutions offering hotel and tourism courses. Their contribution should be monitored by the GTA and any national committee or council,

Private Sector Tertiary Level Hotel and Tourism Educational and Training Institutions

Government, in close collaboration with the private sector, should encourage private enterprise to take appropriate training initiatives. Existing private sector schools should be encouraged to improve their physical facilities, teaching materials and equipment, as well as the standards of their teaching.

If there is a shortage of training programmes, the government may wish to encourage the creation of new institutions. It may therefore provide some guidelines for the location, size and student capacity for any new hotel training centre or centres, specifying the categories and levels of personnel to be trained. It may also offer incentives to set up such new institutions.

Universities

Universities generally have not all recognized tourism as a serious field for academic study and research and for assistance to the local community. Yet the universities play a key leadership role in the formulation of values related to overall socioeconomic development. In this sense they not only educate the future generation of technocrats, but condition attitudes to development options. For tourism to be viewed favourably, and for a wide range of graduates to have developed an awareness of its needs and potential contribution, the study of tourism should be included across a wide range of university programmes. This means not only full-time courses in various tourism specializations, but the inclusion of tourism in the social sciences, business studies, architectural, environmental and physical planning studies, and, lahguage and communications studies.

The role of the universities in relation to tourism should be studied:

(a) Identify and review current university programmes and activities, in support of the tourism sector.

(b) Identify ways in which the universities can develop or improve this support.

Universities should be surveyed to review the following questions:

(a) University perspectives in developing postgraduate programmes related to various aspects of tourism, and particularly tourism development planning.

(b) The development of tourism options within the social sciences curriculum. Any MBA programme might have a tourism option, and even the possibility of a major in tourism.

(c) The intention and capacity to develop tourism as a subject for research, relating this to the specific university faculties and departments. The integration of tourism in any current university research programmes.

(d) Involvement with local government in studies related to the monitoring and development of the touism sector, for example, the economic and employment impacts of tourism, the physical planning aspects, and the management and marketing aspects.

(e) The range of short courses in tourism-related subjects which a university might feel able to organize, related to the needs of a particular region.

(f) The links with community development and public awareness programmes, and the role of the university in these areas.

(g) The development of any programmes for small enterprises.

(h) The possibilities of using university resources in the training and upgrading of tourist guides.

(i) Any role that universities are able to play in foreign language teaching programmes, directed specifically at the needs of tourism.

University activities base themselves on the link between teaching, research and documentation and the concept of service, to the community,

Post-employment Education and Training

A Supervisory and Management Development Programme

The public and private sector training institutions should offer, often in collaboration with the trade associations, a variety of upgrading and recycling courses particularly for supervisors. However, these are often fragmented, and of varying standards, certification and scope.

A national committee or council, as described 'can play important part in identifying the precise needs for these types of course. It can then encourage their organization.

There may be a case for one centrally coordinated and controlled sector-wide management and supervisory development programme, endorsed by the appropriate government bodies. Such a scheme might best be organized by the professional and trade associations, under the auspices of any national committee or council.

Training for Small Hotel and Tourism Enterprises

Small and medium-sized tourism enterprises offer an important source for new jobs and income generation in rural areas. New business activity of this kind can also create more opportunities for the employment of women.

Assistance will focus on those areas considered essential for successful business establishment and growth, namely:

(a) The identification of business opportunities.

(b) Technical assistance in project formulation and feasibility studies.

(c) Training in the basic skills and knowledge necessary for starting and running a business enterprise. Assistance in obtaining appropriate loan finance.

(d) Ongoing technical assistance and advice.

(e) Development of support networks for small businesses.

Cooperatives

The development of cooperatives also relates to the area of small and micro-tourism enterprises. There is a strong case for the creation of cooperatives among these operations, particularly small hotels, with a focus on marketing and training.

Other Educational and Training Courses and Programmes

Tourism Documentation and Publications

The tourism sector needs access to tourism texts, reference material, and teaching material. These needs may be met by private sector initiatives. If not, the GTA may promote and assist the production of various texts and material.

Vocational Teachers

In many countries there is a shortage of qualified vocational teachers for hotel and tourism studies in both the private sector and public sector.

Some teachers can be drawn from senior personnel working in the sector, interested in becoming teachers. They can be given the teaching skills through specially organized intensive courses. However, where the sector is not as yet highly developed, this source of recruitment may be limited. Alternatively a number of hotel and tourism school graduates may be interested, after a few years of appropriate experience, in a teaching career. They will just need to acquire the necessary teaching skills.

Another course of action is to offer three-year courses at the tertiary level, designed to produce vocational teachers in tourism specializations.

Government Tourism Officials

Highly skilled technicians are essential to the effectiveness of a GTA. It is important that these personnel be kept up-to-date on various tourism management techniques and approaches.

Tourist Guides

Many visitors form their impressions of a country through the tourist guide, The skills of these personnel are therefore a major influence on the quality of the overall tourism product.

Tourist guide standards may be developed for general tourist guides and tour leaders, with a separate category for various special interest guides. This latter category represents a guide specialized in one aspect of tourism or one tourism attraction. To designate the different categories, a system of badges can be introduced. A major problem affecting the standards of guides is the level of foreign language proficiency, and the proportion of guides available in each particular language. While English has become the major international language, its importance and widespread use has not replaced the need for proficiency in other languages; for example, in Japanese or Korean.

Tourist guide should be included among the occupational skill standards and national system of trade testing and certification.

Language Training

The ability to communicate effectively with tourists is fundamental to a successful tourism sector. The introduction of specified standards for foreign language competence is essential, together with a range of comprehensive courses and programmes. A number of occupational skill standards for tourism should include a foreign language component.

Human Resources Development Activities

Many of the activities have already been discussed and explained during the course of this chapter. The following summary can therefore act as a checklist. In accordance with the results planned, the first group of activities addresses the identification of existing workforce characteristics and future needs. It also assesses existing and future training needs. The second group tackles the planning and implementation of a programme to respond to these needs.

Result I—Future workforce and training needs

The following activities, described earlier in the chapter, enable estimates of future workforce and training needs:

— Design surveys of the existing workforce; questionnaires, interviewing and survey methods employee.

— Conduct surveys of the existing workforce including profiles and characteristics, occupations held, levels of skill, and any training received.

— Analyse data and process the results.

— Incorporate survey results, on a continuing basis, within the MIS.

— Institute a system for the regular collection and updating of workforce statistics.

— Review the expected development and expansion of the sector, the number of hotels under construction and the addition of other tourism facilities and services.

— Prepare, on the basis of the above, forecasts for future workforce needs.

— Review the future workforce needs by occupation, level of skill, and area of the country and identify future training needs.

— Discuss the workforce characteristics, and future workforce and training needs with any national committee or council, or similar consultative body.

Result 2-Human resources development strategy

The following activities reflect the various components of the strategy discussed earlier in the chapter:

— Survey the existing education and training institutions and evaluate their contribution to human resources development; the quality of programmes and the capacity and output of trainees and students.

— Assess the capacity and quality of the existing education and training system and identify any training gaps.

— Prepare proposals for the improvement, expansion and development of the network of educational and training institutions and centres to meet future needs.

— Review inservice training programmes, and other Post-employment training, in relation to the identified needs.

— Identify future needs for specialized teachers and training staff, and formulate proposals for the necessary teacher training programmes.

— Formulate programmes for all specialized training, including, for example, government tourism officials, tourist guides, and planning and marketing specialists.

— Outline the proposals for the development of a comprehensive set of occupational skill standards for the sector.

— Consult with the universities on the development of their role in relation to both tourism studies and research.

— Review with the educational authorities the introduction of tourism-related education and training in existing educational institutions.

— Develop initiatives to assist the private sector in playing a more active part in training, including the development of more and/or better inservice training programmes.

— Integrate all proposals with other areas of the plan, namely, GTA management and organizational development, regulation and control, research, marketing, product development and public awareness programmes.

— Draft, review and finalize, or update and finalize as the case may be, the tourism human resources development strategy.

— Consult extensively with any national committee or council, or similar body, on all aspects of the strategy.

HUMAN RESOURCE DEVELOPMENT IN TOURISM INDUSTRY IN INDIA

In recent years increasing relevance is being placed on development of human resources in the process of socio-economic advancement. Human resource is one of the basic inputs as well as an active factor of production. However, as an important resource, it assumed prominence only during the last quarter of the twentieth century. Instead of treating as an ordinary thing, human labour is being viewed now as an important asset leading to improved profitability and increased production.

Thus, specific problems of Human Resources Development in tourism need to be analysed to help develop necessary strategies and programmes for HRD. Due emphasis should be placed on research in manpower planning activities and strategies.

Nature and Scope of HRD

In any society, economic development and prosperity depend upon industrial advancement which is possible through an optimum combination and utilization of the factors of production especially its human factor, which is undoubtedly the most important. Most difficult it is to inspire, control and motivate man with his ability to feel to think, to conceive and to plan. Therefore, the responsibilities of personnel department in any organization are far-reaching and wide, *viz.*, they must identify, anticipate far ahead and manage them both within and outside their organization. Human resources are still the most important, complex and expensive in an organization even in the context of increased mechanization, automation and assembly line techniques of production. Yet, this has not received in actual management practices the due attention it deserves. Human Resources Development is of vital importance in a service industry like tourism. People engaged in this trade deal with people and cater to their needs. They are the ones which determine the quality of the 'product offer' to the tourist. Crores of rupees are spent on building infrastructure but it is the service personnel who alone can make them come alive. It is they who create the ambience that lures or repels the tourists. A lot, therefore, depends on the right selection, training and development of the personnel engaged in tourist services.

The total tourism infrastructure, which generates direct. employment of about six million people and indirectly employs another eight million, needs overhauling in view of the scale of international tourism.

Human Resource Development has acquired paramount importance in the processes and problems of development both in the case of the developed and developing nations of the world. It has acquired special importance in the case of tourism and travel management, as man to man contacts are more vital in creating permanent and better image in the minds of tourists coming with specific perceptions and motivation. Further, it is a complex phenomenon with many equally important components, each requiring special skills and talents.

Significance of HRD

The economic significance of appropriate manpower supply to the industry is obvious and without this resource the potential for development and expansion of tourism would be considerable limited. On the other hand, the employment factor, *i.e.*, production of jobs and employment offering remuneration, satisfaction and dignity to people, is also very important economic and social contribution. The success of the tourism industry primarily depends on whether or not a country can upgrade the level of training for those engaged in the tourism industries, while at the same time design new training approaches for those entering the industry. Consequently, education and training will play an important role in developing professionalism in tourism, which is necessarily a people-to-people business.

The introduction of the professional course on tourism and travel in the mainstream of University education in India represents the major step towards imparting knowledge and developing skills oriented to the nature and needs of the tourism and travel industry. These are helping overcome the constraint of lack of formally structured tourism education programmes in the country. Therefore, the Government of India appointed the National Committee on Tourism observed that "in the absence of any training facilities worth the name in the travel and tourism trade, the outrun of trained personnel is meagre—the requirements of personnel in this area have been placed at 2000-6000 per year."

The progress and innovation are so fast that in the absence of continuous training and development programme, a number of the existing employees will be rendered obsolete and the country will run short of employable persons in future. If obsolete machinery is dangerous, obsolete people are disastrous to the country and its economy. As a result, personnel have to be developed for not only today's requirement, but also of tomorrow's. An effective human resource training and development creates opportunities for people to express and develop their talents and competence. The development of human skills in creases business and industrial productivity and thereby economic development of the country.

It may be said that the system of human resource training and development in a country is like a bank on which the nation draws a cheque whenever it requires efficient reliable and skilled workers. If it becomes bankrupt it is a national disaster. The moment has come when every country has to frame its own training and development programmes of human resources in the area of Hotel Management, Catering and Nutrition in order to meet the challenges of the time.

AIMS and Objectives HRD

(i) To develop the individual intellectually as well as materially to enable him to lead a fuller life by developing his capacity to learn and earn;

(ii) To enhance the contribution which individuals can make in the collective tourism endeavour which is needed to enlarge the availability of services which the nation as a whole needs.

(iii) To develop an organizational culture in which supervisors subordinate relationship, team work, and collaboration among different sub-units is strong and contribute to the organizational wealth, dynamism, professional well-being, motivation and pride of the employees in travel and tourism organizations.

(iv) To acquire/sharpen capabilities required to perform various obligations in the tourism sector and the tasks and functions associated with their present or expected future roles;

(v) To impart knowledge and develop skills oriented to the nature and needs of the tourism and travel industry for present and future needs.

Problems of HRD

1. It will be necessary to train workers to appreciate the limits of modern equipment. Otherwise, it will result in equipment breakdowns.

2. There is need to educate tourism both managers and union leaders in the intricacies of developing and operating a modern Industrial system.

3. Tourism organizations will have to develop relevant, relations realistic and fair method for objectively evaluating the performance of employees at all levels.

4. Tourism organizations which do not have effective and comprehensive training programmes will find it difficult to adopt and grow.

5. Infrastructure deficiencies (goods, communication, electricity, water, etc.) will severely hamper some operations and totally cripple others.

6. Pressures for more efficient allocation and utilization of organizational resources will require the use of far more effective techniques in such tourism areas as job design, cost analysis and productivity measurement.

7. Numerous decision activities (*e.g.* planning, control, investment, product mix, etc.) will be hampered by a growing shortage of relevant, reliable and timely statistical data on both the micro and macro levels.

Strategies to Meet Challenges

Because of regular changing socio-economic and political conditions, the industrial environments are bound to change. The HRD managers of the future shall have to face the problems like increasing size of workforce, changing psycho-social system satisfaction of higher-level needs, equalitarian social system, technological advances, computerised information system, mobility of professional personnel, changes in legal environment and management of human relations etc. in the management of labour.

HRD is a system approach to managing human beings in the organizational context. HRD has a unique way of working in which each of its components are so well equipped with the other that ignoring anyone with not fulfil the desired objectives. HRD does no only means a wide range of strategies for improvement of human resources, but it is actually concerned with vitalising activating and renewing an organization though human resources with special emphasis on the prevailing patterns of activities, attitude, values etc. of formal and informal systems. It is an essential function of management, and pre requisites for its success, we should consider the following points:

Human Resource Planning. Human Resource Planning maintains and improves the organization's ability to achieve its goal by developing strategies that will lead to optimum contribution of human resources. It is a basic function which provides the necessary framework and parameters for the job of HRD. Urgent measures for needed to ensure the adequate supply of manpower in quantitative and qualitative terms in all the organizations. The ultimate purpose of Human Resource Planning is to relate future human resources to future enterprise needs as to maximise the future return on investment in human resources.

Recruitment and Selection. Recruitment refers to the process of searching for prospective employees and encouraging them to apply for jobs in an organization, while selection procedure refers to secure relevant information about an applicant. The objectives of selection process is to determine whether an applicant meets the qualifications for a specific job. The selection of employees involves certain important steps like job analysis followed by the preparation of the job-description and man specification, determination of the success of recruitment, preparation of the application form, conducting the interview, placing the applicant through tests according to necessity checking the references, conducting the medical examination of the applicant etc.

Training and Development. The present system of training and development programme suffers from several weaknesses, both, in quantitative and qualitative dimensions. Ability is a prerequisite to achievement but unless this ability is built in, motivated, schooled and properly guided towards achievement of specific objectives, goals will not be fulfilled. It is important to make a distinction between the mere availability of training programmes and their effectiveness for promotion of HRD objectives. Formal training programmes in our country are excessively traditional and frequently of little operational value. Some are only system maintenance and are not directed towards HRD. The emphasis should be laid on scientific and objective training to trainers and trainees. A training programme should aim fostering honesty, integrity and incorruptibility and social discipline. Training can be effective, if the knowledge and skills acquired by the trainees are actually used for performance improvement and also of successful training is really helping the trainees in their career and human resource development.

Reward System. A reward attracts a worker's attention and stimulates him to work. An incentive programme is most frequently based on monetary rewards but may also include non-monetary rewards or prizes.

In a country like India, the role of financial incentives as a primary tool for motivating workers cannot be overemphasised. The only practicable and self-sustaining means of improving and utilizing human resources is to introduce incentive schemes and stimulate human efforts to provide a positive motivation to greater output. The efficiency of worker is very low, and needs to be raised.

Career Development and Counselling. A major thrust of the HRD process is career and growth aspirations of all organization members. It is essential to increase opportunities for internal mobility and the development of 'Career Ladders'. Career counselling and short duration programmes should be organised frequently for updating the knowledge and skills of those employed at the gross roots and supervisory levels. HRD can be achieved and strengthened in tourism industry through this particular tool of management.

Performance Appraisal System. HRD looks at performance appraisal system as a tool to help employees to overcome his weaknesses, improve his strengths and contribute to the growth and development of an employee. It is essential to evaluate the potential of the employee so that he may take up responsibilities of higher level also. The knowledge of performance and potential data helps in taking appropriate steps for employees development. Performance appraisal also aims at identifying whether a change of duties is advisable and finding out whether this could be linked with salary revisions. Human resource development can be planned more effectively if the performance appraisals are followed by periodic counselling. Of the various methods employed for performance appraisal, fixed review, confidential report and submission of period reports on staff for periodic appraisal constitute the most common forms of staff appraisal.

Organizational Culture and Effectiveness. With the globalization of manpower, technology, culture, capital and other important factors of production, organizational culture is bound to get affected and so will work culture.

The organizational effectiveness is the outcome of the interplay of the elements such as the external variables, the internal variables and the HRD climate in the organization. External variables *i.e.* environment, technology, availability of resources, nature of business and Government policies etc. are beyond control of any organization. Internal variables such as personnel policies, financial position, management styles, previous history of business etc. are boundary walls for the organization in which it grows.

Hotel Management and Catering Technology Education Programme

Presently, there are 13 institutes of Hotel Management with a turnover of 2160 trained personnel at the craft and diploma level and another 13 Foodcraft Institutes with a capacity for training 2240 students annually at the craft level. While the intake of candidates for the first year of the 3-year Diploma course in Hotel Management was of the order of 855 till last year, this number has been increased to 1000 from the current year. Having regard to the increasing demand for the courses, efforts are on to augment this number to 2000 by the year 1995, *i.e.* by the end of the 8th Five-Year Plan.

Oberoi School of Hotel Management and Welcome—Group Graduate School of Hotel Administration

In case of private sector also the Oberoi School of Hotel Management has a capacity to train 70 students in craft and management diploma courses while the Welcomegroup Graduate School of Hotel Administration has started training 30 students annually for a degree course in this discipline.

India Tourism Development Corporation (ITDC)

In case of Public Sector, The Indian Tourism Development Corporation has an annual capacity of training 55 management trainees. During the year (up to January 1990), 88 programmes for non-Executives and 50 programmes for Executives have been conducted providing training inputs to 1459 non-Executives and 1112 Executives. In addition, 112 personnel (Executives and non-Executives) have been deputed to specialized need-based management workshops conducted by the professionals in the field?

Indian Institute of Tourism and Travel Management (IITTM)

In a short span of just over three years, the IITIM has completed 14 Management Development Programmes at New Delhi in which 460 participants have been successfully trained. Simultaneously the Institute has launched a wide range of academic programmes and courses at various levels directly and collaboratively with Universities. These include Foreign Language Training Programmes, Tourism Orientation Courses, Professional Ticketing Courses, Tourism Awareness Programmes and the Master of Tourism Administration (MTA), Post Graduate Diploma in Destination

Management (PGDDM) for Tourist Guides and Post-Graduate Diploma in Tourism Management (PGDTM) in sponsored Universities.

Indian Institute of Skiing and Mountaineering (IIS&M), Gulmarg and Institute of Water Sports

With the diversification of tourist traffic, specialized training is needed for certain types of activities such as development of beach resorts, winter sports, mountaineering, trekking. Wildlife tourism, etc. At present, the Institute for Skiing and Mountaineering at Gulmarg has been established. There is also a proposal to set up an Institute of Water Sports as an Institute of Wildlife Management. But, there is need to work out modalities of the programmes as well as identify skill requirements and develop training facilities for the same.

World Tourism Organisation (WTO)

The World Tourism industry provides direct employment to 19 million persons and generates indirect employment to 38 million persons, according to the estimates published by the World Tourism Organization. The WTO considers that the success of the tourism industry primarily depends on whether or not a country can upgrade the level of training for those already engaged in the tourism-related industries, while at the same time design new training approaches for those entering the industry. Education and training will, therefore, play a crucial role in developing professionalism in tourism, which is essentially a people-to-people business. In four decades of Independence, no University in India considered it worth its while to develop a post-graduate degree programme in tourism.

The National Committee On Tourism (NCT)

The National Committee on Tourism appointed by the Government of India in 1987 has identified several weaknesses. Firstly, the combined outturn of trained personnel from the ongoing training programmes in the accommodation and hospitality sector is just a small percentage of the huge requirement of the industry. Secondly, in the travel and tourism trade, there is absence of proper training facilities, whereas the requirements of trained personnel in these areas have been estimated to be of the order of 20,000 persons per year. Thirdly, training facilities at the degree and post-graduate levels even in the accommodation sector are negligible. Fourthly, the training facilities provided through statutory Apprenticeship Act are not adequate. And finally, the quality of training facilities provided through present arrangements is not up to the mark.

It also pointed out that the present system of tourism training programmes suffers from several weaknesses, both in its qualitative and quantitative dimensions. These are:

(i) The combined outturn of 8500 trained personnel from the ongoing programmes in the accommodation and hospitality sector, falls short of the requirements of about 28,000 trained manpower each year.

(ii) In the absence of any training facilities, worth the name in the travel and tourism trade, the outturn of the trained personnel is meagre. The requirements of personnel in this area have been placed at 20,000-26,000 per year.

(iii) Institutes of Hotel Management and Foodcraft Institutes generally provide training at the craft and diploma levels. Training facilities at the degree and postgraduate levels which constitute junior and senior management levels in the hotel industry are negligible.

(iv) The training facilities arranged through statutory Apprenticeship Act are nowhere near the requirements.

(v) The quality of training facilities is not up to the standard required for an internationally competitive industry.

India Tourism Development Corporation

India Tourism Development Corporation was established on October 1, 1966. It has been the prime mover in the progressive development and expansion of tourism infrastructure in the country. It has, nowadays, emerged as the largest multiunit tourism undertaking in the country. It provides tourist facilities *i.e.* accommodation, travel services, surface transport, duty free shopping, tourist literature, entertainment and consultancy services.

Presently, the ITDC Board consists of three Directors including Chairman-cum-Managing Director.

Organizational Structure. At the corporate level, the organisational set-up consists of various business groups headed by Senior-Vice Presidents and Vice-Presidents.

It has four regional offices at New Delhi, Bombay, Madras, and Calcutta. It maintains no overseas offices.

Product Mix. The ITDC product mix comprises own units and managed units. Own units relates to 25 hotels, 1 travellers lodge, 7 restaurants, 11 travel/transport units, 1 service station, 11 duty free shops and 1 sound and light show and managed units comprises 6 hotels, 1 forest lodge, 2 restaurants, catering services at 3 Delhi-Based government establishments and 2 sound and light shows.

Human Resource Development

The total number of employees in the Corporation as on 31 March 1989 was 8945 as against 8927 on 31 March 1988. Out of this, 2299 employees belong to scheduled caste and 131 to scheduled tribes.

During 1989-90, a special recruitment drive for increasing the intake of SC/ST candidate at all levels, has been undertaken.

The scope of the Ashok Training Centre has been enlarged keeping in view the need to provide training to personnel at various levels and in different disciplines. Apart from imparting professional training to executives and management trainees and trainees under the career development scheme, training is provided to apprentices under the Apprenticeship Act. The Ashok Training Centre has been renamed as Manpower Development Centre.

During the year (up to January 1990), 88 programmes for non-Executives and 50 programmes for Executives have been conducted providing training inputs to 1459 non-Executives and 1112 Executives. In addition, 112 personnel (Executives and non-Executives) have been deputed to specialized needbased management workshops conducted by the professionals in the field. To facilitate availability of personnel trained in foreign languages, the Manpower Development Centre is conducting classes in conjunction with Jawaharlal Nehru University leading to proficiency in Japanese, Russian, German and French in the first phase. 65 personnel from diverse departments are attending these language courses.

To provide continuity of 'On the Job' training, nominated line Managers have undergone a specialized training' programme and designated as trainers in 9 hotels units imparting training for the shop floor level.

Industrial relations continued to be cordial and satisfactory during the year. It is a matter of satisfaction that for the fourth consecutive year there has been no loss of mandays during 1988-89.

❐

17

Structuring the Demand for Tourism

The chapter goes on to discuss whether tourism is supply or demand led. It then explains different levels of demand, and the concept of price elasticity of demand. Structuring the demand for tourism is discussed, and the chapter moves on to explain various approaches to market segmentation. The chapter concludes with visitor surveys and market information systems.

The marketing concept can be expressed very simply as the matching of the product with the needs and desires of the market. People should be offered what they want to buy. One must also develop the right product at an acceptable price. Potential buyers have to be told that this has been done. Then they have to see the product in the right way and they have to be stimulated to buy it. Finally its purchase has to be made as easy as possible. The key to successful marketing ties in understanding the market and creating the products to satisfy its needs. To know what people want requires the analysis of two types of data:

Who are the people who travel?—what are their characteristics? *e.g.*, social class and profile, age, sex, marital status. Second, what are the motivations of these different groups?—what do they want? what are they looking for?—why are they travelling?

It is important for the GTA, in collaboration with the private sector, to adopt a complete markeing, role Apart from promotion it should play a key part in product development. It should also act as the catalyst in the formulation of the destination's marketing strategy.

And it should also monitor the effectiveness of sales programmes, lending its support as necessary. The term marketing is best understood in a wide context embracing market product development, promotion and sales.

Why People Travel

People travel for two reasons:

(a) by obligation having to go somewhere on business, or feeling an obligation for religious reasons, or for reasons of family or friendship, or for medical reasons.

(b) for pleasure choosing to go somewhere for pleasure the pleasure, for example, of rest, adventure, escape, discovery, excitement, sport or romance, or any other pleasure seeking motivations. These may differ from person to person. Taken altogether they comprise leisure tourism.

The purposes of travel were listed according to the WTO. They were: leisure, recreation and holiday; visiting friends and relatives; business and professional; health treatment; religion/pilgrimages; and other. Travel for leisure is central to our understanding of tourism. It is linked to the growth in leisure which has accompanied social and economic progress. It is a major contributor to contemporary culture, a part of any modern concept of individual freedom of expression, and the subject of intensive and competitive international market forces. Travel for leisure as a broad category can be broken down into mainstream tourism, special interest tourism and alternative tourism.

Mainstream Tourism

Although the overall market may become more diverse, its mainstream changes little. This solid major market segment, by far the largest, is made up of people looking for rest and recreation. They want comfortable holiday hotels and other types of smart tourist accommodation on a beach or elsewhere. Many may prefer to be in a resort complex offering a full range of shopping, recreation, restaurants, entertainment and other facilities and services. This is the traditional holiday market which changes only according to contemporary fashions, tastes and values. It can be segmented mainly on the basis of nationality, social class, spending power and age.

Special Interest Tourism

The following are examples of special interest markets,

— Nature tourism in all of its specialized forms

— Trekking

— Fishing

— Cultural interest in various specialized forms

— Photography

— Deep sea diving

— While water rafting

— River cruising

— Adventure tourism—based on camping expeditions

— Game watching

— Youth tourism—outdoors and adventure

These markets are formed through the common special interest possessed by the people who make them up. It is this interest—this motivation—which is more important than other characteristics *e.g.*, age, Cultural background, etc. A passion for archery, or photography, or ornithology, or deep sea diving, or military history or archaeology, may unite a highly heterogeneous group of people with otherwise dissimilar backgrounds and characteristics.

Another market may be composed of naturalists. These may be people with a passion for such subjects as ornithology, etymology or botany. In a similar way, hobbyists can be divided into a wide range of segments, for example pastimes like painting, photography or ceramics. Another segment of the market may be looking for soft adventure. This kind of holiday will capture excitement and thrills, while providing a certain level of security and comfort, for example a safari staying at comfortable game lodges or a canoeing trip, again with good food and comfortable accommodation.

Alternative Tourism

It can be questioned whether alternative tourism should exist as a separate category at all, or whether it should just be included as another special interest segment. Tourism marketers tend to talk about the new traveller. The new traveller is described as better educated, more culturally aware, more environmentally and culturally sensitive and more curious and analytical,

Such people are looking for an alternative to the mainstream trends of the large Mass tourism markets. They do not want large, modern hotels constructed and equipped according to international norms. Alternative tourism is usually based on small locally owned accommodation units, very much a part of the local community and reflecting local values and ways of life. Alternative tourism seeks to feature and protect local Culture, and to involve the community in such ways that local people benefit fully. It is a tourism which aims to be better assimilated and more supportive of local needs and aspirations.

Alternative tourism promotes local cuisine, the use of local materials and handicrafts, and the development of a whole range of other participating tourism services, *e.g.* local folkloric performances, trekking, handicrafts demonstrations, and cultural and recreational activities. It also fosters the creation and development of tourism enterprises operated and owned by local people.

Is Tourism Demand or Supply Led?

In business travel, or visiting friends or relatives, or going on pilgrimages, or for health reasons, or for conventions, the traveller's destination tends to be pre-selected by the purpose of his or her journey: going to New York on business, going to Lourdes on pilgrimage, going to Florida to see one's mother, going to Singapore to participate in a convention, or to Zurich for a particular medical treatment.

As already noted, these kinds of travel tend to be motivated by a sense of obligation. This obligatory travel is obviously driven by demand. The number of pilgrims is generated by the strength of a particular religion. There is a correlation between business traffic, economic growth, trade and commercial activity. Visiting friends and relatives is related to the ethnic ties between communities in different countries.

By contrast, travellers motivated by pleasure are free to choose their destination. There is no obligation to visit a particular place, except perhaps for people who may own a holiday home there. It is a question of choice, People choose the destination which, they believe, will best meet their needs. One can go anywhere. In this sense tourism is supply led. It is the destination with the most attractive product which draws the visitors. Obviously, unless a destination possesses the natural, scenic and cultural attractions, it is difficult to create a demand. In this sense tourism is, always supply led. A place has to be attractive to even consider developing leisure tourism.

For a destination to be demand led given that it has the right natural and other attractions requires a marketing approach. This means the complete analysis of all marketing opportunities, and the selection of certain markets. It means the development of an appropriate product to satisfy these markets, with the pursuit of particular types of tourist.

However, the capacity must then exist (in both resources and professional knowledge and skills) to create and operate facilities of the required category and standard to satisfy these tourists.

Levels of Demand

One can talk of four levels of demand basic, displacement, created and future. The basic demand is an existing demand which is not being completely satisfied, for example, there is a demand to stay in a destination but there are still too few hotels. Displacement demand occurs when people are persuaded to stop using one product in favour of another product which better fulfils their needs, for example, new and better hotels are opened in one destination and displace demand from other destinations. Created demand is when the creation of a new product creates a demand which did not exist before, for example, new hotels in a certain destination create a completely new demand. Future demand will be brought about by future changes and developments, for example, by increases in standards of living, by economic growth, increases in population, and by a general growth in tourism. Future demand eventually becomes a part of the basic demand.

These levels to demand are well illustrated, for example, by the countries of South East Asia. The basic level of demand has tended to exceed the supply of the right kinds of facilities. Rapid regional growth has brought future demand on stream at a steady rate. As countries have added facilities, so they have displaced demand from other destinations. Arid they have created demand particularly from short haul tourism within the region price, demand is said to be price elastic.

Total demand consists of different groups of people, with different preferences, tastes and spending power. There may be lots of different market segments each seeking a particular product with distinctive characteristics. Demand has to be analysed and the market for a destination segmented accordingly. The product should then be developed to meet the various needs of these segments. This means that the product will be segmented in a matching way.

Elasticity of Demand

Sometimes when prices are lowered it results in people buying more. Sometimes it has little effect. When the sales of an item are very sensitive to any changes in price, demand is said to be price elastic. When sales are insensitive and demand remains the same it is price inelastic.

Even small changes in price may result in a substantial effect on demand (elasticity), while quite large changes may have little effect (inelasticity). Leisure travel of the popular mainstream type tends to be price elastic. In contrast, business travel people must travel regardless of cost tends to be price inelastic.

The price elasticity in relation to marginal costing and the need to fill up empty space at the last minute, is an important factor. When prices are greatly reduced to encourage last minute travel, the market tends to respond quickly. However, price is also linked to the image of a product. The value attached to a product, its prestige and desirability, may depend largely on how much one has to pay for it.

Marginal cost is the cost of producing one more unit or as is the case in tourism, of accommodating or serving one more visitor. If the cost is low it may be tempting to cut prices to fill up space on aeroplanes and in hotels. Such a strategy takes advantage of the price elasticity of demand.

Structuring the Demand for Tourism

Countries market a tourism product according to its diversity. The product may subdivide into many different places and experiences. Separately these may attract both large and small markets domestic and international.

When confronted with this complexity of products and markets, there is a need to try and structure them in a sensible way. Large countries have a very diverse tourism product indeed appealing to a huge spectrum of market segments, one ran almost say a continuum of segments; for example, countries such as France or Italy.

However, to make sense of large countries they may have to be broken down into regions, areas, counties, provinces, cities, towns and resorts. Each one has first to be studied separately. They are then all brought together and viewed as a whole.

The product is differentiated according to market segments. And markets are segmented according to the entire range of products offered. This is how supply and demand are matched.

Each market segment has to be well understood and analysed according to its characteristics. As noted, product segments are discussed in the next chapter.

Market Segmentation

Each market segment represents people with different characteristics and needs. Segments then sub-segment and sub-segment on down according to these criteria. For example:

— Nationality or place of cultural origin, and gender

— Stage of life

— Social grade

— Psychographics

— Motivation and interests

— Mode of travel/distance travelled

If one was selling clothes people's physical characteristics would matter. Are people tall or short, fat or thin? If it was shoes, do they have big or small feet and what shape are their feet? If it was golf gloves how many are left handed or right handed. How big or small are their hands? Markets can be segmented in any way, using any criteria, that make sense in identifying the characteristics and patterns of consumer behaviour and needs.

For example, American women, single, between 30 and 40 years old, in the professional group, successful, innovating individuals, who play tennis and golf. A particular resort specializing in these two games might target this market segment. There are three basic reasons for segmenting markets:

(a) to develop the product to satisfy specific needs

(b) to identify where and how to sell the product

(c) to judge if and how to mix different segments together.

The following describes typical sets of criteria in the segmentation of markets.

Nationality and Gender

It is obviously important for a resort to know whether visitors are, for example, Japanese, French or Italian. Each nationality has its own language and many distinctive preferences and patterns of behaviour.

A particular resort or hotel has to judge the extent to which it can mix nationalities. Few studies have been done which can assist operators in this decision. Operators go by experience. They know that if they exceed 50 per cent of resort or hotel capacity for one nationality alone, say Japanese, it may be difficult for other nationalities to blend in. Many consider that 50 per cent is already too high. It is sometimes held that once 50 percent is exceeded it is better to aim at 100 per cent for the one nationality. Doing this however, makes the resort dependent on one market only. This has obvious dangers.

Similarly there may be dangers in mixing sub cultures from the same country. There has to be a good understanding of the ways in which groups of people differ and how well they will mix together. People from different regions, with variations in educational and cultural levels and incomes, may not go well together. It may depend on the precise proportions and the nature of the holiday. Gender is also an important variable, Men and Women may have some different travel preferences and needs, These have to be, identified.

Social Grade Groupings

The following breakdown, from the Institute of Practitioners in Advertising, is now used as the Social Grade Profile of the UK's National Readership Survey sample and serves as an example of social grade grouping.

The basis of this sccial grading was originally based on the Head of Household concept, but this has now been changed to Chief Income Earners. This has had the effect of shifting the social class profile more up market. People's incomes help to indicate the price they may be able and willing to pay for a particular product. Some groups, however, may be willing to pay different proportions of their discretionary income for travel. Pricing policy may be developed accordingly. Generally, however, one does not segment markets according to price level; one prices according to each market segment.

The marketing mix as a whole is formulated to target particular segments.

In most countries there are numerous sources of demographic data characterizing segments of society according to criteria such as age, sex, occupation, educational level, income and place of residence. Alone these data allow for crude segmentation only, representing an inflexible way of categorizing society. Marketing specialists have tried to identify more complete ways of explaining consumer behavior, and have used psychographics. This is a technique which relates personality to social values and lifestyles.

Psychographics

Different psychographic profiles may describe inward and outward looking people, adventurers and play-it-safers, leaders and followers and so on. Some of the thinking described may be useful to apply. It may also be based on studies with some validity, and it may increase understanding of the particular appeal of various tourist experiences.

Sometimes, however, the concepts tend to be too glib and fail to recognize all the complexities of human behaviour, People categorized according to one particular profile, may suddenly demonstrate a range of behavioural inconsistencies, They do not always behave as they are supposed to behave.

The main examples of the psychographic approach are:

— Stanford Research's Values and Lifestyles Programme (VALS).

These are four value groups divided into nine lifestyle categories—Survivors, Sustainers Belongers, Emulators,

Achievers, I-am-Me, Experiential, Societally Conscious and Integrated.

— Yankelovich Clancy Shulman's Monitor.

These, are seven lifestyle categories Self-explorer, Social Resister, Experimentalist, Conspicuous consumer, Belonger, Survivor and Aimless.

Both these approaches have been widely used internationally. In the United Kingdom, Young and Rubicam's 4Cs-Cross Cultural Consumer Classification reflects the VALS approach. It uses the following categories and groups.

Three basic categories:

Survivors
Internal values
External values

Beth Salmon covers these various systems in her short guide Psychographics and Lifestyles. She points out that they have many common threads. 'The major inner-directed/outer-directed axis always seems to be present; the 4Cs 11 "succeeders" and "reformers" seem to bear more than a passing resemblance to Monitor's "conspicuous Consumers" and self explorers"!

She indicates that most systems have some sort of mass market moral majority at their core. Whether they call them belongers or mainstreamers is riot of crucial importance. In tourism, as noted, it is this mainstream demand which sustains most destinations.

Mode of Transport/Distance Travelled

People will choose to travel by air, sea, rail or road, and they will travel independently-alone or with family or friends or in groups.

Access can usually be described as follows:

(a) Long haul access by air 6000 kilometres or more usually more than about seven hours flying time.

(b) Medium haul access by air between 3000 and 6000 kilometres from, about four hours flying time up to about six to seven hours.

(c) Access by train mostly national or intraregional.

(d) Access by road also mostly national or intraregional from neighbouring countries.

(e) Short haul access by air under 3000 kilometers or up to about three to four hours flying time. This will usually include the major regional markets.

(f) Access by sea mainly from neighbouring and other countries in the region. This does not include cruise ships.

Tourists can be differentiated according to the mode of transport chosen, the distance travelled and whether they are travelling independently or in a group.

The Complexity of Human Behaviour

The various means of categorizing tourists illustrate the complexity of human behaviour, People share the common characteristics of the species. Beyond this, however, they appear to be infinitely variable. As noted, some of the differences originate in their genetic make-up and sex, some in the major cultural influences that play upon them, some in their age and marital status, some in their previous education and experience, some in their economic and social status, some in their spiritual and inner life, some in their simple likes and dislikes, their interests and passions, and some in a variety of other ways. It is important to keep analysing demand. To be sensitive to every clue about behaviour, and to never stop asking questions. One needs a constant flow of market information; keeping track of people, of who exactly they are, and what exactly they want and need.

Some of the psychographic ways of classifying tourists may seem, at times, to be too superficial or fanciful. However, they are still helpful in the review and discussion of tourist behaviour and in shaping future research projects.

Successful segmentation, enabling clearly defined marketing targets, is assisted by interconnecting various kinds of data and criteria. As data is built up age, nationality, gender, occupation, income, motivations and interests, needs and preferences, lifestyles, stage of life, etc. the picture formed becomes clearer and sharper and more particularized.

Visitor Surveys

Visitor surveys are conducted to supplement the market information obtained from routine tourism statistics. In designing a survey questionnaire, the following points should be noted:

(a) The purpose should be explained and people thanked for their participation.

(b) The meaning of questions should be clear and free of any ambiguit.

(c) It has to be easy to understand and complete.

(d) It should be well laid out, organized into clear sections, printed in large clear typeface allowing plenty of space to write answers and comments.

(e) It should be presented in a logical sequence.

(a) Questions should not lead the respondent, *i.e.* suggest or imply an expected answer.

The length of a questionnaire depends partly on the time people have to complete it. It also depends on people's goodwill and the time they are prepared to spend. If tour groups are being asked, they will generally spend some time in the departure lounge before their return journey. They may have to sit and wait for as long as 30 minutes- given that last minute or duty free shopping has been completed. This may be the ideal time to complete a questionnaire.

Ideally each questionnaire should be collected and checked by a survey assistant. Any part not filled out or not clear can be clarified immediately with the respondent.

The design of the questionnaire will also depend on the survey methodology and the size of the sample. As noted, the questionnaire has to permit the collection of accurate and useful feedback. But it must also facilitate the subsequent correlation and analysis of the data. The more extensive the comments and assessments made by respondents, the harder this is. But it is often worth the effort. It will provide more complete answers about the respondents.

(a) Not only who they are and what they do

(b) But also where they stayed

(c) How long they stayed

(d) What they did

(e) Where they went

(f) How much they spent

(g) And what they liked or didn't like and why.

It is this last assessment which is essential in improving and developing the product. There are usually no other reliable sources for data on tourist expenditures. Banks and currency exchange agencies can give some data on foreign exchange earnings but not enough to build up an accurate and complete picture.

Surveys can help identify and define market segments. Knowledge has to be built up on each market segment, to provide information on how to develop the product and how to promote and sell more effectively. When segments are lumped together the value of a visitor survey is seriously diminished. However, it may not be practical to define and isolate segments in too detailed a way.

The sampling method used can take account of a number of the major variables, for example, seasonality and time of the year, the nationality of visitors, age, and whether travelling independently or in a group. With mainstream leisure tourism there may be quite pronounced differences between people of different nationalities cultures. And there will obviously be major differences between age groups. Some market segments can be determined by the reason for travel; for example, it is easy to identify and survey separately business and official travellers and visiting friends and family traffic.

Purpose of Visit

The definition of tourist is wide-ranging and when tourism demand is broken down according to purpose of visit, the following categories can be identified: holidays, business trips, visits to friends and relatives (VFR) and miscellaneous visits. About 70 per cent of world international tourist arrivals are for holiday purposes, and of the remaining 30 per cent of tourist trips approximately one-half are made for business purposes.

Holidays

Holidays are the most important tourism market overall. This market is characterized by freedom of choice on the part of the individual in terms of selection of destination, transport mode, and so on, and by strong competition among the various segments of the tourism industry (including the destinations) that supply the market. Unlike, say, business travel, where the existence of business contacts largely determines the destination to be visited, in the case of holiday tourism the individual can select from among a wide variety of destinations; thus considerations such as price become very important. Holidaymakers can be divided into those who are conservative and risk-averse and those who wish to try something new and are willing to accept some risk. The conservatives tend to take the same type of holiday year after year often returning to the same country once they have found one they enjoy (and even to the same resort or hotel), whereas the risk-takers seek out new experiences in terms of climate, culture, scenery, and so on.

Many different types of holiday exist. For example, in terms of the mass-market, Mediterranean destinations offer 'sun/sea/sand' holidays (where the norm is to lie on a beach), whereas Austria and Switzerland offer lakes and mountains holidays, which concentrate on scenic attractions in the summer and skiing holidays in the winter. There are now also many 'exotic' long-haul destinations on offer to places such as South America and Southeast Asia, where the emphasis is very much on experiencing something different. A range of special-interest holidays also exists pony-trekking, rambling, cycling, yachting, bird watching, farm tourism, canal cruising, and so on. The short-break sightseeing holiday is also proving increasingly popular.

Business Trips

Business travel is an important segment of the tourism market, and in certain sectors it plays the major role. Although only about 15 per cent of tourist arrivals are for business purposes, tourist spending on a business trip is likely to be much higher than on a holiday, so the contribution of business tourism to the total will be higher in value terms. Furthermore, as far as transport is concerned, business travellers comprise a disproportionately high proportion of air travellers (of the order of 50 per cent), and as far as accommodation is concerned they comprise a disproportionately high proportion of hotel guests, particularly in the four and five-star range where the figure is of the order of 60 per cent.

The business travel market is characterized by relative lack of seasonality, last-minute booking and inelastic response to price. To the extent that seasonality exists at all, the demand for business tourism is likely to be lower at times of peak holiday demand, because the businessmen themselves may well be on holiday. An important attribute, of short business trips is that they usually take place during the week, so hotel accommodation tends to be little used for business purposes at weekends. As business travel is often large town/city-oriented, hotels in these business centres usually offer very attractive rates at weekends to encourage holidaymakers to stay. The facts that many business trips are booked only a short time ahead and that business travellers usually wish to spend the minimum amount of time away on their trips to achieve the required results means that business tourists require maximum flexibility in particular, they do not want restrictive conditions attached to flight tickets and are prepared to pay a premium for this. Furthermore, they usually require good quality accommodation, both in order to be able to function well and also to create the right image with the business contact being visited.

A particular form of business tourism is conference/ congress/ convention tourism, and considerable attention has been focused on this form of tourism in recent years with the development of large purpose-built conference centres in many cities and seaside resorts. However, most conferences take place in hotels, and educational establishments (universities, colleges) also play an important role. Conference tourism is not as predetermined as other forms of business tourism, in that the conference organizers can choose the location for the conference on the basis of facilities, price, and so on. Thus conference destinations are in strong competition with each other to attract conferences. Friel identifies the following criteria, which are censidered desirable if a conference destination is to be successful:

1. It should be attractive to tourists.
2. It should have a variety of meeting facilities.
3. It should have a range of good accommodation.
4. There should be good access by air/road/rail.
5. There should be a civic commitment to hosting delegates.
6. There should be a coordinated approach to destination marketing and visitor servicing.

Visits to Friends and Relatives

Tourists visiting friends and relatives tend to spend much less per day while in the destination than do holidaymakers. They often stay with their friends/ relatives and, therefore, do not make use of commercial accommodation. Similarly, daily expenditure on food and drink in restaurants, etc., is likely to be considerably lower than would be the case for holidaymakers. However, VFR tourists often stay longer than holidaymakers, and thus the total trip expenditure may, in some cases, be higher for the former than for the latter category of tourists.

Furthermore, VFR traffic almost certainly generates additional local resident spending on food, drink, attractions, and so on. In addition, although daily destination expenditure is likely to be relatively low, the VFR component of the tourism market still needs to reach the destination and is likely to use similar means of transport to holiday makers. In fact, tourists visiting friends and relatives may face higher travel costs than those incurred by inclusive tour holidaymakers, who benefit from the bulk-purchasing power of tour operators.

Miscellaneous Visits

This purpose of visit includes tourism for reasons such as study, health, religion, shopping and to attend sporting events. Miscellaneous visits form a small proportion of overall tourism demand, but for certain destinations they can be quite important. For example, visits for religious reasons are dominant in the case of Vatican City, and visits to spas for health purposes form a significant segment of tourism demand in certain European countries such as Germany and Hungary.

Seasonality in Tourism Demand

'Seasonality' refers to the tendency of tourist flows to be concentrated into relatively short periods of the year (Allcock, 1989b) In Europe and North America, for example, the summer months of July and August are when a large proportion of the population goes on holiday. This is mainly due to natural features such as climate (the best holiday destination weather often occurs during these months), but also partly due to institutional features such as restrictions on when employees may take holiday leave and school holidays.

In recent years ski holidays have grown enormously in popularity, which spreads the tourist season into the winter months for appropriate destinations. Furthermore, many holidaymakers now go on 'winter sun' holidays. Sesonality causes particular problems for employment, in that workers employed in the tourism industry for part of the year may have no opportunities for employment during the rest of the year, and this may cause resentment among employees. In addition, the seasonal nature of employment inhibits training and career progress. Seasonality can result in overcrowding and overuse of facilities in destinations during part of the year, while for the remainder of the year facilities may be considerably under-used or not used at all, resulting in inefficient use of resources and loss of profit potential.

There are four principal strategies for managing seasonality: changing the product-mix, market diversification, differential pricing and encouragement/facilitation by the state of the staggering of holidays. Changing the product-mix involves the creation and marketing of new different attractions; thus, a summer beach resort may set out to attract the conference trade in the off season, or it may decide to stage some special event, or to promote special-interest holidays that would be appropriate out of season.

The construction of all-weather facilities, such as covered leisure complexes for year-round use are a means of extending the season. A highly successful example in Northern Europe is the development of Centre Parcs, where accommodation is clustered around an all-weather leisure area incorporating wave-pool, water slides, and so on. Diversification of the market to reach new potential customers may also be used successfully to counteract the effects of seasonality North Americans, particularly from the northeast of the USA and Canada, have been travelling to Florida for winter holidays for some considerable time. The desire to escape the harsh winters for the warmth, and sun of Florida has been a strong pull; and many retired North Americans spend several months there each winter. More recently, however, Florida has been marketed as a summer destination to UK residents, and the British have travelled there in increasing numbers. Pricing policies can also be used to reduce seasonality. By the introduction of price, reductions in the off-season, tourists can be encouraged to take holidays during this period. Similarly, if tourist resorts become overcrowded during peak periods, price rises can be used to reduce the seasonal congestion. State-initiated measures to stagger holidays can also be successful in reducing the seasonality problem for example, the staggering of school summer holidays over a longer period and the encouragement of the staggering of industrial holidays.

Tourism Demand Functions

Tourism demand functions embody the relationship between the demand for international tourism and those factors that influence this demand. They are economic relationships that, when estimated, permit the impact of each of these factors on tourism demand to be identified. Clearly, the group of variables that influences international tourism demand will depend upon the purpose of visit under consideration. For example, the demand for business travel will depend upon where major business centres are located, whereas the demand for visits to friends and relatives will depend upon where close historical, cultural, etc., ties exist, which give rise to the location of friends/relatives in foreign countries. As by far the majority of international tourist trips take place for holiday purposes (approximateiy 70 per cent), and it is only for holiday trips that individuals are completely free to choose the destination, transport mode, and so on, we shall just concentrate on demand functions that explain the demand for international holiday tourism.

Demand Variable

The demand for international tourism is measured in terms of the number of holiday visits from an origin country to a foreign destination country, or in terms of holiday expenditures by visitors from the origin country in the destination country. As the level of foreign tourism from a given origin is expected to depend upon the origin population (the higher the number of people resident in a country, the greater the number of trips taken abroad, ceteris paribus), the demand variable is usually expressed in per capita form. Occasionally, however, population features as a separate explanatory variable rather than demand being expressed in percapita form.

Income

In general, income is included as an explanatory variable. Income usually enters model as origin country real income per capita (corresponding to the specification of demand in per capita terms). As holiday visits are under consideration, the appropriate form of the variable is personal disposable income.

Own Price

Price is usually included in demand functions. For international tourism there are two elements of price: those costs incurred in reaching the destination, and those costs to be met while at the destination. Transport cost can be measured by using representative air fares between the origin and destination for air travel and representative ferry fares and/ or petrol costs for surface travel, Transport cost should enter model in real terms in origin country currency.

It may be possible to measure the cost of tourism in the destination by a specific tourists' cost of living variable if appropriate data available. Otherwise, the consumer price index in a country may be used to represent tourists' cost of living, and Martin and Witt have shown that this is likely to be a reasonable proxy for the cost of tourism variable. Tourists' cost of living should be specified in real terms in origin currency. It is sometimes suggested that exchange rate should also appear as an explanatory variable influencing, international tourism demand; although exchange rates are already incorporated to some extent in the other price variables, in practice people may be more aware of exchange rates than relative costs of living for tourists in the origin and destination countries, and thus pay considerable attention to this price indicator.

Substitute Prices

Economic theory suggests that the prices of substitutes may be important determinants of demand. Potential tourists compare the price of a foreign holiday with the price of a domestic holiday in reaching their holiday decision. However, they also compare the costs of holidaying in a particular foreign destination with the costs involved in visiting other foreign countries. Thus, substitute travel costs and substitute tourists' living costs may be important determinants of the demand for international tourism to a given destination from a particular origin. Substitute prices can be accommodated in model through the inclusion of:

(a) a weighted average substitute transport cost variable, and

(b) a weighted average substitute tourists' cost of living variable.

The weights should reflect the relative attractiveness of the various destinations to residents of the origin under consideration, and are often based on previous market shares.

Promotional Activity

National tourist offices often spend considerable sums in foreign countries on promoting the particular country as a tourist destination, as do carriers, particularly airlines. Hence, promotional expenditure is expected to play a role in determining the level of international tourism demand and thus should feature as an explanatory variable in the demand function. The appropriate form of the variable is promotional expenditure for the destination in the origin, expressed in origin country currency and real terms.

A major problem regarding the inclusion of promotional variables as determinants of tourism demand relates to difficulties in obtaining the relevant data. A further problem concerns the form of the relationship; the impact of advertising on tourism demand may be distributed over time, so that advertising in a given period is likely to influence not only demand in that period but also in subsequent Periods, although the effect will diminish with the passage of time. In addition, the effectiveness of a given level of advertising expenditure in influencing the level of international tourism demand may vary across media.

Lagged Dependent Variable

A lagged dependent variable is sometimes included in tourism demand functions to allow for habit persistence and supply rigidities.

Once people have been on holiday to a particular country and liked it, they tend to return to that destination. Furthermore, knowledge about the destination spreads as people talk about their holidays and show photographs, thereby reducing risk for potential visitors to that country. In fact, this word of mouth recommendation may well play a more important role in destination selection than does commercial advertising.

Supply constraints may take the form of shortages of hotel accommodation, passenger transportation capacity and trained staff, and these often cannot be increased rapidly. Time is also required to build up contacts among tour operators, hotels, airlines and travel agencies. Similarly, once the tourist industry to a country has become highly developed it is unlikely to dwindle rapidly. The hotel industry will have invested large sums of money in the country and tour operators will have built up contacts there.

Estimation and Testing of Demand Functions

The tourism demand function may be estimated by regression analysis using historic data. The empirical results obtained show the estimated. quantitative relationship between foreign holiday demand and the influencing factors. The estimation process is as follows:

1. Specify the demand function in mathematical form (say, linear, or more commonly log-linear).
2. Assemble data relevant to the model.
3. Use the data to estimate by regression the quantitative effects of the influencing variables on demand in the past.
4. Carry out tests on the estimated model to see if it is sufficiently realistic.

When the tourism demand function is specified in log-linear form, a resulting characteristic is that the estimated coefficients may be interpreted directly as elasticities. It is necessary to evaluate the parameter estimate obtained in a regression model in terms of both sign and magnitude in order to determine whether these estimates are theoretically meaningful. Economic theory imposes restrictions on the signs and values of the parameters in demand functions, and the estimates need to be examined to see whether they satisfy these constraints. For example, foreign holidays are 'superior' goods and thus a positive income elasticity is expected. In fact, most foreign holidays are regarded as 'luxuries' and in such cases the magnitude of the income elasticity is expected to exceed unity. Similarly, the own-price elasticity of demand should be negative and cross-price ties for substitutes positive. Changes in consumer tastes may move towards or away from a particular holiday and therefore the variable could have a positive or negative coefficient. The Promotional expenditure and lagged dependent variable coefficients are both expected to be positive. If an estimated parameter has an incorrect, sign or does not satisfy the restrictions on magnitude it should be rejected, as it is theoretically implausible. In general, an unexpected parameter sign or size is the result of deficiencies in the model.

The empirical results may also be evaluated in terms of statistical measures of accuracy and significance of the forecasting equations. For example, the test can be employed to examine the hypothesis that a particular explanatory variable coefficient is significantly, different from zero, or whether the estimated value may simply have been generated by chance. If the hypothesis that a coefficient is equal to zero is true, then the corresponding explanatory variable does not influence the dependent variable and should be excluded from the tourism demand function. However, when a parameter is not statistically significant, this does not prove that there is no relationship between the explanatory and dependent variables; the insignificance of the parameter may be a result of statistical problems. Prior belief plays a vital role in the decision regarding which explanatory variables should be retained in the equation in view of the statistical evidence. If there are strong theoretical grounds for expecting a particular explanatory variable to influence the dependent variable and a 'correct' coefficient sign is estimated but the parameter is insignificant, the explanatory variable should not be eliminated from the equation, as weak support has been obtained for the hypothesis. If the correct sign is estimated for a coefficient and it is statistically significant, this provides strong support for the hypothesis that the variable has an impact on the dependent variable.

Empirical Results

The magnitudes of the various elasticities are of interest. For example, if the demand for tourism is price inelastic, then a price reduction reduces total expenditure on tourism and a price rise increase expenditure. If, however, the absolute value of the price elasticity exceeds unity (that is, demand is price elastic), then a price reduction increases expenditure and a price rise reduces expenditure. Clearly therefore, the impact of a price change on total expenditure on the tourism product depends critically on the magnitude of the elasticity.

Martin and Witt have estimated model for tourism, flows from four major generating countries West Germany, USA, UK, France to their important destinations, using data for the period 1965 to 1980. It is clear that the importance of a particular variable in explaining tourist flows varies considerably with the origin-destination pair under consideration. Building models for USA outward tourism proved difficult, with the result that several of these are rather simplistic, and in general contain fewer explanatory variables that the models for UK outward tourism. The main factors affecting tourism demand by USA residents appear to be income and absolute costs. Most overseas holidays seem to be regarded as luxuries with high income coefficients. The exception is Italy, which may be on account of strong ethnic/family ties or the pull for Roman Catholics to visit the country in either case such motivations would tend to cause these visits to be necessities rather than luxuries. The price elasticities vary considerably. In terms of tourist' living costs, tourism demand is price elastic for travel from the USA to France and West Germany, but price inelastic for travel to Canada and the UK. In terms of transport costs, demand is price inelastic. In the models explaining UK outward tourism, not only do the costs of competing holidays play a more important role than for the USA, but also the exchange rate now enters into some models. The 1974 oil crisis appears to have had a marked impact on international tourism demand by UK residents, featuring in five out of six models, and the currency restrictions appear to have affected those destinations with relatively high tourists' living costs (as expected). All income elasticities exceed unity with the exception of Greece, which has a surprisingly low coefficient value. The co-efficients estimated for tourists living costs suggest that demand is price elastic for travel from the UK to Greece and Italy, but price inelastic for travel to Austria, France and West Germany. Air travel costs do not feature in the models, but the estimated surface travel cost elasticities show that demand is price elastic for West Germany and price inelastic for Greece, Italy and Spain.

Long-term Influences on Tourism Demand

Major demographic changes are taking place in the main tourism generating countries, and this is likely to affect both the volume and types of holidays undertaken. For example, in general an increasing proportion of the population will consist of retired people couples with young children, and a declining proportion will consist of young singles. Also, changes in consumer preferences say, away, from sun/sea/sand holiday may have a profound towards activity holidays such as rambling impact on tourism demand over the long term. Clearly, substantial, changes in the amount of holiday entitlement will also influence the level of demand.

Tourism Forecasting

It is widely recognized that one of the most important functions of the manager at all levels in an organization is planning, and planning creates a substantial need for forecasts. Reliable forecasts of tourism, demand are essential for efficient planning by airlines, shipping, companies, railways, coach operators, hoteliers, tour operators, food and catering establishments, providers of entertainment facilities, manufacturers producing goods primarily for sale to tourists, and other industries connected with the tourism market. Such forecasts are also of great interest to governments in origin and destination countries, and to national tourist organizations.

Both the need for forecasts and the importance of reliable forecasts have been stressed by several authors working in the tourism field. For example, Wandner and Van Erden point out that:

> Since governments and private industry must plan for expected tourism demand and provide tourism investment goods and infrastructure, the availability of accurate estimates of international tourism demand has important economic consequences.

Also, Archer states that:

> No manager can avoid the need for some form of forecasting: a manager must plan for the future in order to minimize the risk off, failure or, more optimistically, to maximize the possibilities of success. In order to plan, he must use forecasts. Forecasts will always be made, whether by guesswork, teamwork or the use complex models, and the accuracy of the forecasts will affect the quality of the management decision.

Considerable benefits derive from an accurate forecasting system. If forecasts of tourism demand are too high, then firms in related industries will suffer; for example, there may be empty seats on aeroplanes and coaches, empty rooms in hotels, unoccupied apartments, unused hire cars, and so on. It is likely that in general capital investment will be excessive, the labour force will be too big and excess stocks will be held of goods normally sold directly to or used by tourists. If, on the other hand, forecasts of demand are too low, then firms will lose opportunities: for example, there may be insufficient hotel accommodation or too few flights to cater for all those wishing to visit a certain area at a given time. Even if supply can be expanded to a limited extent at short notice, this is likely to impose additional costs on firms as, say, less efficient aircraft are used, and excessive overtime is worked. A broad range of techniques is available for demand forecasting in tourism and the main quantitative methods are now reviewed.

Univariate Time Series Methods

Univariate time series methods are non-causal quantitative techniques, *i.e.* they assume that a variable may be forecast without reference to the factors that determine the level of the variable past history on the forecast variable is simply extrapolated. Univariate time series methods determine future values for a single variable through a process of identifying a relationship for past values of the variable. Thus, a great problem with forecasting by extrapolation is that it presupposes that the factors that were the main cause of growth in the past will continue to be the main cause in the future, which may not be the case. In an industry as highly volatile as international tourism, and one that is influenced by so many factors, trend extrapolation is a technique that should be used with extreme caution. It is rarely possible to justify time series models on the basis of theory. The reasons for their use are essentially pragmatic: they often, generate acceptable forecasts at low cost. Furthermore, univariate time series methods may be used where causal models are inappropriate on account of lack of data or incomplete knowledge regarding the causal structure.

Although time series extrapolation models are 'naive' in the sense that the impacts of the forces that determine the behaviour of the time series are not taken into account, they often predict relatively well. Several of these methods are considered below:

Moving Average (Arithmetic)

The arithmetic moving average forecast is very easy and cheap to compute; the data for previous periods are added together an divided by the number of observations to give an average figure, and then as a new data point becomes available this is included in the set the oldest observation is removed, and a new average is calculated.

For seasonal data with seasonality of *s* periods (for example, quarterly data has four-period seasonality), a moving average is periods long is free of seasonal effects. The moving average forecast for periods t + 1, t + 2, etc., is given by:

$$F_{t+2} \sim= F_{t+1} [X_t + X_{t+1} + ... + X_{t-S+1}]/s$$

where

X_t is the value of a time series in period t

F_{1+j} is the moving average forecast of x_{t+i} (*i.e.* the forecast for periods ahead), and

S is the length of the seasonal cycle.

The moving average model attempts to estimate the non-seasonal portion of a time series. It is not applicable to series containing steps or trends, as these would cause the I moving average to lag behind the movement of the data. Thus, for example, if tourism demand were increasing the method would underforecast.

Exponential Smoothing

Exponential smoothing models provide a relatively simple set of forecasting methods that tend to perform well in practice. The single exponential smoothing model in effect attempts to reduce forecast error by correcting last period's forecast by a proportion of last period's error:

$$F_{t+1} = F_t + k(x_t - F_t)$$

where

x_t is the value of a time series in period t

F_{t+1} is the single exponential smoothing forecast of xt+, (*i.e.* the!, forecast for one period ahead), and

k is a constant, such that $0 < k < 1$.

Equation states that the forecast for period t + 1 is given by the forecast for period t plus a proportion (k) of the forecast error for period t. This equation may be rewritten to give:

$$F_{t+1} = kx_t + (1 - k)F_t$$

Single exponential smoothing methods are only applicable to stationary series, *i.e.* to data without steps, trend or seasonality components, and with constant variance. For non-stationary series other exponential smoothing models can be used. Adaptive smoothing models can accommodate sudden upward or downward steps in a series; Brown's double exponential smoothing model can be used for time series containing a trend, and the Holt-Winters' double exponential smoothing method is specifically designed for time series exhibiting seasonality (in addition to a trend).

Trend Curve Analysis

Trend curve analysis is widely used in tourism forecasting situations. In general, regression analysis is used to find a curve of best fit through time series data, which is then projected forward into the future. Trend curve analysis is relatively quick and easy to use and, using transformations, can be employed to produce forecasts from data showing a range of patterns for example, straight line progressions, exponential growth, or patterns that display a gradual approach to a saturation level.

Decomposition Methods

The observed values of a time series are usually the result of several influences, and here we are concerned with isolating and measuring those parts of the time series that are attributable to each of the components. Customarily, time series variations are considered to be the result of three or four basic influences: secular trend, seasonal variations, irregular or random changes, and possibly cyclical fluctuations.

The classical decomposition approach assumes that the observation of the time series at period t, x, can be represented as:

$$Xt = T_t \times S_t \times I_t$$

where

T represents the trend value

S represents the seasonal component

I represents the irregular (unpredictable) component, and

t represents the time period.

Sometimes an additional longer-term cycle component is added to the classical decomposition model, but often this factor is ignored. This can be justified if there are insufficient data to detect it, which may well be the case with tourism series. Classical decomposition is best suited where trend or seasonality, and preferably both, are marked.

An alternative (though considerably more complex) approach to decomposition is provided by the Census XII model originally devised for the US Bureau of Census. This extends the basic decomposition model of equation by allowing the trend term Tt, to be non-linear.

Box-Jenkins Univariate Method

The Box-Jenkins univariate forecasting method is a highly sophisticated technique and is rather more difficult to apply than the other univariate time series methods considered. The models usually incorporate auto-regressive and moving average terms; the autoregressive component implies that the forecast variable depends on its own past values, and the moving average component implies that the forecast variable depends on previous values of the error term. These autoregressive integrated moving average (ARIMA) models are very flexible they can represent many types of stationary and non-stationary time, series. Furthermore, the models contain few parameters. The Box-Jenkins model-building approach can provide relatively accurate forecasts, but it involves complex mathematical and statistical algorithms, and subjective judgements on the part of the modeller. Experience is an essential prerequisite for improving the final models in the analysis of a time series and thus for successful application of the technique.

❐